H✡PPINESS
THE JEWISH WAY

A Practical Guide to Happiness through the Lens of Jewish Wisdom

Olga Gilburd

Happiness the Jewish Way :

A Practical Guide to Happiness through the Lens of Jewish Wisdom

For information contact the author at
www.oglagilburd.com

ISBN-13: 978-1514111246

ISBN-10: 1514111241

First Edition: June 2015

To my daughters Rachel and Rebecca

TABLE OF CONTENTS

PREFACE

*"Joy is the goal of existence, and joy is not to be stumbled upon,
but to be achieved,
and the act of treason is to let its vision drown in the swamp of
the moment's torture."*

—**Ayn Rand**, *Atlas Shrugged*

WHY HAPPINESS?

There was no sign of trouble at the local playground. Birds and kids chirped cheerfully among themselves, a light breeze caressed the trees, and my daughter gleefully swooshed down the slides. So I was not prepared for her crying when it was time to go home. I tried to talk her into a better mood, but nothing worked. She felt genuinely unhappy, and I felt frustrated and, even more so, helpless.

This rather trivial incident got me thinking about coping skills, attitudes, and above all, happiness. Why wasn't my daughter happy to have had the two fun-filled hours of playtime? Was I a bad mom because I hadn't been able to instill a more positive attitude in my child, or was she born the glass-half-empty kind of girl? And was her reaction an indication of how she will deal with future trivial disappointments that are common in everyone's lives?

I resolved to look around and find some classes that teach kids how to focus on the good things and deal with adversity, however small and insignificant. There was bound to be something like that in New York City, right? Wrong. I saw listings for all kinds of classes: math, music, dance, gymnastics, art, drama, horseback riding, fashion, karate, fencing, etiquette, and juggling while tightrope walking. But not one character-building class.

That got me even more puzzled. I believe that knowing how to grow up happy is far more important than any other skill. But it seemed like society must value the benefits of math much more than happiness. Or maybe the absence of such classes meant that you can improve your math through practice, but you can't improve your happiness this way? Perhaps other parents did not need help teaching their kids how to grow up to be happy adults? That thought brought my guilt back full circle.

From then on, I started consciously cultivating a positive attitude in my child. I would bring up the need for a positive attitude at opportune moments, point out examples, role-play. It got me really thinking about the notion of happiness. I thought of myself as a regular person, mostly happy, but of course, that depended on the circumstances. To enhance my efforts to teach my daughter to be happy, I began to research happiness in the biggest data resource of all—the Internet.

I found a multitude of slogans about happiness, such as "Take chances!" "Dance in the rain!" "Laugh hard!" "Whatever you decide to do, make sure it makes you happy," and "There is light inside of you. Do not hoard it." Some of those phrases made me smile; others left me confused or just plain clueless about what they meant. Most of them did not help me understand more about happiness or how to cultivate a positive attitude.

I read a lot of specialized literature on the subject, signed up for psychology forums, listened to presentations, and attended self-help classes. The more I immersed myself in the subject of happiness, the more I came to realize several things: (1) happiness is a skill that can be practiced and mastered; and (2) kids are not the only ones who need classes on happiness—most adults do too.

We become wiser as we get older, but we don't necessarily become happier just by virtue of growing up, just as we don't miraculously start playing piano when we become adults. As with piano, kids who don't know how to practice a positive attitude become unskilled adolescents and then unskilled adults, who are left needing to teach their own kids something they have never learned themselves. And that brings me back to realization number one—happiness is a skill that requires practice.

Together with two of my friends I organized a group for our kids to discuss happiness skills. I started to post my thoughts and ideas in a blog about happiness (www.olgarythm.blogspot.com). I was invited to speak at conferences and give workshops on positive attitude.

Through my own experience, I saw that teaching kids and adults about happiness really does change their attitude toward things. I wanted to share this experience with you.

WHY THE JEWISH WAY

Sometimes the phrase "Jewish happiness" is used in a sarcastic or self-depreciating way.

"What is happiness?" one Jew asks another.

"Happiness is the life I have, of course!"

"Then what is unhappiness?"

"Unhappiness is to have such happiness . . ."

When I was younger, I associated the Jewish culture with many things: tragic history, which included slavery, persecution, the Holocaust, anti-Semitism, and the never-ending Arab-Israeli conflict; strong traditions that kept the Jewish nation true to itself and distinct from the host nations throughout thousands of years in diaspora; multifaceted talent and intelligence, which contributed to the world's literature, philosophy, art, and science. I just didn't think of Jewish culture as particularly happy.

As I discovered more about Jewish history and traditions, however, I was surprised to learn that there is a strong happiness tradition in Judaism, that Jews are among the happiest ethnicities residing in the United States, that Jews have affected and continue to affect our shared understanding of happiness enormously, and that Jewish history, culture, folklore, and religion are full of examples of zest, resilience, and love of life.

I hope this book will provide you with a changed perception of happiness the Jewish way too.

INTRODUCTION

"We are born to be happy, all of us."

—Alfred Sutro

W hat is happiness? How important is it in life? What makes us happy? These are not your everyday questions. We do not hear them discussed in the subway or by the water cooler, nor in the school yard, nor in regular family conversations. We tend to get more concerned with them when something in our lives goes wrong.

Unfortunately, a lot can go wrong. A 2011 report from the British counseling organization Relate lists the serious emotional problems an average class of thirty children will have faced by the time they reach their sixteenth birthdays:

- 10 of them will have witnessed their parents separate

- 3 will have suffered from mental health problems

- 8 will have experienced severe physical violence, sexual abuse or neglect

- 3 will be living in a step family

- 1 will have experienced the death of a parent

- 7 will report having been bullied[1]

These statistics are about kids, who have not even ventured into the adult world yet. Grown-ups have to deal with even more negative experiences.

In their struggle to stay happy in the face of minor and major problems, most people are equipped only with their inborn disposition. But while this determines the baseline of our happiness level, everyone can cultivate more joy by learning and practicing happiness skills.

Jews face their share of difficulties and tragedies just as everybody else does. However, the Gallup-Healthways Well-Being Index, which measures the components of "the good life," including happiness, ranked Jews highest in well-being among their counterparts in every other major faith in America.[2] Given this assessment, the Jewish wisdom about happiness, accumulated over thousands of years, warrants a closer look.

Happiness the Jewish Way is a practical guide to happiness illustrated with examples from the rich wisdom, stories, history, humor, and traditions of the Jewish people. The first part of the book is dedicated to clarifying the definition of happiness. It is very difficult to cultivate happiness if we do not know exactly what it is (and what it is not). The second part briefly introduces Jewish thought on happiness and it's influence on the western civilization. The third part discusses skills that people can cultivate to make themselves happier, followed by several easy and effective exercises.

Names of the Jewish terms and persons are highlighted in bold when they are mentioned in the text for the first time. They are listed in the glossary at the end of the book.

You can read *Happiness, the Jewish Way* in or out of sequence. You can practice all the exercises or just a few. Either way, the earlier you start practicing, the happier the rest of your life will be!

Congratulations on starting your journey to happiness! Mazel Tov!

DISCLAIMERS

1. This book is not a replacement for professional help.

Happiness the Jewish Way is intended for self-improvement, not treatment of emotional disorders or mental illness. If your emotional condition feels like something much more than a bad mood or a general dissatisfaction, seek a professional advice.

2. There are many paths to the same destination.

This book offers invaluable paths to a happier you. But keep in mind that it is not the one and only guide to your happiness. There is more than one valid approach to any personal quest. Even the same person may prefer one method now but like a different one better later. Jews display a great diversity in views— you may have heard that every two Jews have three opinions! Certainly no theory of happiness can provide a single true methodology that will fit all people despite their vastly different personalities, worldviews, cultures, and beliefs.

As you are reading this book, apply the parts that speak to you. Do not be alarmed if some things do not touch you or seem wrong. But keep an open mind. Remember that our worldviews are little more than habits.

3. This wisdom can be used with any belief system.

Although many of the Jewish teachings used throughout this book mention God, you can benefit from them even if you do not consider yourself a highly spiritual or a religious person. Whether you believe the world is ruled by another force, by our own will, or by chance, you can apply the same principles to the concepts discussed in this book.

4. It does not matter whether you agree or disagree with the contents of this book.

Either way, it is still beneficial to read about happiness, because it helps you understand your own attitude better. Whether you agree or disagree with the ideas in this book, it will help you to crystalize who you are and to become more self-aware and, eventually, happier.

5. Repetition is the mother of learning.

Throughout this book, some themes may be repeated or discussed multiple times from slightly different angles. Since our brains learn something better the more we repeat it, it is beneficial to go over the same things more than once. In fact, I recommend re-reading this book from time to time to refresh your mind on the concepts it discusses and to get a new boost of enthusiasm about working on happiness!

6. *Lefum tzara agra*: according to the effort is the reward [3]

Sorry, no miracles.

I wish this book worked like a magic spell: you read it and—boom!—you are happy. Although Jewish culture has its tradition of magic, this is not such an example. Instead, think of it as a map to happiness. It shows you the destination, points to the best routes and shortcuts, and offers tips, but you have to make the trip yourself.

It took each of us many years to become who we are today, so any adjustment will take time and effort. Such adjustment is in many ways similar to improving our bodies. It takes several months of diligence, effort, and persistence to get the desired results. But anyone can do it. Our inner change may not be so clearly visible. There is no scale or clothes size to give us clear indication that our efforts are working, but it does happen.

So expect great things—happiness, contentment, and joy—but don't expect them to happen by magic!

7. Use common sense.

Even water and oxygen can be toxic in excess. And any self-improvement technique can turn into self-impairment if it is taken to extremes. Follow the middle path and enjoy the journey!

PART I

WHAT IS HAPPINESS?

CHAPTER 1

INTRODUCTION TO THE SECTION

In different languages, the word for "happiness" has varying roots that shows different notions about what it meant in different cultures.

In English, the word *happy* came from Old Norse *happ* (chance, fortune). *Happy* replaced the previous term *eadig* that originated from the Old English *ead* (wealth, riches)[4].

In Russian and related Slavic languages, the word *happiness* (счастье, pronounced *schastje*) goes back to the ancient Indian *sčęstj*, meaning good destiny or part of a joint share.

The Hebrew word for happiness, *simcha*, means gladness or joy. *Naches* is a Yiddish word for pleasure, satisfaction, delight, and proud enjoyment. It derives from the verb *lanuach*—to rest, be at ease[5].

Happiness. One word, the universal human longing and the reason for most everything we do. The desire to be happy is what all humans have in common. Yet people disagree on what that means. Formulating something is half the success for understanding its true meaning. When such an important concept as happiness is left undefined, we can get confused or worse, misguided in our search for it.

How would you explain human happiness to some friendly aliens? Here are some definitions to choose from, some of them quotations, some of them common ideas, and some of them my own:

- "Happiness is a mental or emotional state of well-being characterized by positive or pleasant emotions ranging from contentment to intense joy."[6]

- Happiness is the freedom from emotions. It is the state of complete union with the Universe unobstructed by own feelings or thoughts.[7]

- Happiness is the art of living.

- Happiness is a habit.

- Happiness is attainment of goals.

- Happiness is a state of needing nothing.

- Happiness is a choice.

- Happiness is a lucky accident, it happens when it happens but it cannot be found.

- Happiness is a form of self-discipline, a contentment with your situation no matter what you have or do not have.

- Happiness is good fortune, good luck, possession of the highest advantages and blessings.

- Happiness is harmony with yourself, the feeling of completeness.

- Happiness is a state of mind based on the present, a memory, or an expectation.

- Happiness is living out one's perceived purpose or destiny as a human being.

- Happiness is (1) the goal of life and (2) a chimera.[8]

- Happiness is transitory.

- Happiness is not a reaction to some good news; it is not a moment; it is a state of being.

- Happiness is the highest good—a complete, self-worthy, self-sufficient state of life.

- Happiness is the ultimate subjective goal of human activity.

If we were to list all of the above definitions to our friendly aliens, probably all they would conclude is that happiness is a fuzzy concept. And earthlings clearly like it.

CHAPTER 2

WHICH THEORY OF HAPPINESS IS THE RIGHT ONE?

"Whatever we do [for self-improvement] is good, as long as we do no wrong."

—Rebbe **Nachman of Breslov**[9]

As we can see, people understand happiness very different-ly. Some theories argue for achieving happiness through worldly pleasures, others through detachment from the worldly matters; some through faith and religion, others through aboli-tion of religion; some through selflessness, others through self-ishness. Some theories propose specific steps to achieve happi-ness. Others insist that looking for happiness prevents us from getting it altogether.

All in all, these approaches are rather contradictory. Still, each theory is confirmed by supporting information and has been claimed to work for some, making all of them valid.

This diversity, as frustrating as it may be for not offering a clear answer, makes sense. There are so many people, and we all are so very unique. We come from societies with different cultures, traditions, and beliefs. Even within the same culture, each person has a unique background and upbringing. On top of all this social diversity, we all have different inclinations and temperaments.

To each his own. Each of us, including the most respected theorists on happiness, is limited by his or her own experiences and beliefs. And since we perceive all information through the lens of our worldview, we tend to like and choose theories that align with our existing opinions and beliefs and disregard or disagree with the rest. Understanding that, Jewish sages encourage telling the **Passover** story about the liberation from Egyptian slavery in different ways to ensure it is understood by four different kinds of people.

Besides, practicing happiness is an art. In the same way that two chefs who use the same recipe will not end up with exactly the same cakes, or two students of the same teacher will not develop the same handwriting, our happiness will be unique even when we follow the same set of instructions as others.

Given the abundance of opinions, which happiness theory is the right one? Which one should you study and practice, and which can you disregard? The answer is there is no theory that is right for everyone. There cannot be a universal instruction on how to be happier that will fit everyone or work without fail. Each person will connect with a different teaching, use dissimilar tools to achieve the goal of happiness, and progress at his or her own pace. The right theory for each one of us is the one that is working.

Still, the **Lubavitcher Rebbe**, Menachem Mendel Schneerson, taught that "it is a **mitzvah** to direct someone onto the path where he belongs."[10] Therefore, in this book I offer an approach inspired by Jewish wisdom that may lead you onto your path to happiness.

CHAPTER 3

THE GOOD, THE GREAT AND THE AWESOME: THE BENEFITS OF HAPPINESS

Being happy is terrific. In order to be happy, we usually work on improving our life circumstances because we are used to thinking that the good life leads to happiness. But it works the other way around as well: being happy first actually helps us to achieve our other goals and, in turn, leads to the good life.

By redirecting our efforts to mastering happiness in ways described in the following chapters, we can automatically achieve many other enjoyable benefits:

LOOKING GOOD

Probably the most obvious benefit of being happy is the instant improvement in appearance. Whether it is a radiant smile, a cheerful light in the eyes, or just an expression of calm and contentment, happiness brings visible changes to facial features and posture. We look younger, more confident, and more beautiful when we smile and hold our heads high.

BECOMING A BETTER VERSION OF OURSELVES

When we are happy, we are better people: we are kinder, more active, and even wiser. Rabbi **Shloma Majeski** writes, "When a person is happy, he stands above all his personal limitations and weaknesses. He can do things that he ordinarily could not do. He can forgive his worst enemy. His joy generates inner energy that breaks through and shatters any barrier that stands in his way."[11]

IMPROVED RELATIONSHIPS

Happiness attracts people like a magnet: happy people are more sociable and well liked, enjoy stronger friendships, and have more social support.[12]

When it comes to our personal lives, many of us expect happiness to ensue if and when we find the right partner. Unfortunately, when we rely on another for our happiness, we are bound to be disappointed. However, when we take charge of our own happiness, we become more self-reliant, enjoy marriages more, and have fewer divorces.[13]

HIGHER PRODUCTIVITY

Happiness may help us realize our dreams of prosperity. Studies find that happiness results in better productivity at home and work. Happy children make better students, and happy adults display greater creativity and may produce higher income.[14]

RESILIENCE

Happiness helps us deal with life's challenges. Happy children and adults are optimistic and are more likely to exhibit greater self-control and have better coping skills.[15] They are less prone to depression and anxiety.[16]

IMPROVED PHYSICAL HEALTH AND LONGEVITY

The Hebrew Bible states, "A happy heart is good medicine."[17] In the twelfth century, **Moses Maimonides** elaborated: "Emotional experiences produce distinct changes in the body. . . . Emotions also have an effect on the circulation of the blood and the functioning of one's organs. . . . They affect the body and they in turn are affected by the constitution of the body."[18]

The strong connection between our mind and body is becoming more evident due to medical research. Our feelings, thoughts, and emotions trigger the release of hormones by glands in the brain. With these chemicals the mind affects nearly every cell in our body and, thus, our physical health: positive thoughts and emotions promote balance and health, whereas negative emotions may lead to illness. In fact, positive emotions are so powerful that they can protect us from diseases that range from the common cold to cancer.[19] Happier people have stronger immune systems and a lower risk of stroke and heart disease,[20] and they are more fit and energetic.[21] These are benefits that will continue to pay off for a long time, as happy people are more likely to live longer.[22]

SPIRITUALITY

Jews believe that joy has tremendous spiritual power. The **Baal Shem Tov**, founder of **Hasidism**, taught that it is essential to be joyful to make spiritual progress[23] and that joy draws us closer to God.[24]

Additionally, Jews believe that we attract more of what we are, and so happiness leads to more blessings. The **Zohar**, a seminal book of **Kabbalah** says, "The upper world provides in accordance with the state below. If the state is joyous, then, correspondingly, abundance flows from above; but when the state below is one of sadness, then correspondingly, the flow of blessing is constricted."[25] When we are happy, we attract goodness, positively affecting our situations, as illustrated by a story about Rebbe **Sholom Dovber Schneersohn.**

> One time, a man came to Rebbe Schneersohn. The man cried and asked the Rebbe for a blessing to help with his problem. But the problem was so grave that the Rebbe said that even he could not do anything to improve the situation. This happened in the middle of a celebration for **Simchat Torah**, a festive Jewish holiday. The man stayed and little by little he could not help but get involved in the celebration, slowly getting into dancing and singing (which, by the way, are mitzvot—the plural of mitzvah—on Simchat Torah). Afterward, the Rebbe unexpectedly called the man and blessed him. He explained to the delighted but surprised man that his situation was so serious that nothing could have helped . . . except the power of joy.[26]

IMPROVING SOCIETY

Our happiness benefits not only us personally but also society at large. On a social level, happy people of all ages are more cooperative and less antagonistic, resulting in less bullying at school and less negativity in the workplace. Happier individuals provide stronger social and emotional support to their friends. Happy adults have better family dynamics, which benefits their spouses and leads to happier, more well-adjusted children.

Happiness positively affects national economics as well. Happier children perform better at school, and happier adults perform better at work,[27] improving the well-being of society. In addition, as I have already discussed, happier people are healthier, which means they use fewer sick days and contribute to driving the overall cost of healthcare down.

Happier people are also likely to get directly involved in helping others. They donate money to charity and volunteer.[28]

Moreover, happiness is contagious. People tend to get in a better mood when they are in the company of happy people.

* * *

As we can see, happiness does not merely feel good. It tends to improve our impact on the world, as well as our own appearance, creativity, productivity, marriages, friendships, resilience, health, and longevity. So instead of focusing on improving our circumstances first, let's focus on being happy first—it will improve not only our moods, but our lives too.

CHAPTER 4

OUR HAPPINESS DELUSIONS (OR WHY HAPPINESS DOES NOT MAKE US HAPPY)

Where do we find a little, at least a little—
Where do we find some happiness?

People, they try hard by day and by night.
To make just as much as they can,
Each one of them thinks.
They run and they run
All around and around.

No matter what they have—
It's never enough.
People are jealous of everyone else,
But I ask just one thing from God:
Where do we find a little luck?

—"Vu Nemt Men A Bissele Mazl?"
(Where Do We Find a Little Luck?),
a Yiddish song,
attributed to Ben Zion Wittler, popularized by Mike Burstyn

Before we go any further, it is crucial to define the notion of happiness. To pursue it, we need to know what we think it is, because we seek happiness according to the definition of it that we accept. A Jew who believes that happiness is in unity with God will study the **Torah**. Someone who believes that happiness is in financial success will study business instead. And someone else for whom happiness is in simple pleasures may just eat some chocolate. If we don't define what happiness is, how will we know what to do to get it?

There is a lot of disagreement between philosophers on how to achieve the state of happiness. And of course a concept as abstract as happiness will evoke different feelings and thoughts in each of us. So what do you picture when you think "happiness"? We know everyone will think of something different, because we are all unique.

But philosopher Alan Watts points out a commonality in our thoughts: "We seldom realize that our private thoughts and emotions are not actually our own. For we think in terms of languages and images which we did not invent, but which were given to us by our society."[29]

It is undeniable that even our most private thoughts are at least partially (sometimes majorly) affected by our culture and the society we live in. That includes our idea of happiness. The conventional notions, the generally accepted priorities, and the images of happy people in the media enter our subconscious, unavoidably defining happiness for us.

There are several concepts that modern Western culture strongly identifies with happiness. One is enjoying the life pleasures and with feeling good. Another is that there are certain conditions that lead to happiness or, as I call them, happiness prerequisites. The most popular "happiness prerequisites" is success, which is usually associated with wealth (and the comfort it can buy), career and power, love, family, children, and popularity (via fame, beauty, achievements, etc.). Although most people wouldn't say that happiness *is* wealth or popularity, these goals are seen as so desirable that somewhere in our brains they become strongly associated with happiness, and most of us think of them immediately when we dream about it. Other slightly less common but still prevalent happiness prerequisite is closeness to nature. It's also a common belief that we need to wait for the right circumstances for happiness: a lucky break, a fast lane, a great bargain, a fortuitous meeting, the right person. Additionally, it is often understood that happiness should be deserved, as we believe it is bestowed on good, hard-working people.

We spend our lives in pursuit of all these factors. And yet many people feel that they still are not quite happy. Why is that? Let's briefly examine our common beliefs and see which ones are really just happiness delusions.

HAPPINESS AND PLEASURE

Our society tends to define happiness as having pleasurable experiences.[30] By the same token, we believe that whatever brings us pleasure makes us happy. It seems that we think pleasures are the stepping stones to happiness, and we end up chasing pleasures believing that we are looking for happiness.

Let's consider some everyday examples of what might bring us pleasure. Eating a satisfying meal is a pleasure; so is watching a good movie or entering an air-conditioned building on a hot day.

But do these things give us lasting, authentic happiness?

The Dalai Lama writes that pleasure is simply replacing one kind of suffering with another.[31] For example, after we've been standing for a long time, sitting is a pleasure. But after a while we will start feeling uncomfortable and want to stand up and move around. When we are hungry, to eat is a pleasure indeed. But if we keep eating past the point of fullness, it will become unpleasant. When hot, we derive pleasure from cooling down. But eventually we get cold and yearn for warmth. The pleasures we crave are actually the very beginnings of suffering of one kind or another and as such cannot be sustained for a long time. That is one difference between pleasure and happiness.

The other difference is that pleasure mostly comes from outside sources. It comes from food, the climate, money, friends, technology, and so on. And these only bring us pleasure in the moment when we are experiencing them. As soon as we don't get the next scheduled meal, or we don't have enough money, or the friends leave, the pleasure rapidly subsides.

That is the distinction between pleasure and happiness: pleasure is subject to change according to extraneous conditions, is transitory, and is more physical in nature than happiness. Happiness is a sustainable, lasting psychological state that comes from our intrinsic frame of mind.

In no way do I want to devalue pleasure. Enjoying life is great! Let's just keep in mind that pleasure is not the exact same thing as happiness.

HAPPINESS PREREQUISITE: SUCCESS

"Try not to become a man of success, but rather try to become a man of value."

—Albert Einstein

The feeling of achieving success is wonderful and rewarding! We associate success with happiness to such an extent that they are listed as synonyms by Dictionary.com.[32] Our society loves success and cheers for it. And who does our society deem successful? People who have achieved a lot in life, those who are powerful, affluent, and famous. Who do we consider most successful? Whoever has achieved more. Thus, "A-list" celebrities are more successful than "B-listers," the owner of a restaurant chain is more successful than an owner of a single restaurant, and the first-place winner is the only successful athlete in the race.

This sense of competition thwarts the happiness we get from our achievements. If you have earned two million dollars, you are still not as successful as your neighbor who has earned four million, and if you have published one book, you are not as successful as an author who has published five. **Irving Berlin**, an American composer and lyricist of Russian-Jewish origin, noted, "The toughest thing about being a success is that you've got to keep on being a success."

We do not have much tolerance for any outcomes other than our traditional ideas of success—anything else we label as failure. It is obvious that we all want to achieve success, and we teach our kids to want the same. In cities like New York, even toddlers are expected to compete with each other on exams and interviews for preschools. Older kids are expected to make it onto teams and win competitions. Teenagers have to deal with increasing parents' expectations, the process of college admissions as well as peer pressure. Suddenly they need to be popular and involved in romantic relationships, or else they are made to feel like failures. Gradually they grow into adults caught up in the race for success, believing that the winners will achieve contentment and happiness.

But when there is no moderation, any good thing starts to turn into something else. When our actions are judged by the world in terms of success or failure, the joy of working for our goals turns into fear of failing, healthy incentives transform into sickening stress, and excitement becomes anxiety. Instead of ending up happy, many end up taking antianxiety medications.

It is not bad at all that society preaches and praises success. The problem is that it insists on a very particular type of success. Another problem is that it does not preach the idea that any level of success is ever enough. **Henry Kissinger**, a German-born Jew and a recipient of the Nobel Peace Prize, lamented, "Each success only buys an admission ticket to a more difficult problem."[33]

There are two kinds of success. There is a commonly accepted type of success, a vague standard by which we measure each other's achievements. It is judged by visible outcomes and the bottom line, such as financial stability, career growth, and celebrity status, without paying close attention to how they were achieved. This outward prosperity is the type of success our society recognizes.

The other type of success is based on the process rather than the result. It acknowledges our efforts regardless of the final outcome or what others think, neither of which are entirely within our control. This type of success is the internal satisfaction we feel as a result of the effort we put into working toward a goal, and it is often invisible to others. This success if very relative and cannot be compared to the success of others. For some, success is winning gold in the Olympic Games. For others, it is making it to the Olympics. And for others still, success is being able to walk across a room. In the eyes of the people who overcome hardships to achieve these successes, none of them are less successful than any of the others.

Jewish thought insists that becoming a good and happy person is a bigger success than getting high marks on a test.[34] It advises us to encourage children to become the best version of themselves, not just chase someone else's idea of success. As a Hasidic proverb puts it, "If your child has a talent to be a baker, don't ask him to be a doctor."[35]

When we reach for goals that are meaningful for us and do not let the world judge whether our outcomes are successes or failures, that is the success that matters the most and leads to genuine happiness.

HAPPINESS PREREQUISITE: MONEY

You gotta have a little mazel.
Mazel means good luck,
'Cause with a little mazel
You always make a buck.

—"Mazel," Yiddish jazz song

Money, undoubtedly, is a very powerful and desirable object in our society and for each of us individually. It shapes our lives. We choose careers because of it. We spend most of our precious waking hours working instead of doing something else that we may enjoy more because of it. Money grants unbelievable opportunities, inspires hideous crimes, and spurs amazing scientific and artistic achievements. Money is one of the major engines of our world, whether we like it or not.

And despite the popular saying that money can't buy happiness, the majority of us tie money closely to our happiness levels. Our consumerist culture nurtures the idea of being able to buy some happiness with money. It is in the news, ads, popular songs, and movies. People on game shows always jump up and down with exaggerated joy when they win cash (or a dining set). The word "happiness" is plastered across marketing campaigns for cars, shampoos, and soft drinks. And these campaigns are targeted not only at adults, but at kids too. They distort and devalue the true meaning of happiness. They also contribute to our confusing happiness and pleasure.

In fairness, although money can't really buy happiness, it can procure conditions that are conductive to happiness: it can give us a sense of financial security, of indulgence, of the ability to help others, ability to be free to do what we choose and not toil at a job we do not enjoy. Money grants us opportunities to learn what makes us happy and the ability to do it.

But even if we have it, we can still feel dissatisfied, like the saying goes, some complain that their soup is too watery, others complain that their diamonds are too small. So money can help with our levels of happiness, but it does not guarantee it. Prosperity can bring different kinds of problems with it, and researchers say that some of the richest countries have the highest rates of depression.[36] A study that compared tenth-grade students from affluent suburban families with students from low-income inner-city families reported significantly higher levels of anxiety and greater depression among the affluent youth. It also reported significantly higher use of substances such as tobacco, alcohol, marijuana, and other illicit drugs among the affluent students compared to the inner-city students.[37]

Moreover, money has the ability to make us unhappy. Just think about investing and managing money, the fear of the potential of losing it because of either our own mistakes or the market, the long hours and sleepless nights the rich put into planning and worrying about competition, preserving capital, growing capital, and so on. What a headache! **Ethics of our Fathers,** Jewish ethical teachings also called *Pirkei Avot* confirms, "More possessions, more worry."[38]

Money also can lead to excessive permissiveness. And once we dispense with moderation, the many bad habits available to us can turn into addictions and into broken lives. If they didn't have so much money, a lot of good people would not get into a lot of trouble.

So the same powerful object—money—may make us happy, make us unhappy, or have no impact on our happiness levels. As Ayn Rand summed it up, "Money is only a tool. It will take you wherever you wish, but it will not replace you as the driver."[39]

HAPPINESS PREREQUESITE: CHILDREN

"Kinder brengen glik, kinder brengen umglik."

(Children bring good fortune, children bring misfortune.)

—A Yiddish proverb

Parenthood and children are sacred topics in the wider discussion about happiness. Modern society has a widespread and strong emphasis on parenthood as one of the most important components of happiness. So when at times kids evoke the opposite feeling in us, we may feel inadequate and guilty.

Certainly children make us happy. They are our continuation, our legacies, our pride and joy, the most important work of our lives. They bring meaning to our lives, make us feel fulfilled. They give us love and admiration. They are among the closest people to us. Kids brighten our days with their wonder, their smiles, and their achievements.

But they also make us miserable, angry, and frustrated. Parenthood is a package deal. It does not feel a lot like happiness when our children defy us, disrespect us, forget to call, never clean their rooms—the list goes on and on. **Barbara Walters** once said, "Motherhood is tough. If you just want a wonderful little creature to love, you can get a puppy."

Some kids are more difficult than others; some have personality traits we do not like; some are missing traits we would like; some have physical or mental disabilities that are challenging for their parents. And that is on top of the baseline stress of worrying about their future and well-being.

Contrary to our deeply ingrained beliefs, research shows that parents are less happy overall than childless couples, and children are one of the top reasons for marital dissatisfaction.[40] Parents are more likely to be depressed, suffer from stress and anxiety, and experience more dissatisfaction with their life in general than people without children. In fact, **Daniel Gilbert**, a professor of psychology at Harvard University, states that when couples have children, happiness levels plummet. Couples only recover their blissful existence once their offspring have left the nest.[41]

It is indisputable that parenthood leads to lots of emotions in all parents (both positive and negative). Children have the power to make us happy, but they do not necessarily do so. If people do not have children, their lives are not devoid of meaning and happiness (although it may feel this way to some). And the fact that people have children does not automatically indicate that they are happy and their lives are meaningful (although it may feel this way to some).

Ultimately, our true happiness does not depend on others. Not even such important people as our children, husbands and wives, or friends. True happiness depends on us: our attitude toward life and everything in it. Nothing can make us happy (or miserable) except ourselves, not even our kids.

HAPPINESS PREREQUISITE: NATURE

"Only then does one feel that all is as it should be and that God wishes to see people happy, amidst the simple beauty of nature."

—Anne Frank

Nature is another thing that is commonly regarded as happiness inducing, although our culture emphasizes it less than money or success. We are part of nature, and it feels good to be one with it. Magnificent, awe-inspiring views, a cute kitten, or just warm sunshine on our faces all undoubtedly induce feelings of harmony, spirituality, and happiness.

But nature is also capable of inducing other feelings. We get annoyed when we get bitten by a mosquito, uncomfortable when it's hot and humid, depressed when it's cold and gloomy, and scared when we're faced with natural disasters. Somewhat ironically, humans have done a lot to distance themselves from nature in order to gain some comfort and happiness.

Nature, therefore, is not a source for our unconditional happiness. Once again, the feeling of happiness comes from our own mindset our attitude toward the things around us. As Horace Friess, author and philosophy professor, said, "All seasons are beautiful for the person who carries happiness within."

WAITING FOR A LUCKY BREAK

It practically goes without saying that normally we are happy when all is well. When things do not go right, what reasonable person feels happy?

Overall, our moods are justified by the way our day is going. So if our bus arrives as soon as we come to the station, the cafeteria carries our favorite kind of cake, or we get the best tickets for a great concert, then we probably find ourselves in a good mood.

On the other hand, if we notice a scratch on our car, get stuck in traffic jam, or learn that our nosy neighbor is talking about us behind our back, it's natural for our mood to sour, right? Anyone who still feels happy under unpleasant circumstances or for no good reason seems eccentric at best, bizarre at worst.

Since we cannot control such circumstances, we may think that our happiness is out of our own control and at the complete mercy of the capricious fate. But in fact, people have the ability to identify and manage emotions regardless of circumstances. Jewish American psychologist **Peter Salovey**, along with John D. Mayer, called this emotional intelligence.[42]

Nothing and no one can spoil our mood without our consent. And, as was taught by Rebbe **Naftali of Ropshitz,** we don't need a special reason to be happy.[43] We do not control our circumstances, but we can control our emotions. Our reaction to life circumstances is our own responsibility.

DESERVING HAPPINESS

Some believe that happiness must be earned. Some religious leaders teach that people have to pass some life tests to be rewarded with a good and happy life (or afterlife). The theory of karma holds that we may be paying for some digressions from past lives and have to clear that bad karma by doing good deeds. And some people believe they must earn approval in the eyes of society before they permit themselves to be happy.

The feeling of not being good enough to have a happy life may lead to guilt and self-depreciation. If we tell ourselves that we do not deserve happiness, if we doubt ourselves, then we are the ones who preclude it, who make it harder for us to feel happy. We dig a bigger hole by feeling bad about feeling bad.

THE PURSUIT OF HAPPINESS

The Founding Fathers of the United States of America listed the pursuit of happiness as one of the unalienable human rights, along with life and liberty. The US government was instituted in the way that was believed to be best able to attain safety and happiness for its citizens.[44]

We spend our lives in pursuit of happiness. Mostly we pursue it by trying to attain the dreams suggested by our society and upbringing. Sometimes we may disagree with certain common happiness "prerequisites." We may believe that the key to our happiness lies in different things. So we go in a different direction according to our personal understanding of happiness.

More often than not, we do achieve our goals to varying degrees. We become financially secure; hold a job; have a family, kids, and friends; and spend time in nature. But as we saw, any of these factors may or may not make us happy; none of them guarantees our happiness.

Wealth, success, love, and beauty are all good goals to strive for. But the pursuit of happiness cultivated by our culture implies that happiness comes from these and other external sources. We believe they have the power to make us happier. If only I had more money . . . if only I met my soul mate . . . if only my kids listened to me . . . then I would be happy for sure.

The pursuit of happiness does not yield the desired results, because it connects happiness to the circumstances of our lives. In reality, as psychologist and author **Martin Seligman** found, externalities such as weather, money, health, marriage, and religion together account for no more than 15 percent of the variance in life satisfaction,[45] and some say it's even less.

... AND THEY LIVED HAPPILY EVER AFTER

Many fairy tales, movies, books, and success stories finish with a happy ending: after much struggle, the characters finally achieve their goals, find true love, outsmart their enemies, attain great fortunes, or win the war and come back home to start a life of peace and harmony.

This pattern gets ingrained into our brains from the childhood. We tend not to look beyond the end of the story. We just sort of assume that Cinderella was always joyous at the palace with the prince, that Elsa from *Frozen* completely accepted herself and her amazing but dangerous ability to command ice, and that Harry

Potter felt happy settling down for family life.

As we grow up, the childhood belief in the everlasting happiness of our favorite characters becomes an assumption that, once we achieve happiness, it will stay with us forever. Interestingly, we do not think this way about many other things vital to our lives. We do not believe that one big breath will last us forever. We do not become disappointed that one shower does not last us a lifetime. We do not mind eating and sleeping daily to sustain ourselves. We would never expect a fairy tale to end with "and after they had the best feast of their lives, they were sated ever after." But for some reason we balk when we are faced with the idea that we need to put in a daily effort in order to sustain our happiness.

The result is that, while there is an abundance of cooking classes that teach creative ways to prepare our daily meals, there are very few happiness classes that teach how to sustain joy on a daily basis long after our dreams come true.

THE DEFINITION OF HAPPINESS

The foolish man seeks happiness in the distance;
The wise grows it under his feet.

—James Oppenheim

As it turns out, the definition of happiness prevalent in our society is misleading, because it identifies happiness with specific objects or milestones, and we begin thinking they are "happiness." And we spend a lifetime working to achieve these milestones in hopes of becoming happier.

It may actually be easier to think that happiness is "out there" to be searched and struggled for rather than to know that it is contained within us. We rarely accept that our own thinking and habits are the cause of our happiness or misery. It takes more strength and courage to acknowledge that we are the ones responsible, not anyone or anything else. Besides, "pursuit of happiness" sounds nobler, more romantic, and more inspiring than just "contentment".

Jewish mystics teach that we can never find permanent happiness in impermanent worldly pleasures. Instead, we will be forever thrown back and forth between gratification and dissatisfaction in this ever-changing world. The ultimate source of joy and happiness lies within us, and it is constant and immune to any worldly changes.[46] That is the kind of joy we should tap into.

Happiness is not success, money, or children. Happiness is our reaction to all of these things happening or not happening. Lasting happiness is dispositional rather than situational. That means that it takes residence in our souls when we cultivate happiness inside ourselves and learn to be happy regardless of whoever or whatever is around us.

* * *

Now that we've defined what happiness is and where it comes from, the next step is cultivating it by practicing simple skills like the ones listed in this book. Do not get sidetracked by conventional ideas about happiness. In time you will notice how the world around you changes. And then you will realize it is not the world around you that has changed. The world is its old self, as it will always be. The change is coming from you! You have the power to feel happy anytime, anywhere, in any situation!

CHAPTER 5

HAPPINESS PARADOXES

Sometimes, happiness requires us to embrace and unite apparent contradictions. For example, we are born predisposed to a certain level of happiness, but we may change our level of happiness anyway. To be happier we should be mindful but not pay too much attention to details, to want more and have goals in life but also be content with what we have, to have relationships with others but be self-sufficient. Below are some additional examples of the seeming contradictions in our quest for happiness.

WORKING TOO HARD TO ACHIEVE HAPPINESS MAY IMPEDE IT

A very strong desire to be happy can prevent us from actually being happy. Striving for happiness sometimes drives it further out of reach. Instead of struggling in pursuit of happiness, we have to learn to just let ourselves be happy.

For some of us, thinking about our happiness levels only brings us down and sours our mood. We stress ourselves out too much over not being as happy as we want, and that makes us even less happy with ourselves. If you feel you are that person, then for you, the way to uncover happiness is not to concentrate on the pursuit of it too much, not to stress or fret about it.

For others, thinking about happiness and formulating what it means to them opens their eyes to it and helps them focus on the right priorities in life. If you are that person, then by all means, contemplate happiness and the best way to cultivate it in your soul.

OVERDOSING ON "HAPPINESS"

There has been an increase of interest in happiness in recent years. On one side, the benefit of this is that the newly founded science of positive psychology is making strides in bringing attention to the importance of happiness. On another side, the drawback is that the entertainment and advertising industries now also exploit the concept of happiness more than ever. Too often we see and hear the word "happiness" used to describe corny situations or to sell products. The more we see happiness portrayed in a superficial way in the media, the more its true meaning gets diluted. So we should take into consideration the advances in the study of happiness but try to avoid buying into the way happiness is portrayed in the media.

VARIETY IS THE SPICE OF LIFE

Humans have a periodic need to change emotional states. People are known to do unnecessary and even dangerous things to experience more intense emotions than they do in their day-to-day life. Some endanger themselves or take recreational drugs. Most of us turn to art, such as music, theater, and movies, for this additional burst of emotions. So even as we strive to be content and happy, sometimes we may find ourselves discontent with the continuous contentment and unhappy even with happiness.

Do these contradictions make happiness seem too complicated? Here is another paradox: being happy is really rather easy.

CHAPTER 6

FOUR SECRETS OF HAPPINESS

1. IT'S ALWAYS RIGHT THERE

Have you ever been to a large airport where there is a moving walkway in the middle of a long corridor, and some people prefer to ride it while others walk next to it in the same direction? Happiness is like that moving walkway, running alongside us all the time, whether we experience a big change, no change, pleasant moments, or stressful circumstances.

The possibility of being happier is always there. All we have to do is allow ourselves to step into the "happiness lane." To change our lane, we just have to start noticing good things and not focus too much on the bad. Once we do this, we will continue to go in the same direction, but the experience will be different.

2. HAPPINESS FLOWS FROM THE INSIDE OUT

We go through life letting the circumstances of our days determine the level of our happiness or dejection, joy or frustration. We react to things that happen to us, to the way others treat us, to the daily shifts in our luck.

In fact, no people, possessions, or events hold the key to our happiness. Lasting, sustainable happiness does not flow into us from the outside. Moreover, it does not result from what we do. Happiness comes from our souls, from deep inside of us: our perception, attitude, beliefs, and mental habits.

Gerald Epstein, a psychiatrist, founder of The American Institute for Mental Imagery, and author, has said, "We always seem to think that our circumstances determine our inner state. Yet we are in charge of our inner state and have the capacity to create our own circumstances. Our beliefs create our experiences, rather than the other way around".[47]

3. WE CAN ONLY CHANGE ONE PERSON

"No one's happiness but my own is in my power to achieve or to destroy."

—Ayn Rand, *Atlas Shrugged*

Here is one of the most important things to understand in our search for happiness: despite our lifelong wishes and efforts, we cannot control what happens to us or change others. There's a Yiddish proverb that goes, *"Nit mit shelten un nit mit lachen ken men di velt ibermachen,"* which means "Neither with curses nor with laughter can you change the world." We do not know what will happen in a year, in a week, or even tomorrow. And we cannot control how other people, even those closest to us, behave. If other people change, it is not because we made them but because they wished to themselves.

Still, we wish, pray, plan, work, expect our families to behave a certain way, and try to direct our lives onto the paths we want them to take. We spend years trying our best to change our lives and the lives of others. But the secret is that we should change ourselves. In fact, that is the only thing we *can* change. We are only in complete charge of our own thoughts, words, and actions. We cannot change how others behave, but we can change our own behavior. And when we change ourselves, we change the whole situation.

> Rabbi **Simcha Bunim**, a Hasidic leader in Poland, shared that when he was young and ambitious, he set out to reform the world. After years he realized he couldn't do it, so he resolved to change just his community. As time went on, he realized that changing a community was beyond his grasp, and he decided to concentrate on improving his family. As he got older and wiser, he saw that he could not change even his family. So he finally decided that he could only change himself. But once he had changed himself, it affected and changed his family too. And when his family had changed, his community changed, and as his community changed, the world changed as well.[48]

The secret of happiness is to stop trying to control what we can't and instead focus on controlling the only person we can.

4. HAPPINESS IS A HABIT

Our happiness depends a lot on how we are used to reacting to situations we are presented with. Do we usually focus on the negatives, or do we enjoy the positive aspects of things? Do we appreciate little things or tend not to notice them? We think happiness is a part of our personality that we are born with. But it is in large part a habit. Our behavior and attitude are matters of habit in many facets of our lives, and practicing happiness is one habit we can cultivate.

Some people describe their approach to happiness as similar to the habit of flossing—something you have to practice daily in order to reap desired benefits.[49] So let's get in habit of being happy.

CHAPTER 7

WHAT HAPPINESS IS MADE OF

In order to know what we have to do to be happier, let's consider what happiness is made of. Just as buildings are made of blocks and not of little buildings, happiness too is made of other components.

To understand why happiness is not made of just happy occasions, let's use the analogy of trees. Trees don't grow out of trees. They need roots, which don't look anything like the trees we see above the ground. The roots are hidden inside the soil and nourish every little leaf and flower above. Without the roots, trees would not exist.

Similarly, the feelings of lasting elation, joy, delight, and bliss that we call "happiness" do not produce themselves. These feelings are manifestations of something deeper, something more fundamental and important. Something that makes these feelings of happiness possible.

The way to be happy is to find out what that thing is and to cultivate it.

Let's continue with the tree analogy. As long as we have the necessary roots, happiness will manifest itself, but it will do so differently for different people. There are hundreds kinds of trees and as many ways that happiness looks and feels to us. Trees grow in different kinds of terrain, not only fertile soil. The stronger the roots, the more beautiful, healthy, strong, and grand the trees are. And the more greenery it produces, the more vital oxygen a tree generates for those around it. Similarly, happiness can be found in any circumstances, and happy individuals spread positive energy to everyone around them.

So what makes happiness possible? What are the very roots without which it does not flourish? They are **contentment** and **moderation.** These are the building blocks, the things below the surface that keep us grounded and happy.

Contentment to enjoy what we have or don't have. Moderation to regulate any excess or shortage in our actions, emotions, desires, and in our contentment.

When we think of happiness, we may not think about contentment and moderation. But when we have them at the core of our being, happiness will sprout and grow into something vital, beautiful, and strong.

CHAPTER 8

CONTENTMENT AND MODERATION: THE BUILDING BLOCKS OF HAPPINESS

"Who is rich? The one who is happy with his portion."

—*Pirkei Avot* 4:1

"The best path lies midway."

—**Judah Bar Ilai**

Once upon a time, a king's son became ill from sadness and depression. The king sought out many doctors, but none of them were able to cure the prince until one doctor assured the king that the boy would be cured if he wore the shirt of a happy man.

The king himself was not happy because of the problems he had in his kingdom and in his family. He sent his servants to the wealthiest men who lived in big mansions, thinking that they certainly must be happy. But they told the servants that they were not happy as they had worries, anxieties, and unfulfilled desires in their lives. The king sent the servants to other successful men, traders and builders, but the servants returned with the same answer. Finally they found a shepherd, who told them that, yes, he is truly content with his lot and happy. But when they asked him for his shirt, he opened his jacket and showed them that he did not have one.[50]

The root of happiness, and its main ingredient, is *contentment*—the state of mental or emotional satisfaction free from stress, anxiety, fear, worry, or anger. This meaning can be seen in the Hebrew phrase for contentment, *sameach b'chelko*, which literally means "happy with one's lot." This Jewish concept of contentment encourages us to accept and enjoy the present circumstances as they are and ourselves as we are. Contentment is the knowledge that life is good as it is and nothing is lacking for us to be happy today. A traditional prayer recited three times a day includes the words: "Happy are they who dwell in Your house" (Psalms 84:5). Judaism repeatedly reminds us that we can be happy by simply being in the world.

Throughout recorded history, a big part of humanity has seemed generally disgruntled with most everything in life. The discontented part of mankind finds itself in constant struggle for a better life and at war with others over land, power, resources, religious differences, and so on. This dissatisfaction propels the progress of mankind, but it also keeps us from our individual happiness.

We live in a culture that does not promote contentment; in fact, it scorns it. We are conditioned to struggle for success and to believe that what we have is never enough. It seems strange not to want to have bigger and better things in life, doesn't it? The struggle to amass more becomes, in essence, a rat race—a competitive, unremitting, and exhausting routine. But if we are not happy now with what we already have, we will probably not be happy after we get whatever we want. We may still experience bursts of joy when something goes exceptionally well. But these bursts do not last for a long time; they are transient feelings of pleasure, not enduring state of happiness.

If we are not content with our lots or ourselves, we cannot be happy. However, if we take the notion of contentment to the extreme, what is to prevent us from lying in dirt under the sky, wanting nothing and doing nothing?[51] Just as we may overdo the drive to succeed to ridiculous and sometimes dangerous levels, so we may overdo our efforts to be content in the pursuit of happiness. There is a fine line between being content and apathetic.

That's where the second component of happiness, *moderation*, comes in. Moderation is a cornerstone principle of Jewish living.[52] Moderation means striking the right balance, the golden mean, the happy medium, in every aspect of life, embracing the world passionately, but also exercising self-discipline. Maimonides calls it *kav ha-emtza*, or the middle path. He teaches that we should follow the middle path in all qualities known to man, not veering to either extreme.[53]

Jewish tradition prescribes moderation in every aspect of life. For starters, it affirms that humans are godlike because we have free will, but it also limits our behavior with a set of rules – commandments. It requires us to be neither too generous nor too cheap, neither too kind nor too strict. Similarly, we should keep the desire to succeed strong enough to spur us on but not so strong that it gets in the way of our happiness.

How to achieve moderation? Rabbi Simcha Bunim famously taught that everyone must carry two notes with them. When feeling lowly, depressed, discouraged, or disconsolate, one should reach into the right pocket and find the words "For my sake was the world created." But when feeling overly self-important, one should reach into the left pocket and find the words "I am but dust and ashes."[54]

Maimonides believed that, if we have an extreme quality, we should work on behaving in a way that is the opposite extreme. So if we are very stingy, we should work on being very generous. One extreme will uproot the other, and the person will be able to follow the middle path.[55]

We will discuss many ways to achieve contentment and moderation in this book. Contentment with our world, our lives, and ourselves gives way to positive emotions, joy, and serenity. Moderation ensures the right balance for everything. It allows us to have goals in life to aspire to while also being content with the present. Contentment and moderation are the biggest building blocks of happiness, the foundation underlying all the other happiness skills, such as self-esteem, gratitude, and mindfulness.

PART II

THE JEWISH WAY

CHAPTER 9

INTRODUCTION TO THE SECTION

"It is a great mitzvah to be happy all the time."

—Rebbe Nachman of Breslov, *Likutei Moharan* 2:24

The influence of the Jewish people on Western civilization is enormous. From the **Tanakh**, or the Old Testament, which introduced monotheism and became the foundation of Judeo-Christian civilization, to Ayn Rand, who founded objectivism, a philosophical system that had a profound impact on the Republican Party, Jewish thought is the source of influential values and views on many subjects, including human happiness. We will explore some of these views in this section.

According to Jewish mystics, happiness is not just an important aspect of Jewish teachings, but one of our main goals as humans. Enjoying life and being happy are not only desirable but also essential.

Throughout this book I will use religious and secular Jewish texts, tales, songs, and humor to illustrate ways of cultivating a happy and joyous living. These valuable lessons offered in Judaism will benefit you in the journey toward happiness regardless of your ethnicity or faith status.

CHAPTER 10

JUDAISM ON HAPPINESS

"Always remember: Joy is not merely incidental to your spiritual quest. It is vital."

—Rebbe Nachman of Breslov[56]

"According to the ideas of real Judaism, all the inhabitants of the earth are destined to felicity."

—**Moses Mendelssohn**, *Jerusalem*

Religious Jews find the source of happiness in the Torah. As Proverbs says, "She [the Torah] is the tree of life to those who grasp her; and happy is everyone who holds her fast."[57] The Torah sets forth principles that encourage living in harmony with the forces of the universe instead of struggling against them. It instills attitudes of awe, purpose, gratitude, appreciation, hopefulness, and love of life. Living in accordance with Torah's commandments promotes happiness, as attested by the words of a morning worship service: "Happy are we, how goodly is our portion, how pleasant is our lot, and how beautiful our heritage!"[58]

Jews believe that together with God, who is constantly involved in our lives, we too have a tremendous influence on our destiny. We affect the higher planes with our mood and behavior, and our happiness creates joy in the spiritual realm and brings us great blessings in the material realm. It is told that even on this death-bed, the first Lubavitcher Rebbe taught that happiness attracts good fortune. He asked his family, who were crying and praying around him, to lighten up, explaining that happiness would draw God's blessings to them. Besides, he added, seeing their happiness would make him feel better as well.[59]

Our level of happiness can change not only our own lives, but the entire world. The Hebrew word for joy, *simcha*, contains the same letters—s*hin*, *mem*, and *het*—as the word *moshiach*, which refers to the messiah who will signify the beginning of a new era of peace and harmony. Rabbis interpret this to mean that by increasing the level of our personal happiness we can hasten the arrival of the messianic era on earth.

Besides, Judaism teaches that God wants us to be happy![60] Contrary to the popular belief that the more we suffer the holier we are, Judaism tells us that happiness is our essence and duty. It inspires and empowers us to become the happiest we can be. Jewish mystics hold that attaining the bliss that God intends for us is the ultimate human aim.[61] According to the **Talmud**, one of the questions we have to answer at the heavenly tribunal is, "Did you enjoy My world?"[62] Such a question from God indicates that everyone should be happy. Even more important, it means that everyone *can* be happy!

Although the state of happiness does not always come naturally, the sages interpret the line "Teach me, God, your ways" from Psalms[63] as an indication that happiness can be taught and achieved with practice. Rabbi **Moishe Winner** teaches that if we work at it we can develop a "taste" for happiness, much as we have to practice to develop taste and appreciation for a fine wine, poetry, music, or art.

Kabbalists, Jewish mystics, say that we already carry happiness and bliss in our souls, but we forget it when we are born, distracted by other things. Thus, all we have to do is learn to unlock what we already know.[64]

The teachings of Judaism promote happiness in many ways. They boost our self-esteem by telling us that each person is immeasurably valuable due to having a unique particle of divine inside of us—a soul. Judaism takes the stress off by teaching that humans are not created to be perfect, and happiness comes when we are who we are supposed to be, imperfections included.[65]

It also increases happiness by focusing our attention on the good via ritualized gratitude and celebration of life. Each prayer and blessing draws our attention to the wonderful things and events in our life, routine and extraordinary. Most Jewish holidays and every Shabbat, observant families gather around a table, sing, and remember the good things that have happened to them and to their ancestors, thereby creating joy and gratitude.

With rituals and blessings, Judaism also teaches us to acknowledge the holiness in everyday actions and events, to see the divine reality of the world, and to relish it. It sanctifies simple moments of our lives, elevating them to a higher level, turning simple activities like waking up and eating into meaningful and happy experiences.

As we learned earlier, one of the main components of happiness is moderation, which is also one of the cornerstones of the

Jewish living. Judaism teaches that humans are different from the animals, who act on instinct. We must partake in earthy pleasures but also exercise self-discipline. We should enjoy and appreciate this beautiful world but also help improve it.

Additionally, Jewish teachings are filled with the idea that our happiness comes through connection to the present. It is not about what happens in the future or what has happened in the past. It is about connecting to and participating in creating the present moment and, with it, our reality.[66]

In the chapters that follow, we will discuss these and other values and skills that Judaism promotes, such as finding purpose, increasing optimism, and turning troubles into moments of meaningful growth.

CHAPTER 11

JEWISH THINKERS ON HAPPINESS

Religious texts are the major basis of Jewish thought on hap-piness, but the whole body of Jewish wisdom extends to in-clude much more. Philosophers, scholars, atheists, mystics, scien-tists, and ordinary Jewish men and women have also introduced many ideas about happiness that contributed to shaping Western thought, affected our lives, and still inspire many people. Here are some of them:

Philo Judaeus (15-10 BCE–45-50 CE), a leader of Alexandrian Jewry and an important Jewish philosopher, laid the foundations for the later philosophical and theological development of Chris-tianity.[67] On the subject of happiness, he reasoned that perfect happiness comes not through man's own efforts to achieve virtue but only through the grace of God.[68] He also held that "hope is the source of all happiness."[69]

Moses Maimonides (also called Rambam, 1135–1204) was a me-dieval rabbi and philosopher whose ideas had immense reach within the Jewish world and beyond, influencing such non-Jewish thinkers as Thomas Aquinas, G. W. Leibniz, and Sir Isaac New-ton.[70] According to Maimonides, the ultimate goal of creation is man, and the ultimate goal of man is happiness. He taught that this can be achieved through exercise of the intellect and understanding of truth and that the highest understanding is that of God and his unity.[71]

Baruch Spinoza (1632–1677), a Dutch-born Jew, was one of the most important philosophers of the early modern period. His philosophy is centered on the idea that controlling the passions leads to virtue and happiness. He urged "not to laugh, not to lament, not to detest, but to understand."[72] Spinoza held that "happiness is a virtue, not its reward," and that "all happiness or unhappiness solely depends upon the quality of the object to which we are attached by love."[73]

Soviet Jewry was probably most affected by **Karl Marx** (1818–1883), a German-born Jew and one of the authors of *The Communist Manifesto*, who declared that "the first requisite for the happiness of the people is the abolition of religion."[74]

Sigmund Freud (1856–1939) was another influential Jewish philosopher, known as the father of psychoanalysis. Freud argued that the only purpose of life people agree upon is to be happy but that this goal is largely unattainable. As Freud put it, "One feels inclined to say that the intention that man should be 'happy' is not included in the plan of 'Creation.'"[75] In Freud's view, in its purest form, happiness can only be achieved through pleasure and the satisfaction of all needs. But if we satisfy each desire as soon as it arises, the happiness is lessened. Freud argued that the very best sort of happiness can only be had when there is "a sudden satisfaction of needs" that have been pent up for some time. On the other hand, our world presents extreme possibilities for suffering. Therefore, if an individual has escaped suffering, he must consider himself happy.[76]

We have already heard a little bit about Ayn Rand (1905–1982), a Russian-born Jew who was the founder of a philosophical system called objectivism. In 1990, the Library of Congress named her book *Atlas Shrugged* the most influential book in the US after the Bible. For Rand, happiness proceeded from the achievement of one's values. In *Atlas Shrugged*, she wrote, "By the grace of reality and the nature of life, man—every man—is an end in himself, he exists for his own sake, and the achievement of his own happiness is his highest moral purpose."[77]

Sonja Lyubomirsky is another Russian-born Jew. She is a leading expert in positive psychology who believes that happiness skills can be learned and improved. Her research on the possibility of permanently increasing happiness has been honored with various grants, including a million-dollar grant from the National Institute of Mental Health.[78]

Tal Ben-Shahar is an American and Israeli author and lecturer in the areas of positive psychology and leadership. He teaches how to apply psychological research to everyday life as a way to achieve happiness. In 2006, his positive psychology course The Science of Happiness became the most popular course in the history of Harvard University, beating even Introductory Economics.[79]

As these examples show, the Jewish heritage contains a lot of differences of opinions on happiness and its sources. What's clear, though, is that in the thousands of years since the receipt of Torah at Mount Sinai, Jewish thought has continued to influence the world by shaping our understanding of human happiness, and we will draw on this thought in our quest to achieve happiness of our own.

PART III

PUT HAPPINESS TO PRACTICE

CHAPTER 12

HOW TO BECOME HAPPY

"We cannot solve our problems with the same thinking we used when we created them."

—Albert Einstein

Since all of us are born with different dispositions, we may feel that we are "stuck" the way we are for the rest of our lives because a trait such as the capacity for happiness cannot be changed: we are who we are. However, the Tanakh (the Hebrew Bible), some prominent thinkers, and positive psychologists insist that we can learn to be happy. Renowned happiness psychologists such as Martin Seligman and Sonja Lyubomirsky estimate that about 50 percent of our happiness is due to genetic predisposition, about 10 percent is affected by our circumstances, and the other 40 percent is under our voluntary control. This means that we can become much happier if we change a few things.

Usually we try to improve our lives by spending time and energy on efforts to change our circumstances and to convince others to behave differently. But if we really think about it, we will realize that we cannot control the circumstances that arise in our lives. However painstakingly we may plan things out, we really cannot account for the weather, the traffic, the mood of our boss, the news we get, or other things that happen to us. Despite all our efforts and all out planning, we cannot know what will happen in a year or even tomorrow. And therefore, if we try to change all these things or wait for something wonderful to happen to bring us lasting happiness, we are left at the complete mercy of the unknown.

But there are things that we have complete power over. Whatever happens to us, we are in control of our thoughts, words, and actions. Adjusting our attitudes and behavior is how we become happier.

Our personality is an intricate mix of character traits. Some are inborn; others are acquired. Most are influenced by our upbringing, our circumstances, and our choices. Our personalities are not static; as we age and gain experience, we may see our priorities shift; we may become more or less patient, more or less kind, more or less content. We are not the same people we were ten years ago. Often these changes are subtle and practically imperceptible on a day-to-day basis, but they happen nonetheless.

We can change our personality in a similar way to how we can change our body. We all are born with different physiques determined by our genes. Some people are naturally fit and do not have to do anything to stay in shape. Others have to put in effort, change their lifestyle, diet, and exercise to get the desired results. It takes time and constant work, but it is possible. There are people who are puny and become muscular or who are overweight and become slender.

Perhaps personality changes are not as clearly visible as physical ones, but they are completely within our reach. Happiness is not the only personality trait that can be managed. On the other end of our personality spectrum, there is anger. As with happiness, anger is partially an aspect of our disposition, partially an emotion that depends on our circumstances, and partially a matter of choice and behavior. And if we put our minds to it, we can successfully control anger with anger-management classes. In the same way, we can learn to build happiness skills.

We can tweak our attitude and boost our contentment in several ways. The chapters that follow each target a different set of happiness skills. Every skill is a part of a complete approach to happiness, like an ingredient in a recipe or a brick in a wall.

Practicing these skills will benefit readers of any age. Even at a hundred, it is not too late to experience life with joy and contentment. But the sooner we start, the more happy days we will experience. So start practicing as soon as you read each chapter, and teach your children as well.

If it seems too difficult or the results do not show as fast as you would like, remember that you are doing it for the most important person there is—you! Even a minute change in attitude is a reason to celebrate. Our circumstances won't dramatically change for the better, but our lives will change as our take on those circumstances does.

PUT IT INTO PRACTICE

Any time you're working on self-improvement, it's important to stick to the three *P*'s: patience, praise, and perseverance.

- Be patient.

Self-improvement happens at different rates. Sometimes people get so jolted by something that they may change overnight. However, if the circumstances in which you decide to make a change are not very dramatic, self-improvement may take longer: weeks, moths, years, or even decades. To avoid disappointment, do not expect too much change too soon. Although this process is gradual, it is very rewarding.

- Praise or reward yourself.

Validate each of your efforts and achievements. Every time you practice happiness skills, feel happier or less unhappy than you used to, or think about how to react better to your circumstances, that is an improvement, and you should praise yourself for it. Tell yourself, "Six months ago I would have responded so differently, and now I am not bothered! Kudos to me!" You might decide to reward yourself with an actual prize. For example, for every five times you practice happiness skills, you might give yourself a piece of chocolate, an extra five minutes of reading time, or something else you decide is an appropriate positive reinforcement to encourage you to keep up the good work. Or you can just give yourself a mental pat on the back and allow yourself the satisfaction of knowing you are on the sure track to happiness.

- Do not get discouraged.

Sometimes, despite exerting conscious effort to be happier, you may feel that it does not work. Or it does work, but you keep slipping back into old habits. Setbacks are not an indication that you lack intelligence, character, or willpower or that you are doomed to failure. They are normal, temporary, and are to be expected.

Rabbi **Akiva**, who was a semi-illiterate shepherd until the age of forty but became one of the greatest scholars in Jewish history, was inspired to change by observing how water drops make a hole in a rock when they drip persistently. He demonstrated with his life that we can change our hearts and minds as long as we are persistent, too.[80] The more you practice, the more natural the new skills will become. Do not give up and divert your attention elsewhere. Persist as if you know for sure that you can reach your goal, regardless of how long it takes. Relax, keep practicing, and remember to praise yourself at every step on the way to a happier you.

CHAPTER 13

HAPPINESS IS A SKILL

"Real change only comes from consistent, daily practice."

—Rabbi **Shneur Zalman of Liadi,** *Tanya*[81]

A skill is an ability to do something, and the more we practice the skill, the better we are able to put it into practice. Even when we are born with a talent for something, we have to practice a lot in order to master it. While people are born with different dispositions, there are happiness skills that anybody can practice to become happier.

Most of the things we know how to do today, both physical (such as dressing, ballet dancing, or sewing) and intellectual (such as speaking, writing, or problem solving), are skills that we learned at some time. Any skill is acquired in pretty much the same way—through lots of practicing. Usually it helps to learn some theory about the thing we are trying to learn first, although some skills (such as walking) are more intuitive than others. In the beginning we struggle and have to think about getting every minor detail right. If we are not naturally good at something, we may get frustrated and even want to quit. With repetition, several great things happen: we acquire "muscle memory"—that is, the skill becomes automatic; the process becomes easy and, as a result, more enjoyable; and we get a deeper understanding of activity we have mastered.

Let's say we decide to learn to play a musical instrument. We cannot just listen to some music and begin playing at once. Instead we learn the building blocks of the skill—the notes, the terminology, the finger placement and even the correct posture. We start out by playing painstakingly, checking every note and making mistakes. What comes out sounds disjointed and cumbersome. The more we practice, the more quickly playing becomes automatic, sheet music translates into beautiful melodies, and fingers find their correct place without our conscious effort. Learning to play fluently may take a year or ten years. Some people have a talent for it and can learn to play several instruments rather easily. Others may struggle, but even they will play well if they practice a lot.

Becoming happier is similar to mastering any skill. We must define the goal, learn about it, start practicing, and observe the learning curve—in the beginning we will struggle and often slip back into our usual reactions, but the more we practice, the better we will become at it. As with any skill, some people will get it more easily than others, but anyone can learn and become better with practice.

Our level of happiness depends on our attitude toward the world. This attitude is in large part also a product of repetitive behavior of a certain kind. We may have forgotten how we got to feel and behave the way we do today, but little by little, starting in childhood, we formed habits of instantly and automatically reacting a certain way toward certain situations.

From a scientific point of view, every experience, thought, feeling, and physical sensation we experience triggers thousands of neurons in our brain. According to Hebbian theory, neurons that fire together wire together. That means that when we react in a certain way over and over, the brain learns to trigger the same neurons each time, and eventually the same reaction is triggered automatically. This is how we end up with the attitude that we practice most often. But as soon as we start practicing a different attitude, we start forming new neural networks.

The more we exercise happiness skills, the easier it will come each and every time. We will feel happiness instead of just understanding it intellectually, and eventually a positive attitude may become our second nature. The opposite is true as well: if we consistently let ourselves be negative, we can "learn" to be unhappy.

This book provides a theory of happiness and exercises. But in order to actually be happy, you have to practice the skills every day. You may know what goes into riding a bicycle—the movement, the speed, the balance—but you can experience it only if you actually do it. Just like riding a bicycle, happiness is learned through repetition. In both cases, struggling to much to "get it right" can just make it harder, but the moment we let go, we start enjoying it.

The techniques described in this book are simple and doable. But they are powerful. Practice the happiness skills as frequently as possible. Keep a journal in the beginning to write about the effects the exercises have. This will help you to acknowledge and evaluate any changes in your perception, behavior, and mood, to notice and appreciate the benefits, and to want to practice the skills even more. Do not just read about happiness—get involved with it! Eventually you will notice a difference in yourself and in the world around.

CHAPTER 14

THE SHORTCUT:
IF YOU THINK YOU ARE
HAPPY, YOU ARE

"Reality is merely an illusion, albeit a very persistent one."

—Albert Einstein

Before we delve into the secrets of happiness one by one, I want to tell you a shortcut that gets us there directly:

You are happy when you believe you are.

That's it. When you know you are happy, you are. There are no obstacles to happiness except our own point of view on it. Regardless of what is happening in your life at this time, if you feel genuinely blessed and happy, you immediately are happy.

The world is all kinds of things, but we only see and feel them through our perceptions. Our own beliefs are the most powerful force shaping our lives and determining our attitude, actions, lifestyle, and happiness. That is why, while having the exact same experience, one snowflake in the following parable is happy while the other one is not:

> It was snowing in Jerusalem. Two big, fluffy snowflakes were circling together in the air, slowly approaching the earth. One of them said cheerfully, "How I enjoy our flight!"
>
> "We do not fly. We just fall down," the second replied sadly.
>
> "Soon we will touch the ground and turn into a white, fluffy blanket!"
>
> "No, we're going to die; we will be crushed on the ground."
>
> "We will become streams and head out to sea. We will live forever!" said the first one.
>
> "No, we will melt and disappear," objected the second.
>
> And so they flew down to meet the fate that each chose for itself.[82]

Not only our happiness but also our entire life is a product of our perceptions. When a man walking in a forest at night sees a shape across his path that he thinks is a snake, he is terrified and is afraid to move. Does it matter to him at that moment that it is really only a piece of rope? No, he is caught up in his own story. His perception makes him feel genuine terror despite the actual circumstances being rather benign.

We all get caught up in the stories we tell ourselves about our lives. We *are* our stories. Our perceptions make our reality. If we change perceptions, we create a new reality, one in which we are happy.

PUT IT INTO PRACTICE

Believe in your happiness. Start today.

Here are a couple easy approaches you can take:

- Reinforce your perception of yourself as a happy person.

Take a picture of yourself in which you are genuinely laughing, feeling great, or being authentically happy. Put this picture up where you will frequently see it. Every time you glance at it, remind yourself that this is your core—joyous and happy. You are a happy person. Even if sometimes your feel low, happiness is always inside you. In a very short time, you will notice that when you face difficulties in life you now stay happier, because you have embraced your true nature.

Affirm: I am joyful, I am content, I am happy! This is who I am even though I do not always feel this way.

- Reinforce your own perception that life is great.

We are what we think, and our lives are as good or as bad as we believe. According to Kabbalah we bring our thoughts even closer to reality when we speak them out loud. Repeat positive statements about your life and yourself daily, but do not just recite them. Say them with true feeling and genuine belief. You can write your own affirmations, but here are some examples:

- My world loves me. It loves to pleasantly surprise me with good things I did not expect.

- Everyone and everything on my path is good.

- I am at peace with all that has happened, is happening, and will happen.

- I choose to live my life to the fullest, and I smile the entire way.

- I am excited to walk out the door and live the rest of my life.

- I love life.

- Life is great!

* * *

If you are not completely convinced you are outright happy just yet, keep on reading. The following chapters and tips will help you gradually come to realization that you are.

KNOW YOUR HAPPINESS

KNOW YOUR DIABETES

CHAPTER 15

INTRODUCTION TO THE SECTION

Once upon a time, Baruch was walking through the woods and met a woodcutter. His body strained, sweat pouring from his face, the woodcutter was sawing a fallen tree. When Baruch got closer, he has noticed why the other man was exerting so much effort but could not complete his work faster.

"Hey, your saw is quite blunt," he said to the woodcutter. "Why don't you sharpen it?"

"Are you kidding?" exclaimed the woodcutter. "I have absolutely no time for that. I need to cut another twenty trees!"

And with that he went back to work.[83]

This parable illustrates how sometimes spending a little time on planning saves a lot of time and hard work on doing. Rebbe Nachman of Breslov agreed: "You must make sure you set aside a time each day when you can reflect calmly on everything you are doing and the way you are behaving and ask if this is the right way to spend your days."[84]

This section will help us avoid repeating the woodcutter's mistake. Before starting to work on increasing our happiness, we will spend some time organizing our thoughts and deciding what happiness means to us.

CHAPTER 16

WHAT IS GOOD AND WHAT IS BAD

How would you describe a good day, a day when you feel happy? For the majority of people, a good day is when good things happen to us: we win a prize, get a raise, meet good friends, sell a house—things like that. By the same token, a bad day is when bad things happen: the roof leaks, the house gets robbed, or the favorite outfit gets stained. Our understanding of "good" and "bad" days is reflected in our state of happiness or unhappiness: we are happy on a good day and not happy on a bad one. But there is another approach to thinking about what is good and what is bad.

Sara Yoheved Rigler, a Jewish author and an international lecturer, teaches that our lives consist of two flows: the inflow and the outflow. Inflow is everything that happens to us, which we do not have any control over. It's like the Yiddish proverb says, "*Mentsch tracht, Got lakht*" (literally "Man plans, God laughs"). Whether we believe in God and a higher plan or in chaos and randomness, the fact remains: we are not masters of the inflow. But we are in complete control of the second part of our lives, the outflow, which consists of our thoughts, words, and actions.[85]

Our usual definitions of good and bad days has to do entirely with the inflow, which we cannot predict or affect. If, instead, we think of good and bad days in terms of the outflow, our happiness will radically change. A day when we have good thoughts, offer good words, and do good deeds will become a good day, a day to feel happy.

In her book *Holy Woman*, Rigler records a conversation with Rebbetzin **Chaya Sara Kramer**, whose family was murdered in Auschwitz and who was experimented on by the notorious "angel of death," Dr. Mengele. Kramer asserts that, despite all that, Auschwitz was not a bad place. She explains that she was able to keep some mitzvot there. To her, a bad place is a place where one can do good deeds but doesn't.

Sara Rigler writes:

> She had just turned my whole reality upside down. A bad place had nothing to do with bad things happening *to* you. No matter that the Nazis had murdered her whole family. No matter that Dr. Mengele had experimented on her and probably sterilized her. All that really matters is what issues *from* you.

> In a flash I realized how my mind was so busy evaluating the content surging through the [inflow] pipe into my life that I paid scant attention to the [outflow] pipe—the thoughts, words, and actions that flowed from me. The holywoman, on the other hand, evaluated her life only according to the [outflow] pipe.

> No wonder she was always smiling, despite her barrenness, despite her poverty, despite the grueling hardship of her daily life. She was performing *mitzvoth*. She was bonding

with God. She was projecting her own light, both now and before, in the darkness of hell.

I had met many holy masters in India. I had sat at the feet of great swamis and had waited in line for hours to place a garland around the neck of Anandamaya-ma, a woman venerated by millions. But sitting in that bare room with its tin roof, eating cucumbers and farmer's cheese across a rickety table from Rebbetzin Chaya Sara, I felt like I had just emerged from a whole lifetime spent through the looking glass. I had been seeing everything in reverse. Now here I was at the top of the rabbit hole, awakened from the dream, my eyes squinting at the brightness of a world of total spiritual clarity.

I looked long and hard at Rebbetzin Chaya Sara. She gazed back at me, and laughed.[86]

When we revise our understanding of what makes something good and bad, suddenly we gain complete control over happiness. Now this is something we can work with!

PUT IT INTO PRACTICE

At the end of every day, evaluate the day in the light of outflow:

Did you face difficulty and manage to have positive thoughts?

Did you do a good deed?

Did you offer good words?

Did you learn something new?

Did you forgive someone?

Did you put effort into self-improvement?

If you said yes to any of the above, consider it a good day, and feel the happiness of having the opportunity to do good and using it.

CHAPTER 17

RECOGNIZE YOUR HAPPINESS

Happiness is a tricky concept. It is a state of being, like health or a good mood. And yet rather often we think of it as a goal to be reached, an object we want, and not just a condition to be in.

Do you always know when you are happy? This question may sound strange, but sometimes our expectations of happiness preclude us from recognizing actual happiness. Indeed, we sometimes mislabel or doubt our feelings. We feel something, but we are not sure what it is. When your stomach lurches, is it due to a gut feeling, or are you just hungry? When you feel tingling after a yoga class, is it a surge of life energy or just a rush of blood? When you feel a tug in your chest, is it because of love, attraction, or friendship? When you are in a good mood, is it due to happiness, pleasure, or amusement?

Sometimes we dream up an idea of how these states must feel, and when we experience them, we don't always realize it, because we expect something else. If we expect love to feel like fireworks or happiness to be like walking on a cloud, we may dismiss less intense feelings. If we think that happiness is warranted only by special occasions and the most intense positive experiences, we may miss the happiness in small, routine, everyday things.

How do you imagine happiness? Is it a feeling of busting joy or calmness? Ecstasy or harmony? How do you know when you are happy?

Every person experiences and expresses happiness (and other emotions or mental processes) differently. We think differently, we love differently, and we grieve differently. Therefore, we should not expect our happiness to mirror the displays we encounter in other people, on television, or in books. And by the same token, we should not expect our children to express happiness the same way we do.

The feeling of happiness is individual. It can be very visible, expressed with great passion, big smiles, laughter, jumping up and down, or whistling in the shower. Or it can be quieter, peaceful, insightful, and content, but not a bit less intense.

Furthermore, even to the same person, happiness feels different at different times, and the way we experience happiness may change with age.

Happiness is not just a warm, pleasant feeling. Sometimes, happiness happens when we do not notice our feelings at all. People usually only become very aware of their head or a limb when they hurt. A healthy person does not pay much attention his or her limbs. Similarly, rabbis teach that a spiritually healthy person does not usually notice his own emotional state.[87] When we are completely immersed in a physical or mental experience, we do not notice the passage of time or how we are feeling. We just do it, or as Jews say, "Just Jew it," without overthinking how we feel.

We should also keep in mind that a feeling of happiness may even not be centered on us. It may emerge when we expand our consciousness, transcend our selves, and feel oneness and harmony with other people, God, and the universe.

It is very important to recognize when we are happy, whether it feels like a surge of joy, peacefulness and calm, or engrossment in something captivating. Do not shortchange yourself by thinking you are not happy just because you are expecting something more than you usually feel. If we wait to feel happiness in the specific way we imagine it, then in our quest for happiness, we will resemble a thirsty fish surrounded by water without realizing it. Sometimes we experience good feelings without realizing they *are* happiness. All we have to do is to look within, acknowledge our happiness, and enjoy, and we will never be thirsty again.

PUT IT INTO PRACTICE

Listen to yourself and get to know how happiness feels to you. Recognize that happiness does not only feel like intense bliss and delight but also like quiet contentment and peace of mind. Here are a couple easy approaches you can take:

- Acknowledge your feelings of everyday happiness.

Look at something or someone you love (family, pets, nature, art, etc.). Recognize that whatever you are feeling when you look at this is what your happiness feels like.

- Find your happiness baseline.

The sensation of happiness fluctuates all the time. It is more or less intense depending on our outlook at the time. We cannot sustain peak feelings for a long time, but that does not mean that we are no longer happy when they are over.

Think back to a time when your happiness was strongly expressed, when you felt intense pleasure, elation, and joy. When these intense feelings subsided, there usually are less intense pleasant feelings left in their wake. That calmer, milder feeling is also the feeling of happiness.

- Go with the "flow."

Reflect on your day or week and make note of instances when you were so lost in an activity that you did not notice passing of the time or how your body felt. Know that this is happiness as well.

- Recognize and reinforce.

At any moment in your life when you are just living, feeling neither sad nor exceptionally joyful but, rather, neutral and content—let's say when you are brushing your teeth, walking to work, or reading a book—pause, look inward for a moment, and recognize that you are happy. Repeat three times a day.

CHAPTER 18

GET YOUR PRIORITIES STRAIGHT

"Money will not purchase happiness for the man who has no concept of what he wants."

—Ayn Rand, *Atlas Shrugged*

"There is nothing very mysterious about free will. You do what you want to do, and you don't do what you don't want to do."

—Rebbe Nachman of Breslov[88]

Jewish tradition indicates that freedom of choice is the human privilege that sets people apart from all other creations.[89] While animals can only react to their environment, humans are created *b'tselem Elohim*, or in God's image,[90] and can make moral choices.[91] This includes the ability to choose our values, priorities, and our own life path. Having the choice makes life difficult, but it also gives it meaning.

What are your goals in life? What do you imagine in the perfect future for yourself and your children? Is there a beautiful house?

A big, loving family? Prosperity? Health? A satisfying career? Do you think of yourself as having a calling to fulfill? When you think about your ideal future, do you consider the state of your mind, feelings, and emotions? Do you wish for inner peace and joy? What is most important in your vision of the perfect life? What can you give up, and what will you always strive for?

Often when we dream of the future, especially when we are younger, we think in terms of what we are going to possess— money, position, power, success, family. We concentrate on more palpable, quantifiable goals and make choices accordingly. With age we gain experience, become more established, secure, and, we hope, wiser, and some of our life priorities change. We may begin to value our emotional state over material gains or social standing.

Many philosophers think that our ultimate goal, whether we are conscious of it or not, is always happiness, and anything we dream about and want to achieve is a pathway to that ultimate goal. If we dream of a beautiful house, it is because we want to be comfortable and happy. If we dream of a big, loving family, it is because that is what makes us happy. If we dream of health, prosperity, career, world peace, or anything and everything else, it is because we believe these things will make us happy.

Surprisingly, however, not all the choices we make are based on this principle. According to American economist Edward Glaeser, people constantly make choices that decrease their happiness, because they believe that they have more important aims.[92] Our own happiness may come second to the happiness of our loved ones, the call of duty, or even the fear of changing the status quo. Or we may believe that we simply do not have a choice about doing something that makes us unhappy.

To help us make decisions that bring us closer to our ultimate life goal, we need to get our priorities straight. Confusion in our minds generates chaos in our reality. Unclear life priorities, conflicting desires, and dreams of getting everything at once will not get us where we want to be. To achieve goals, we first need to know exactly what they are. If your goal is to be a pianist, you will not achieve it by practicing violin. It is the same with happiness.

Consider what we do with the lifetime we are granted. Whatever we do in life—eat, sleep, travel, work, quarrel, love, check emails, raise kids, exercise—we pay for it with our finite time. In a workday we may have produced five chairs, or contributed to a project for improving a banking system, or wrote an article, or baked cupcakes, or maybe done something we do not care about just to earn the living. We have exchanged eight hours of our lives for that. If you love what you produce, it is worth it. If you do not really care and just wait for each workday to be over, then you lose those hours of your life forever.

"Without vision, the people become unrestrained," teaches the Tanakh,[93] "but happy is he who keeps the law." As civil and religious laws keep society in order, so our personal priorities add structure to our lives. If we do not have clear priorities in life, we may get pulled in many different directions by the choices we are presented with on a daily basis. When we make decisions according to what feels right at the moment, we may regret them later. For example, people are known to complain on their deathbed that they wish they had spent more time with their family. Not many people say that they wished they had spent more time in the office.[94] It is too bad that many people only realize what their priorities are when it is too late to change anything.

Establishing priorities will help us organize our thoughts, goals, and desires. It will enable us to recognize what we want in life and in what order we want it. Once we are clear about our priorities, we can decide whether to continue in the direction we are moving now or make some changes.

When we know our priorities, it is easier to choose some options in life over others. When we have decided that enjoying a peaceful life is a higher priority, it is easier to decline a higher paying and more stressful job offer and stay content. Or vice versa: if the higher priority in life is having a successful career, it is easier to accept that job despite other drawbacks. Adhering to our priorities makes us happier.

In addition, having clear priorities makes it easier to cope with the minor annoyances in life. When your spouse forgets to put the socks away again, your cherished vase breaks, or somebody cuts in front of you in a line, it may seem like a big deal at the moment. But if you manage to remember what your most important priorities are for that day, that week, and life in general, it will help you to see that the situation at hand is ultimately not too significant and, therefore, not worth getting upset about.

Setting priorities will help us orient ourselves in any situation, pursue the right things, give up others, not get upset over unimportant stuff, simplify our decision-making, and feel good about the choices we make.

We are limited in the amount of things we can dedicate our time to. It is important to choose the essential and meaningful things first, as illustrated by the professor in the following story.

> At the beginning of his philosophy class, a professor picked up an empty jar and proceeded to fill it with golf

balls until it was full. He then picked up a box of pebbles and poured them into the jar. They settled into areas between the golf balls until the jar was finally full. The professor next picked up a box of sand and poured it into the jar until it filled every available space. Now the jar was truly full. The professor then took his cup of tea and poured the entire contents into the jar, effectively filling the empty space between the sand.

"This jar," said the professor to the students, "represents your life: the golf balls are the important things—your family, your children, your health, your friends, your favorite passions—things that, if everything else was lost and only they remained, your life would still be full. The pebbles are the other things that matter like your job, your house, your car. The sand is everything else—the small stuff.

"If you put the sand into the jar first," he continued, "there is no room for the pebbles or the golf balls. The same goes for life. If you spend all your time and energy on the small stuff, you will never have room for the things that are important to you. Pay attention to the things that are critical to your happiness. Play with your children. Take time to get medical checkups. Take your partner out to dinner. Play another eighteen holes of golf. There will always be time to clean the house and fix the disposal.

"Take care of the golf balls first, the things that really matter. Set your priorities. The rest is just sand."

One of the students raised her hand and inquired what the tea represented.

The professor smiled. "I'm glad you asked. It just goes to show you that no matter how full your life may seem, there's always room for a cup of tea."[95]

It is probably impossible to fill each moment with deep meaning and spend all your time working exclusively toward the big goals. As always, everything is good in moderation. But it is necessary to know what your priorities are and live accordingly.

Last but not least, although we should think about our life priorities, we should also recognize that our state of happiness runs parallel to everything that happens in our lives. Granted, it is easier to feel happy in favorable circumstances, when we can choose to do something we are inclined toward. But even in adverse circumstances when we cannot do what we want to, happiness should not be put on hold until better times. We can feel happy anyway, if we only choose to.

PUT IT INTO PRACTICE

- Create a priorities list for your life.

Think about all the major ideas you have about happiness, about success, and about the meaning of your life. Consider all the factors that are important to you. You might use some of these and add anything else that you come up with on your own:

- ❖ Just feeling good about life, contentment
- ❖ Fulfilling relationships
- ❖ Children
- ❖ Spirituality

❖ Health

❖ Physical beauty

❖ Financial status

❖ Amassing knowledge

❖ Amassing quality possessions

❖ Making a difference in the world and creating a legacy

❖ Peer approval and popularity

❖ Good entertainment (computer games, movies, music, electronic media, etc.)

❖ Relaxing

❖ Staying busy

❖ Taking care of others, feeling needed and helpful

❖ Feeling love and care for others

List the most important priorities first.

Do not try to include things that you think are appropriate or constitute the "right answer." This exercise is not for anybody else's judgment; it is just for you, for your self-examination. The appraisal of what is meaningful is very personal. Some may want to impact the world, eliminate hunger, or invent flying cars. Others may want things that impact them personally, for example, to see their kids graduate from college or quit smoking. So just pick whatever you've always wanted in order to be happy.

What list would you create for your children? Would it be the same as yours?

- Narrow your priorities down.

Look at the resulting list carefully. Ask yourself:

❖ Which of these goals are important for my success and which for my happiness?

❖ If I do not achieve these goals, will I still be able to be happy?

❖ If I do achieve them, will I be happy forever?

❖ Do I already have some of the things on the list?

❖ Which of the things on my list depend on outside circumstances and which on my own attitude?

❖ If one of my goals is to be happy, how high a priority is that? Is it higher than success or peer approval?

❖ What five achievements or adjectives would I want to describe me at the end of my life?

Based on the above reflections (which may take a couple of minutes, a day, or months), decide what is essential for you and what is not. Weigh whether you can be happy with less.[96] Add or subtract some goals to create a focused list of things you are ready to dedicate your life to.

Keep in mind that many things we consider goals are really only means to something bigger that we want. For example, if you want to have a lot of money, is it because you like the look and smell of money, because you want to be able to afford a nice lifestyle, or because you want to give generously to charity? Unless it's the first reason, the money is just a means to other goals in your life. List only those end goals.

- Use the "would you rather" exercise.

This exercise will help you test-drive your dedication to sticking to your priorities under trying circumstances. Imagine yourself in a difficult situation in which you have to decide how to react or behave. Based on your life priorities, what would you rather do:

❖ Would you rather be right or happy? When you are faced with people (parents, kids, spouses, friends) who, despite being clearly wrong, insist that they are right, would you rather argue and prove at any cost that you are right, or would you rather forfeit the point and stay loving and close with them anyway?

❖ Would you rather stress out because (insert reason) or be happy?

❖ Would you rather give in to the judgment of others or continue on your chosen path?

❖ Would you rather spend several hours in front of a TV or spend several hours reaching your goals?

You might add some more "would you rather" scenarios of your own. Think about these situations on a philosophical level. Which choice would you suggest that your children, parents, or best friends make? Obviously, there is no right answer, and you do not *have* to choose the "I'd rather be happy" option. Again, the goal of these exercises is to bring to light and crystallize the priorities for your personal life journey.

Now think about the choices you have actually made in similar situations. Thinking about these choices will help you recognize what is most important for you. It also will give you the opportunity to reflect on whether you act in accordance with your own priorities. Possibly, you will have to change your behavior or rethink your priorities.

- Remember the reason for wanting happiness and making it a high priority.

Now that you have identified your priorities, let's look specifically at happiness.

Is the importance and supremacy of happiness self-evident to you? Are you convinced that being happy is your goal and priority?

Think back and try to identify what experiences and thoughts brought you to your current attitude on happiness.

If something made you doubt your priorities (for example, if you got a very lucrative job offer for a position you did not like or you faced losing friends because of your life choices), would you be able to convince yourself of what is most important for you again? What would you say to convince yourself that your priorities are still right?

- Remember your priorities and act on them.

Your priority list is a reminder of what is truly important for you. Review it every month, or even every morning and decide what you are going to work on today. This way you will stay on track to achieving your goals and, along the way, happiness. If you find yourself doing something that conflicts with your life goals—such as getting angry at the world for something; getting stuck at a meaningless, joyless job; or spending hours in front of

TV—then think again about what is most important.

Limit the time you dedicate to nonessential and counterproductive things such as bickering with people you are close to over minor issues or playing computer games. Rededicate your time and energy to something you consider more important, such as enjoying your family, achieving something meaningful, or practicing happiness.

Remember that our time is finite. Therefore, choose to enjoy your life instead of enduring it[97]; choose to celebrate it instead of wasting it on something meaningless.

- Do not get discouraged.

Self-improvement is a lifelong process. Remember that you should not get discouraged if you find yourself sidetracked. Work on improving your situation, and continue getting closer to your goals. And always feel satisfied and happy as you get closer to your goals, even if you are getting there little by little.

CHAPTER 19

CHOICES THAT LEAD TO HAPPINESS

*"Everything can be taken from a man but one thing: the last
of human freedoms—to choose one's attitude in any given set of
circumstances, to choose one's own way."*

—**Victor E. Frankl**, Holocaust survivor

The famous Jewish teacher Rebbe Nachman of Breslov used to say, "Everything in the world—whatever is and whatever happens—is a test, designed to give you freedom of choice. Choose wisely."[98] Every day we are faced with a plethora of choices: important and insignificant, difficult and easy, short-term and long-term. We choose a spouse, a college major, and how to spend a couple of free hours we have in the evening. We choose whether to treat ourselves to a piece of chocolate or to abstain. We choose whether to scold the child struggling with homework or to help her.

Unfortunately, it is impossible to constantly do only what we want. So, among other things, we ascribe our unhappiness to less favorable choices we have to make. How can we be happy when we want to play outside, and instead we have to study or work? When we want to read but have to do the dishes? Or when we want to devour a juicy hamburger, but we are told a carrot is a healthier choice?

Our lives are defined by such decisions. Our happiness, however, depends on another set of choices we make all the time, choices so subtle that most of us do not even notice making them: choices about what attitude to take in every situation. When you get an extra assignment at work, do you choose to feel angry or trusted? When it's raining outside, do you choose to be annoyed or grateful? When called out of bed at night to bring water to your child, do you feel grumpy or needed? If you eat that piece of chocolate, do you feel guilty or enjoy it? And if you abstain from it, do you choose to feel frustrated or proud? Of course, everyone *wants* to always be happy. But that usually slips our minds in the course of the everyday stress and grind, and so we continue with our automatic responses to life, getting upset, frustrated, and grumpy.

Therefore, in any situation, but especially when we are presented with challenging choices and trying circumstances, it is very helpful to remember that we can choose to be happy. Keep in mind the reasons why happiness is a priority above other things. Then extra work assignments, poor weather, having to forgo reading or sweets, and many other circumstances will no longer hold much power over our state of mind. We will be able to transcend them and not let them interfere with our mood.

It also helps to have a clear rationale for *not* being upset or grumpy. For example, every time you find yourself in an unfavorable situation, you may say to yourself, I want to be happy anyway because life is precious and I do not want to waste a day being in a bad mood. Or you may say it's because everything is relative and nothing is as bad as it seems. Or you might come up with your own individual reason to continue to be happy. For example, in the following story, tragedy helps a young man find a reason for lasting happiness.

Once in Jerusalem Rabbi **Noah Weinberg** met a young man with an unusually happy disposition and asked what his secret was.

"When I was eleven years old, God gave me a gift of happiness. I was riding my bicycle when a strong gust of wind blew me onto the ground into the path of an oncoming truck. The truck ran over me and cut off my leg.

"As I lay there bleeding, I realized that I might have to live the rest of my life without a leg. How depressing! But then I realized that being depressed won't get my leg back. So I decided right then and there not to waste my life despairing.

"When my parents arrived at the hospital they were shocked and grieving. I told them, 'I've already adapted. Now you also have to get used to this.'

"Ever since then, I see my friends getting upset over little things: their bus came late, they got a bad grade on a test, somebody insulted them. But I just enjoy life."[99]

When faced with a tragic situation, this young man made a conscious choice to be happy, because he realized that concentrating on what is missing is simply a waste of energy and an impediment to happiness.

All the choices we make are important. They shape our lives. But there is only one choice that affects our happiness—the choice to be happy.

PUT IT INTO PRACTICE

- Exercise your freedom to choose.

Being happy is a choice you can make in any situation. Holocaust survivors Viktor E. Frankl, Chaya Sara Kramer, and others like **Alice Herz-Sommer** attest to the fact that people can make this choice even in death camps. No one can take this human right away from you, except you.

With this in mind, assign an additional meaning to every situation: know that you have the ability to stay positive even in difficult times.

- Give yourself time to make the choice.

Especially in the beginning, when a good mood does not come naturally in challenging situations, give yourself time. The first moment you feel that you are getting upset over something, pause or count to ten. But don't just count. This little moment is a time is for you to remember this chapter and to act on your choice to stay happy. This is the time to remember your priorities, remember the reasons for those priorities, and make an effort to switch to a genuinely happier attitude. This is the time to remind yourself, "Wait a minute, how I want to look at things is my choice," and use this to help yourself feel better and be happier. Count as high as necessary to giver yourself enough time to make a conscious decision about your emotional reaction instead of reacting spontaneously. The more you practice, the less time you will need.

- Find your method.

Pick a simple strategy that will keep you feeling content or even good in an unfavorable situation. It can be reciting an inspirational quote, breathing deeply, remembering past experience, thinking of the bright future, reminding yourself that life is transient, thinking of the divine, meditating, or reminding yourself that you have a duty to yourself to stay happy no matter what.

Use your strategy during the time you give yourself using the previous exercise.

• Practice, practice, practice.

Ultimately, we want to feel happy without having to consciously choose to. Practice will get you there. Make the choice to be happy continuously, in every situation. Every time you practice your "happy" choice, certain neurons "fire together" in your brain. The more you "exercise" these neurons, the sooner they will create new "habits," and the new way of reacting will soon become automatic.

You will slip back into old patterns sometimes, and that is okay. If you find yourself getting upset, frustrated, or angry, it is never too late to retrace your steps and make a new choice. On the contrary, you should congratulate yourself on noticing your reactions now. This is itself a type of progress. Changing habits is not easy, and every step forward is a big deal.

START WITH YOURSELF

CHAPTER 20

INTRODUCTION TO THE SECTION

"The Almighty leads a person along the path that he
wishes to follow."

—The Talmud, Makkot, 10b

Circumstances change; good and bad times replace each other; people come in and out of our lives; even time and space are relative. The one constant we always have and can never escape is ourselves. We live with ourselves every moment of our lives. And nothing we experience and feel comes to us in a pure form. Everything gets filtered through us, through our perception and understanding. We are offered a multitude of paths in our lives, and we follow only the ones that we choose. That makes us rather crucial to our own destiny.

The Talmud says that we are born with some predetermined traits. We do not decide on our height, IQ level, or singing voice. But the choices we make are all up to us.

Sometimes it feels as if we are trapped by our personality and

OLGA GILBURD

cannot behave differently. Judaism teaches that we and we alone
are the authors of our autobiography. We can choose our behavior, as did the prince in the tale called "The Prince Who Thought
He Was a Rooster":

> Once there was a prince who thought he was a rooster.
> He spent his days sitting naked under a table in his room,
> refusing to eat anything except birdseed. The prince's best
> friend tried to coax him from under the table to play. But
> the prince refused to even look at him. The prince's fa-
> vorite tutor came to talk reason with the boy and read a
> book to him. But the prince only turned his head to one
> side and cried, "Cock-a-doodle-doo!" The king and the
> queen were distraught. They announced a reward for any-
> one who could cure their son.
>
> Many people came, tried, and failed. The prince thought
> he was a rooster, and that was it. One day, an old man
> called Ezra arrived at the palace and said that he could
> cure the prince in a week. The king and the queen knew
> that his name meant "help" in Hebrew and took it for a
> good sign. They welcomed Ezra to the palace and intro-
> duced him to the prince.
>
> As soon as he was inside the room, Ezra took off all his
> clothes, crawled under the table next to the prince, and
> began to peck at the floor. "I am a rooster too," he said
> to the surprised prince. After three days sitting under the
> table together, pecking the birdseed, and shouting, "Cock-
> a-doodle-doo!" they became great friends.
>
> On the fourth day, Ezra put his cloths back on. "What are
> you doing?" protested the prince. "You are a rooster like

me, and roosters do not wear clothes. Take them off!"

"Even though I am a rooster," Ezra told the prince, "I prefer to wear clothes. That way I don't feel so cold as I sit on the floor. You can do whatever you like, but this rooster is more comfortable in clothes."

The prince thought for a while and then slowly crawled from under the table and put on his own clothes.

The next morning, the prince was pecking away at the birdseed on the floor as he and Ezra did every morning. This morning, though, Ezra fetched the breakfast tray that the palace servants had left outside the door, as they did every morning. Ezra put some food on a plate, brought it back under the table, and began to eat it.

"What are you doing?" cried the prince. "Roosters eat birdseed, not scrambled eggs and toast. That is people food, and you are a rooster. Put it back!"

But Ezra continued to enjoy the food. "I am a rooster, just like you. But roosters are free to eat whatever food they like. If you prefer the taste of birdseed, then by all means, continue to eat birdseed. But I like eggs and toast and all sorts of other foods."

The prince thought about it and picked some food from the tray. They spent the rest of the day as usual, sitting under the table and shouting, "Cock-a-doodle-doo!" But whenever a meal arrived, they brought it under the table and shared the food.

The next morning, instead of bringing the food back under the table to eat, Ezra sat on a chair at the table. After he had eaten, Ezra began to walk around the room instead of crouching under the table.

"What are you doing now?" the prince asked suspiciously. "How can you be a rooster if you eat your meals at the table and walk upright like a man?"

"Just because I am a rooster does not mean I cannot sit or move around comfortably. Is there any reason why a rooster cannot do that if he prefers it?"

"I suppose not," the prince mumbled after taking some time to think about it. And he too sat down at the table to eat his breakfast.

That day, instead of spending his time yelling, "Cock-a-doodle-doo!" Ezra turned to the prince and asked, "The Sabbath begins this evening. How do you think we should celebrate it? Even though I am a rooster, I prefer to spend my Sabbath praying to God, sharing a fine meal, studying the words of the Torah, and being with my family. Would you like to join me?"

There was a long silence. Then the prince said quietly, "I am still a rooster. But I would like to celebrate together with my family."

When the king and the queen came to the room at the end of the week, the prince walked over and hugged them.

"This is remarkable!" the king exclaimed as he hugged his son in return. "How did you manage it?" he asked, turning to Ezra.

"Nothing has changed," answered Ezra. "Your son is your son. He always has been and always will be. He's still the same inside. The only thing that is different is the way he behaves. All I taught him is that God gives human beings the ability to make choices. No matter how we feel on the inside, we can choose to behave better than we feel."[100]

Our sense of identity plays a major role in our lives. We tend to speak and act in ways that are consistent with our self-image. If we believe we cannot do something, we can't. If we believe we can do anything, we can. And if we believe we are happy, we are.

In the tale above, only the prince himself had the power to change his thinking, behavior, and perception of his life. Ezra only helped to allow himself to make the choice to do so. Similarly, no matter what our personality is and no matter what we believe we are, we can control our thoughts and behavior if we choose to. We are the ones who can make ourselves happy.

Happiness is nothing more than a reaction to life, which is expressed through our thoughts, words, and actions. This makes us the masters of our happiness. Only we can squash it or allow it to flourish.

Therefore, we should begin our quest for happiness by focusing on ourselves: mind, body, and soul.

CHAPTER 21

MASTER OF YOUR HAPPINESS

I asked God to give me happiness,
And God said, "No."
He said He gives blessings,
Happiness is up to me.

—Anonymous, "And God Said No"[101]

"I was always looking outside myself for strength and confidence,
but it comes from within. It is there all the time."

—Anna Freud

Imagine living with a nagger who stresses your inadequacies, diminishes your strengths, predicts a gloomy future, fills you with worry and anxiety, and points out the negative qualities in everything you see, experience, and do. He or she would constantly make you feel miserable and deprived of all enjoyment. On the other hand, someone who always supported you and directed attention to all the great things that were happening to you would make you feel great.

Indeed, you have such powerful person affecting the quality of your life. Allow me to introduce the master of your happiness, the one who defines how much joy you are allowed in any circumstances and how happy you are going to be. This person is you.

That is right: your happiness depends completely on you. So much so that even the Hebrew word for "to pray," *lehitpalel*, is a reflexive verb, which means it describes doing something to the self, not to God. Rabbi **David Aaron** teaches that we do not pray to inform God of our misfortunes and implore Him to change the world and make us happy. Instead, when we pray, we have a chance to change our whole situation by hearing ourselves express our current view of our circumstances and changing our thoughts about them. He instructs us not to ask, "Is God listening to my prayers?" but rather, "Am I listening to my prayers?"[102] God and fate may arrange for different circumstances, but they do not arrange our response to these circumstances. Our reactions are totally up to us. In a way, we pray to ourselves, because we are the masters of our happiness.

Hasidic philosophy maintains that everything comes from the mind, including all happiness and suffering. Modern science has gradually come to a similar conclusion. Psychology demonstrates that the power of the mind is real and highly effective in changing our levels of happiness. A study of the placebo effect in the treatment of depression found that when people who were given "fake" pills not containing a therapeutic substance were convinced that they were taking real medication, their symptoms improved almost as much as with actual antidepressants.[103] New physics experiments are forcing scientists to acknowledge that consciousness creates reality and we can change our lives through the way we observe ourselves and the world.[104]

Psychiatrist Gerald Epstein says that we can change our minds at will.[105] Just as we decide what to let into our homes and what to keep out, so we can choose which thoughts to cultivate and which to curtail.

The thoughts we choose have the power to change the flow of our lives:

> Our thoughts shape our actions;
> Our actions shape our habits;
> Our habits shape our character;
> Our character shapes our destiny.

You and only you have the power to make yourself happy, joyful, and content. In any given situation, you can choose whether to be depressed or hopeful, stressed or excited, sad or content, condescending or encouraging, distracted or mindful. When things don't go as planned, it is up to you to decide whether to think of yourself as failing or as gaining valuable life experience. Choose wisely, because your life depends on it.

PUT IT INTO PRACTICE

It is very liberating to realize that our happiness does not depend on other people or things, and this realization in itself contributes to happiness. Suddenly the world of happiness is ours to master! But this also means that we have to assume full responsibility for our happiness or lack thereof. Here are some tips to help you take on the role of master of your own happiness:

- Assume responsibility.

"The girl who can't dance says the band can't play," observes a Yiddish proverb.[106] Sometimes we too blame outside circumstances for our shortcomings and emotional states. But if you are to successfully master happiness, you must shift responsibility for your happiness from circumstances and other people to yourself. To paraphrase another Yiddish proverb, if you don't want to be happy, one excuse is as good as another.[107] Don't pin your happiness or unhappiness on the events of the day, your spouse, your coworkers, your kids, or strangers. You do not have to be a victim of the universe's whims. You are the one responsible for your mood.

Every time you catch yourself rationalizing your bad mood by blaming it on some outside cause, restate your thought in a way that places the responsibility for your feelings with you. For example, when you feel that everything always goes wrong and the universe is conspiring against you, say to yourself, "I am in a bad mood and getting annoyed at everything." Or instead of complaining that someone hurt your feelings, realize that you care too much about the words or actions of others.

- Correlate your reaction with the importance of the situation.

Adjust your overly negative reactions to unpleasant circumstances and interactions with other people by considering how much importance you attach to them. If your car gets scratched or your husband leaves dirty socks on the floor, weigh how important this is and how much negative reaction it warrants. And if you find yourself in a bad a situation that is truly important, ask yourself how helpful a highly negative reaction would be then.

- Stop predicting the future.

Sometimes we get upset over small things because we think they may become big things. For example, running late for work may be not earth shattering in itself, but we get very upset because we think we might get reprimanded or fired. In case like this, it helps to remind ourselves that we are just imagining worst-case scenarios for a future that we cannot predict.[108] Stay focused on the present, and do not make a mountain out of a molehill.

- Believe in your power.

Finally, do not doubt your ability to make yourself happy. You live with yourself twenty-four hours a day, and you have tremendous power to improve your happiness. Be kind to yourself, be positive, and do not let others have more control over your thoughts than you have.

Praise yourself for every little improvement and every little victory, for every time you could have slipped into a bad mood but didn't.

Repeat this mantra to yourself: "Nothing can ruin my day without my permission or make me happy without my blessing. I am capable. I can control my reactions."

CHAPTER 22

SELF-ESTEEM: LOVE YOURSELF JUST THE WAY YOU ARE

"One must encourage and uplift oneself."

—Rebbe Nachman of Breslov[109]

"The way we perceive ourselves is crucial to happiness."

—The Rohr Jewish Learning Institute,
How Happiness Thinks[110]

One of the essential conditions for happiness is satisfaction with ourselves or self-esteem. It is easier to enjoy the world when we like ourselves and think ourselves worthy of all the miracles it has to offer. Being content with oneself is the key to peace, freedom, and happiness.

Our self-esteem is influenced a lot by things outside ourselves. When others give us admiration, compliments, and appreciative looks, our self-esteem gets boosted. When they disapprove of or judge us, it gets tested. But the biggest influence on self-esteem has little to do with the reactions of others. It comes from the inside, from our biggest critic or a biggest fan—ourselves.

When someone glances your way and laughs, do you feel it is because the person is making fun of you or because of something unrelated to you? If you hear a car horn while driving, do you mentally berate the other driver for honking at you when you did nothing wrong or keep calm because it must be meant for someone else? Of if someone pays you a compliment, do you doubt their words or feel confident that you deserve the praise? Our gut reactions to situations like the ones described above determine our level of happiness at that moment, and these reactions depend on what we think about ourselves much more than on what other people say or do.

Low self-esteem causes all kinds of problems and misery. According to psychologists, people with low self-esteem interpret even benign remarks as insults or cause for jealousy. They crave validation and form unhealthy attachments and codependent relationships. They want to please everyone. As a result, they're afraid to say no to requests, but they then harbor resentment toward others for taking advantage of them. They find situations involving normal levels of stress overwhelming, not because the challenges are so enormous, but because they feel inadequate to cope with them.[111]

Low self-esteem cost the newly liberated Jews the Promised Land. According to the Torah, after escaping from Egypt, the Jews quickly reached the Promised Land. They dispatched twelve spies to explore it, and the spies returned bearing fruits of the land and reported that it was indeed the land of milk and honey. However, there were other tribes living there, and the spies said, "We felt as small as grasshoppers, and that's how we must have looked to them."[112] The Torah does not say what the locals thought. That was what the Jews thought of themselves. Because of this doubt in themselves and in the support of God, the Jews were punished, and the entire nation was made to wander in the desert for forty years, until almost the entire generation of men who had left Egypt had died.

High self-esteem does not mean being arrogant and believing that we are perfect and can do no wrong. It means trusting ourselves and not being deterred by the fear of making mistakes. When we fail, healthy self-esteem allows us to be less defensive, to laugh at ourselves, and to be less concerned about getting everyone else to like us all the time. It enables us to own up to our weaknesses and failures without depreciating ourselves. Nobody is perfect at everything. Napoleon was afraid of cats, Tchaikovsky ate paper and cried up to ten times a day, and Bach threw his wig at a musician who was out of tune. All of us have strengths and shortcomings. That is part of what makes us us.

If sometimes we feel that just being us is not good enough, Judaism begs to differ. It insists that just being you is very good, as that is exactly what you are supposed to be.

Zusya of Hanipol, a nineteenth-century Hasidic rabbi, once commented, "When I am called to give a final account before the Heavenly Throne, I am not afraid of being asked, 'Why were you not like **Abraham**?' for then I will answer, 'Because I am not Abraham.' And if I am asked why was I not like **Moses**, I can answer, 'Because I am not Moses.'"[113] The important thing is to be the best version of yourself and not to try to be anyone else.

Judaism promotes healthy self-esteem in many ways. Its very essence is contingent upon people believing that we are indeed significant and worthy of God's attention.[114]

The Torah says that we are "a ladder that is stood upon earth whose head reaches the heavens,"[115] and all our gestures, engagements, words, and movements have an effect on high. In fact, excessive humility distances us from God, because it leads us to disbelieve that our prayer and Torah study affect the supernal world.[116] The Baal Shem Tov disapproved of self-censure, teaching that it leads to sadness, which is an ugly trait.[117] Besides, disliking the way we are means doubting the ever-purposeful and superior work of God.

The Talmud and the rabbinic writings use three categories to describe people: **tzaddik** (righteous), *rasha* (wicked), and *beinoni* (intermediate). It is believed that there are only thirty-six truly righteous people, called *lamed-vavniks*, in the world at any one time. The *Tanya*, a book which lays down the practical and mystical fundamentals of the **Chabad** philosophy, asserts that God created our world for the *benioni*—an imperfect and conflicted being—and that the purpose of creation is our everyday struggle to overcome the negative aspects of ourselves. Therefore, a person should not feel dejected or depressed that he is not a *tzaddik* and that he struggles with flaws all his life.[118] The *Tanya* teaches us to see that our imperfections are opportunities for improvement and to rejoice in these opportunities, as this is God's purpose in creating us the way we are, the exact way we are supposed to be.

Moreover, the Torah holds that each person is intrinsically special and important because of a *neshama*, a unique soul. Everyone brings to this world something that only he or she can bring. You cannot be anybody different than who you are, and nobody can replace another in his or her unique contribution to the world: you cannot accomplish anybody else's mission, and no one can accomplish yours. Everyone is important and irreplaceable.[119] The following parable shows that even a cracked pot has a special value.

A water bearer in Babylon had two large pots. One pot was perfect and always delivered a full portion of water at the end of the long walk from the stream to the house, while the second pot had a crack and arrived only half full.

The perfect pot was proud of its accomplishments, perfect to the end for which it was made. But the cracked pot was ashamed of its imperfection. One day it said to the water bearer: "I am a failure. Because of my crack the water leaks out all the way back to the house."

The water bearer smiled. "Do you notice that there are beautiful flowers along your side of the path, but not on the other pot's side? Every day while we walk back from the stream, you water them. Thanks to you I have been able to enjoy the sight of these beautiful flowers and to decorate the house. Without you being just the way you are, we would not have this beauty." [120]

Each of us has unique strengths and flaws. We may think, like the cracked pot, that we are inefficient or useless in certain areas, but these flaws can turn out to be blessings in disguise. What makes us great is not the absence of flaws but the presence of merits.

PUT IT INTO PRACTICE

- Be proud of yourself.

Rabbi **Zelig Pliskin** recommends keeping a highlight journal and every day writing down one positive story about yourself. Describe something positive you said or did as if you were writing a biography of someone else. For example, if you said a kind word to someone, describe your act of kindness in glowing terms. You can write about the potential benefits of that kindness. Do not view this as boasting about yourself. Rather, consider it a record of at least one positive thing you did each and every day. Stories about your own strength and positive actions are the most inspiring stories you can read when you are facing challenging times.[121]

Acknowledge any efforts at self-improvement. For example, if you wanted to scream and you didn't (or only screamed a little), congratulate yourself for this. If you have kids, share your victories with the them. They will learn from you.

- Work on self-improvement without self-depreciation.

You are not perfect, but you don't need to be.

Do not condemn yourself for having undesirable character qualities or feeling negative feelings. Love yourself as you are—with your strengths and flaws—without self-judgment or guilt even as you work on self-improvement. Maintain the balance of changing yourself while still accepting yourself.

Know that you are a work-in-progress, gaining new experiences and improving every day. You are working on yourself even now by reading this book.

- Acknowledge your intrinsic meaningfulness and uniqueness.

Every day, notice three things that you do that you consider meaningful.[122] You will become aware that you probably do many more than three meaningful things each day and that your life is very meaningful and you are a valuable person. You will feel better about yourself and your whole life.

Acknowledge and love your uniqueness. Say to yourself, "I am needed: I am needed by the universe because of my uniqueness. I am needed by my family. I am needed by other people." If you are a believer, repeat, "God loves me as I am right now."

- Do not let yourself be too affected by another's opinion of you.

Each of us has felt peer pressure and judgment at some point. People often judge others who are not like them. Meat eaters judge vegetarians. Vegetarians judge meat eaters. People judge each other based on anything and everything, including clothes, choice of music, sexual orientation, and many more things that should not matter to them.

Do not let yourself be too influenced by or get too hung up on either the positive or negative judgments of others. Remember that other people's reality stems from their perception of the world and has more to do with them than with you.

- Do not compare yourself to others.

We are all different. There will always be people with both better and worse qualities than you. Comparing yourself to them will only make you feel worthless or conceited, but ultimately, it will not make any difference—you will still be you, and they will be them.

Besides, we never fully know what is really going on with other people—what their true circumstances are, what is going on in their heads. A man sitting in a bar by himself with an air of importance may seem very cool and self-sufficient, but in reality he may just suffer from social anxiety. Therefore, it is pointless to measure yourself against others.

If you ever find yourself feeling jealous of someone because it seems that they are better than you are, remember that, even though we all are different in our qualities and attributes, no one is any more or less divine in his or her own unique way than anyone else.

Sigmund Freud taught: "The only person with whom you have to compare yourself is you in the past. And the only person you have to be better than is you now."

- Appreciate your potential.

Our self-esteem is built not only on what we have done and what we are today but also on the awareness of our potential, on what we can do and what we can be. The fact that we are imperfect is the precise reason that improvement is possible. Having flaws means a promise of joy ahead as things improve, something to look forward to, a goal.

When your current self-image is lacking, always add a magic word to your thoughts about yourself—*yet*:

I cannot do that . . . yet.

I am not as happy as I want to be . . . yet.

- Boost your self-image.

Chabad rabbis teach: "Just as we have to know the defects, so too, we need to know our strengths."[123] Find your good qualities and rejoice over them. Boost your self-esteem with daily positive affirmations about yourself.[124] You might use some of the affirmations that follow or come up with ones of your own:

❖ I am smart.

❖ I am unique.

❖ Every day I gain more experience and knowledge. Every day I become an even better person.

❖ I am charming. People enjoy my company.

❖ I am what I am. I do what I can. My world loves me, and I love me, too!

Choose some adjectives from the list below to describe your strengths, and add your own:

A: active, adaptable, adventurous, affable, affectionate, amiable, articulate, artistic, athletic, attentive, attractive, _____

B: beautiful, benevolent, bold, brave, bright, brilliant, broad-minded, _____

C: calm, candid, caring, charming, cheerful, clever, communicative, compassionate, conscientious, considerate, courageous, courteous, creative, cultured, curious, cute,

_____

D: decisive, dedicated, delightful, determined, devoted, diligent, discreet, dutiful, dynamic, _____

E: earnest, easygoing, educated, effective, efficient, elegant, eloquent, empathetic, energetic, enthusiastic, extraordinary, exuberant, _____

F: fair, faithful, fearless, flexible, focused, forgiving, frank, friendly, funny, _____

G: gallant, generous, gentle, genuine, goal oriented, good, good-natured, graceful, gracious, grateful, gregarious,

_____

H: hardworking, healthy, helpful, high-spirited, honest, honorable, humble, humorous, _____

I: imaginative, independent, insightful, intelligent, interested, intuitive, inventive, _____

J: jokey, joyous, just, _____

K: kind, knowledgeable, _____

L: lively, logical, lovely, loving, loyal, _____

M: many-sided, mature, mindful, modest, motivated, _____

N: neat, nice, _____

O: objective, observant, open-minded, optimistic, organized, original, _____

P: passionate, patient, peaceful, perceptive, persevering, personable, playful, polite, positive, powerful, practical, proactive, profound, prudent, punctual, _____

Q: quiet, quick-witted, _____

R: radiant, rational, realistic, relaxed, reliable, resourceful, respectful, responsible, romantic, _____

S: self-reliant, sensible, sensitive, sincere, skillful, smart, sociable, straightforward, strong, suave, sweet, _____

T: tasteful, thoughtful, tolerant, trustworthy, _____

U: uncomplaining, understanding, unique, upright, _____

V: versatile, visionary, vivacious, _____

W: warmhearted, well rounded, wise, witty, wonderful, _____

Y: youthful, _____

Z: Zen, zesty, _____

CHAPTER 23

ARE WE TOO LAZY TO FEEL AMAZING?

"It is astonishing how fast the waves of delight subside. We spend hours and days on end gnawing ourselves, tormenting ourselves, nagging and complaining, but rapture comes and goes in a moment."

—**Arkady and Boris Strugatsky**

Why don't we feel our happiest most of the times? One reason is our emotional laziness. Physical and emotional comfort is much easier to ignore than an equal level of discomfort. That is why we get upset when we are running late to a much greater degree than we get happy when we are on schedule.

Even though being upset, annoyed, frustrated, or angry takes a lot of mental energy, many of us find the strength to react or even overreact when we experience these feelings. Sustaining positive emotions also requires some mental energy, and we are often too lazy to exert it, letting the nice things slide by unacknowledged or getting bored without outside stimulation.

Not making our best effort to sustain and express positive emotions affects not only ourselves but others as well. Are we always as loving or as kind as we could be? **Golda Meir** once noted, "There can be no doubt that the average man blames much more than he praises. His instinct is to blame. If he is satisfied he says nothing; if he is not, he most illogically kicks up a row."[125]

Shifting the responsibility for our boredom or bad mood to other people and circumstances is a sign of emotional laziness. We do this automatically when we think, "She annoys me" instead of "I am inpatient with her" or "it was a bad day" instead of "I lost my temper."[126] In a way, slipping into a bad attitude is just easier than putting effort into reacting more positively to the outside world.

One might think that once we've experienced happiness and the pleasant feeling that comes with it, we would want more of it and even work for it. Conversely, one would think that once we've experienced sadness, anger, and, more important, the negative fallout of these emotions in our lives, we would work to keep them away. Surprisingly, it is not so. We often find ourselves falling into a habit of being negative despite the fact that we're harming ourselves with unpleasant emotions.

The Lubavitcher Rebbe taught that our mental ability is a great gift from God, and we should not waste it.[127] Resolve to use this mental ability to express positive feelings with more enthusiasm and feel amazing every day.

PUT IT INTO PRACTICE

- Think of the benefits.

Positive emotions such as pleasure, contentment, and happiness feel great. If you put just a little more effort into them than usual, you get to enjoy them more intensely. Imagine how people around you will feel when you will express your joy more openly and impart kind words and bright smiles on them.

- Get physical.

Our mind and body are very closely connected. Sometimes we are just too tired to even smile, let alone be cheerful.

Take good care of your body to ensure you have enough energy for positive emotions. Get adequate rest, eat healthily, and get your blood flowing with movement. Get up and jump up and down a couple of times. Do it right now and every time you feel too blah to be happy.

- Start small.

Every time you notice something nice, even something small, do not let it slip by. Start by simply putting on a nice smile in response.

- Create an "I feel amazing" team.

Enthusiasm is contagious. Therefore, enlist your family and friends into the antilaziness campaign. Every time you see them expressing positive feelings, you will remember to do the same.

- Seize the opportunity.

When you have a choice either to pay a compliment or just keep silent, choose to say what you're thinking out loud. Do not hesitate to smile and say kind words if you feel the smallest inclination to do so.

CHAPTER 24

CHERISH YOUR BODY

"The well-being of the soul can be obtained only after that of the body has been secured."

—Maimonides, *Guide for the Perplexed*[128]

In addition to fostering positive mind-sets and self-esteem, we should also love and care for our bodies. Most of the things we do and experience have to do with the body. The body can make us feel pleasure or pain, a surge of energy or fatigue. Our bodies can enable or limit our freedom to do what we want—our ability to dance, swim, play musical instruments, manipulate objects, and enjoy the senses of sight, smell, hearing, taste, and touch. Our bodies can put us in the state of joy or suffering. It is possible to enjoy life even with indigestion or pain, but if we take good care of ourselves, we can prevent many physical problems that can cause us unnecessary suffering.

Judaism holds that a relationship with God brings us bliss, and maintaining a healthy body allows for a better connection. "Since it is impossible to have any understanding and knowledge of the Creator when one is sick, it is one's duty to avoid whatever is injurious to the body and to cultivate habits to promote health and vigor," instructed Maimonides.[129] For the first-century scholar, the great sage **Hillel,** keeping the body in pristine and pure condition was a spiritual task.

> It is told that after Hillel finished giving a lecture, he rushed off.
>
> "Master," his disciples asked, "where are you going?"
>
> "To fulfill a religious obligation," Hillel answered.
>
> "What is this deed?" they asked, hoping to learn from him.
>
> Hillel replied, "To take a bath in the bathhouse."[130]

Jewish tradition places major emphasis on keeping the body clean and healthy, as it was created by God in His image, is interconnected with the mind, and contains the precious soul. Taking care of the body is a mitzvah.[131] The Talmud contains much advice on how to stay in good health and even forbids residing in a town with no physician to care for the health of its citizens.[132]

In fact, Jewish sages teach that acts of fulfilling our physical needs, such as eating, can transcend mere sustenance of the body and become spiritual experiences in themselves.[133]

PUT IT INTO PRACTICE

The Hebrew Bible emphasizes the importance of taking care of oneself when it says, "He who does good to his own person is a man of piety."[134] Here is what we can do to take care of our bodies:

- Rest.

"Sleep is the best doctor,"[135] says a Yiddish proverb, and another declares that "a sleepless night is the worst punishment."[136] The amount of sleep we get affects our health, energy, stress level, mood, memory, and weight. Some rabbis even proclaim that getting enough sleep is the secret to any personal and spiritual growth.[137]

On average, an adult requires seven to eight hours a sleep per day.[138] Keeping that in mind, decide on your bedtime and commit to it. The National Sleep Foundation advises that you "put it on your to-do list and cross it off every night."[139] Make getting enough rest a priority. Get to bed on time even if you have to postpone some things till the next day.

If you find it difficult to stick to a decent bedtime, make a chart and mark off which days you get to bed on time. If you get do it for four consecutive nights, give yourself a reward, such as ice cream, a manicure, or a massage. The next week up the ante to six consecutive nights until you're getting to bed on time every night.[140]

- Eat well.

"Eating is an act of holiness. It requires full presence of mind," taught Rebbe Nachman of Breslov.[141] The way we eat affects our health, our weight, and our energy level. Make a habit of choosing healthy food. Transform mundane food consumption into a mindful and joyous experience. Be grateful for every meal. Appreciate its smell, its taste, and its texture. Notice how fast you eat. If you tend to eat quickly, slow down and enjoy every bite. Observe how the taste of food intensifies and becomes more complex the longer you chew it.[142] Think good thoughts, and be grateful for the nourishment the food gives you. Consider how happy you are to have it.

- Move.

Movement is life. Move in any way you like—you might choose to walk, dance, practice yoga, or do any other kind of exercise. Incorporate more movement into your daily routine. Do exercises each morning. Walk to places nearby instead of driving. Use the stairs instead of elevators. Get up and move a little every hour. Enjoy movement and your ability to be active.

- Keep yourself and your home clean.

Cleanliness is next to godliness according to an ancient Hebrew proverb.[143] Cleanliness and good personal hygiene are certainly major contributors to good health. Therefore, it's essential to take good care of all the parts of your body, your clothes, and your dwelling.

- Get attuned to your body.

The body we have now is the only one we've got for the whole duration of our lives. We should not take it for granted. Acknowledge and appreciate what your body does for you. Learn to listen to it. If you feel tired, stop what you are doing and rest; if you feel sleepy, go to bed; if you feel full, put the utensils down.

* * *

Remember that everything is good in moderation. If you exercise, do not work so hard that you can't walk the next day. If you try to eat healthy, do not starve yourself or skip necessary nutrients. Whatever you do, be gentle with yourself. Cherish your body.

PERSPECTIVE

CHAPTER 25

INTRODUCTION TO THE SECTION

"Only in relation to our imagination can things be called beautiful or ugly, well-ordered or confused"

—Baruch Spinoza

The Zohar points out that the letters forming the Hebrew word *besimchah* (with joy) are the same letters that spell *machshavah* (thought),[144] indicating that our happiness comes from our minds. Indeed, our subconscious brains can't tell the difference between what's real and what's in our thoughts. If we pay more attention to the negative, we can miss the positive things that are happening at the same time. If we focus on the positive, it will predominate and fill our lives with joy, despite the negative things around us. The more trifles we deem strokes of good luck, the luckier we become. In short, our happiness fully depends on our view of the world, our perspective. That is how the vendor in the following folktale was able to sell happiness.

Once upon a time a stranger came to a town square and loudly announced:

"Listen up, everyone! I sell happiness! Trade your problems and complaints for joy and contentment! I have enough happiness for everyone!"

People started to gather around, curious to see the stranger, who was now tying a rope to two poles.

"Townspeople! Come and hang all your problems on this rope in exchange for happiness!"

People rushed to get rid of their problems. Old Rebecca hung her arthritic knee. Zeev hung up his ginger hair; Mordecai got rid of his empty purse. People pinned all their complaints to the rope: the town is too gray, the work is too hard, the sun is too hot, and the kids are too loud. Soon the rope was sagging under the weight of everybody's problems.

"Nu, good people, I promised to trade happiness for your troubles, and here it is: you pick any problem from this rope that is smaller than yours; exchange your trouble for a lesser one and be happy!"

Everyone in the square rushed in once again to pick the easiest trouble for themselves. To their surprise, they all saw that their own trouble was the smallest of the bunch! Soon the rope was empty again.

"So, did everyone pick the smallest hardship?" asked the happiness vendor.

"Yes," said Zeev, petting his ginger hair and being glad for it.

"Yes," said Rebecca, gently bending her knee.

"Yes," chimed in everyone else, each one happy to have grabbed his or her own small trouble before anyone else got to it.

"Very well. I kept my promise and provided you with happiness of your own choosing! Now go on and be happy!"

Indeed, the people were smiling and excited. They felt much happier after getting the happiness from this vendor, even though nothing had changed.

The happiness vendor packed up his rope and left for the next town, pondering once again how, by changing perspective and attitude, we control our reality and happiness.[145]

In the following chapters, I will discuss how we can learn to do just this.

CHAPTER 26

THE BIG PICTURE

"This also is vanity and a striving after wind."

—**Ecclesiastes** 2:26

We often let unimportant annoyances that do not play any major role in our lives mar our happiness. A broken car, a harsh word, a breakup, an approaching deadline—these and so many other things seem very significant at the time we experience them. We get emotionally invested in them: upset, angry, or depressed. We get so immersed in the daily hustle and bustle that often we forget how great our lives are overall, or as a Hebrew proverb succinctly summarizes it, we "can't see the forest for the trees."[146]

A rabbi once had many of his students over for a Shabbat dinner. At the end of the meal, he showed them a tray holding an assortment of different cups and invited everyone to pick one as their drink. When everybody had a cup in hand, the rabbi said, *"Al tistakel baqanqan, ela bemah shebetokho*—don't look at the jar but at what's inside it.[147] What you really wanted was a drink, and yet you moved to pick the best-looking cup and got disappointed if you didn't get the one you wanted. But the cup itself adds no quality to your drink. Now consider this: life is the drink; jobs, money, and position in society are the cups. The type of cup we have neither defines nor changes the quality of the life we live. Sometimes, by concentrating only on the cup, we fail to enjoy the drink.[148]

There is another reason not to get too upset. As **King David** taught his son **Solomon**, everything is temporary. The story goes that shortly before his death King David presented his young son with a gold ring. He instructed Solomon to engrave it with the Hebrew letters *gimmel, zayin, yod*, which stood for the words *gam zeh ya'avor*—this too will pass—and to be sure to concentrate on this inscription during any trying circumstances.[149]

We can think of our life as a large painting. From a very close proximity, all we can see are smears of color, individual strokes, and images or shades that may not make sense. But from a distance, we see how it all fits together, how every brushstroke or every charcoal line forms an integral part of a vast, magnificent picture. Often, things that seem very bad or very significant when they happen actually become something else as the big picture develops. We do not always know what is truly good or bad, as the prophet **Elijah** demonstrates in this fairy tale called "Elijah's Wisdom":

> One day, the prophet Elijah paid a visit to Rabbi Joshua, who had prayed to learn why bad things happen to good people and vice versa. They set off to travel together and visit different people along their way.
>
> The first night, they came across a rich man and asked him for a meal and a place to sleep. He refused to give them any food to them or invite them in, but allowed them to

stay one night by a broken wall in his stable. The next morning, the rabbi observed with surprise as Elijah prayed for the wall to repair itself.

The next day, they knocked on the door of a poor old woman. She invited them in and was very hospitable. She only had one cow, and she shared her milk with the visitors and invited them to stay the night in her humble house. Rabbi Joshua expected the prophet to reward the woman for her kindness. But the next morning, Elijah said a prayer over the woman's cow, and it died.

"How can you say such a prayer?" exclaimed Rabbi Joshua. "You've repaired the stable wall for the rich man who was rude and unkind, but you made the only cow of this poor woman die after the way she treated us!"

"My dear Joshua, things are not always as they appear," said the prophet Elijah. "In the rich man's stable, there was treasure buried under that wall, which the rich man did not deserve because he was so ungenerous. So I asked God to repair the wall to make sure that he would not find the treasure beneath it.

"In the second house, the old woman was meant to die on the very day we visited her. Because of her kindness to us, I prayed that God take the cow in her place."

And now, suddenly Rabbi Joshua realized that life is not simple and that he hadn't understood who was being rewarded and who was being punished.

With that, Elijah vanished back up into Heaven, and Rabbi Joshua was left to ponder over this precious bit of wisdom.[150]

Remembering the existence of the big picture will put many things in perspective. It will help us transcend and not have overly negative reactions, bringing us closer to contentment and happiness.

PUT IT INTO PRACTICE

- Recognize that life is such a gift that anything else is trivial by comparison.

If you regard life in this way, everything else instantly becomes less stressful.

- See the big picture.

How do you react to circumstances such as lost luggage? Do you let them spoil your day or maybe even the entire vacation? The way you handle such rather small hiccups can reflect the way you deal with your entire life.

Evaluate the things that upset you in terms of your life priorities.[151] Are they truly important? Are they even on the list? Are they more important than your state of happiness? You do not have to ignore the problems, but deal with them without getting immersed in negative thinking.

- Remember that troubles are temporary.

When upset, remember the inscription on King Solomon's ring. Look past the here and now and consider how important the upsetting thing will still be to you in five or ten years.

- Let the big picture develop.

Often things that seem crucial are in fact inconsequential. For example, Sigmund Freud was booed off of the podium when he first presented his ideas to the scientific community of Europe. It must have felt awful to have his theories rejected by his peers. But that does not seem as horrible now, when we realize he will be forever known as the father of psychoanalysis. Other times, such things may in fact be significant in the larger scheme of our lives, but not in the way we initially thought. **Hilene Flanzbaum**, a poet and English professor, describes having to deal with the diagnosis of breast cancer. This experience, which she says was "horrible" at the time, led her to change her world view, resulting in a much happier life.[152]

You may have had the experience of getting upset over being late to an airport only to find out that the flight has been delayed or cancelled. If only we waited long enough to see how the situation would play out before making ourselves unhappy, stressing out, and getting high blood pressure.

Commit to letting things play out before letting them make you unhappy.

CHAPTER 27

MINDFULNESS

"You are wherever your thoughts are. Make sure your thoughts are where you want to be."

—Rebbe Nachman of Breslov[153]

Being able to conceive of the big picture and not dwelling on unpleasant details does not preclude us from being mindful of the present moment. Neuroscience research correlates increased levels of happiness with exercising the prefrontal cortex, which happens when we focus gently and continuously on whatever we are doing or saying.[154] That means that we are happier when we exercise mindfulness.

Mindfulness is the nonjudgmental awareness of the present moment. It is a skill for fully experiencing life as it happens by focusing on whatever is going on right now. When we say things without really meaning them, attempt to juggle several tasks at the same time, or space out, we are not being mindful.

There are two aspects of mindfulness: concentrating on the here and now and being conscious of our own thoughts and feelings.

FOCUS ON NOW

When rabbis tell schoolchildren what the most important moment in Jewish history is, they teach that it is not the giving of the Torah on Mount Sinai or the parting of the Red Sea. It is right now. *This* is the most important moment in Jewish history.[155] It is the most important moment in your life as well.

"The past is only memories. The future is but illusory hopes. Focus on the present. For that is where your life really is," taught rabbi **Eliyahu Eliezer Dessler**.[156] There is no time like the present. In fact, there is no time except the present. That is why today is the best day of your life: is the only day that ever exists. Now is the only time you can influence your life, the only time you can choose what to think, say, and do.

Often we are not as happy as we could be because we are distracted from the present. Thinking of the negative events of the past can make us feel regret, guilt, and anger. Reliving the positive events can cause wistfulness and nostalgia. Learn from past experiences, but focus on the now. Similarly, fretting about an uncertain future causes anxiety and fear, while dreaming about a great future only takes away from experiencing the present. Do not overthink the future: it may not happen the way you imagine.

Rebbe Nachman of Breslov instructed, "Every day is an entirely new creation. Take as much as you can from what each new day has to offer."[157] Enjoying the present moment and everything around us is the key to happiness. Rabbi Pliskin notes that we don't even have to be positive and happy all day. We only have to be positive and happy now.[158]

The Lubavitcher Rebbe taught that mindfulness makes the fullest use of our limited time. We cannot add actual time to the length of a day or night, and all we ever have is a present moment. If this moment, brief as it is, is free of all irrelevant thoughts about the past or the future, we will have the ability to utilize it to the highest degree. Therefore, when we are engaged in a particular activity, we should treat anything that is not pertinent to the matter at hand—whether it is something that we have previously done or that we need to later do—as if it does not exist. The Rebbe called this "success in time."[159]

BE CONSCIOUS

Judaism holds that "the mind rules the heart."[160] Thoughts precede and create our emotions, including happiness: if we think everything is good and will get even better, we feel very different than if we think it's all bad and may get worse. So it's rather important to be aware of our thought processes.

Ayn Rand identifies lack of mindfulness as one of the biggest failings one can have: "Man's basic vice, the source of all his evils, is the act of unfocusing his mind, the suspension of his consciousness, which is not blindness, but the refusal to see, not ignorance, but the refusal to know."[161]

Cognitive psychologists estimate that we spend 95 percent of the time in the automatic thinking mode. This is the habitual way of thinking and behaving in which our reactions to circumstances take less than a second. Our other mode, called rational thinking, is a bit slower because in this mode we do not just do something or say something but consider it first. It involves being mindful of our thoughts, feelings, and consequently, behavior.

Such mindfulness helps us develop both self-awareness and general awareness as we notice the fine details about ourselves and the world around us. Being conscientious about our decisions allows us to be in a better control of our life choices. Practicing mindfulness helps us recognize our mental patterns and gives us an opportunity to choose a happier attitude instead of just automatically slipping into a routine.

Practicing mindfulness also means avoiding multitasking. Scientists say that when we multitask, dividing our attention between many tasks, it takes away from all of them. As Albert Einstein noted, "Any man who can drive safely while kissing a pretty girl is simply not giving the kiss the attention it deserves." Multitasking leads to high stress and frustration, while mindful engagement leads to calmer moods and decreased stress levels.

PUT IT INTO PRACTICE

- Engage.

Focus on now and what you actually think, say, and do. Concentrate on the present moment, and do everything wholeheartedly. When listening to someone, focus your total attention on what that person is saying. When reading, do not just glance through the text but absorb every word. Trace each line with your finger to help yourself focus. When praying, focus your total attention on the words you are saying. Put your heart and soul into it.[162]

If you catch yourself getting distracted, Rabbi Pliskin recommends calmly repeating the word "Focus" in your mind,[163] or be more specific and say:

❖ Right now, I am aware of the sounds I am hearing.

❖ Right now, I am aware of what I am seeing.

❖ Right now, I am aware of the thoughts I am thinking.

- Notice everything.

Recognize the nice things in the world around you and in your-self, even if you are used to them. Notice the taste of an orange, the smiles of your loved ones, the feel of the wind on your face, the beautiful color of your own eyes. Feel good about it. Consciously do this at least once per hour. The opportunities are endless.

- Be in control of your thoughts.

Our positive and negative emotions are sustained by our thoughts. Jewish sages teach that the solution for dealing with negative feelings is not to stop thinking negatively but to replace negative thoughts with positive. As Rabbi Menachem Mendel of Lubavitch puts it, "The primary method of removing negative thoughts from your mind is by directing your mind toward other matters."[164]

Use mindfulness to not only be aware of your thoughts and re-sulting feelings but to control them. When you have negative feelings, consciously think about something positive, something that makes you happy. In any given situation, choose not the im-mediate reaction but the more mindful one. The more you prac-tice, the better you will become at generating different emotions.

- Meditate.

Meditation happens when we consciously concentrate on one image, one thought, or one task. Meditation helps us exercise mindfulness. Dr. **Richard Davidson**, director of the Laboratory for Affective Neuroscience at the University of Wisconsin, be-lieves that meditation can mold our brains to develop a happier temperament.[165]

For the simplest meditation practice, take a comfortable seat, close your eyes, and pay attention to your breathing, to each inhale and exhale. When your attention wanders, return it to the breath. Start by doing this for two minutes at a time.

CHAPTER 28

ATTITUDE IS
EVERYTHING

"Our attitudes control our lives. Attitudes are a secret power
working twenty-four hours a day, for good or bad. It is of
paramount importance that we know how to harness and control
this great force."

—Irving Berlin

E ven when we practice mindfulness, our brains have a limited
capacity for attention. They filter out a lot of incoming information. What we pay attention to and what gets overlooked
depends a lot on our attitude. Basically, we see only what we want
to see or what we are used to seeing. The rest goes unnoticed.
Once we let the selected information in, our attitude also colors
our reaction to it, whether we think of it as good or bad, and
whether we are happy or not.

The Torah indicates that the attitude we choose has the power
to change the flow of our lives.[166] Attitudes manipulate our reality: they determine which details we focus on, and those details
get bigger while the things we ignore get smaller or disappear.

For example, when we get vaccinated, if we focus on preventing a highly dangerous illness, we will appreciate this opportunity, while if we concentrate on the discomfort of the prick, we will be anxious or upset. Similarly, if we focus on what we don't have in life or what is wrong with it, we will become miserable and unhappy. Complaining perpetuates the problems that we are complaining about. If we focus on what we do have, we will become grateful, content, and happy.

Another way our attitudes affect the way we perceive situations is by determining whether or not we take things personally. When someone (a spouse, a child, a boss, or a stranger) is unkind, we may believe their behavior has to do with us (that it means they do not appreciate us or we really did something wrong) and take offense or feel guilty. Or we may allow for other explanations (that the person is hungry or suffering from a toothache, for example) and stay in a good mood.

As Ayn Rand pointed out, "Emotions are inherent in your nature, but their content is dictated by your mind. Your emotional capacity is an empty motor, and your values are the fuel with which your mind fills it."[167] Nothing in the world comes emotionally precharged. We bring different thoughts and emotions with us everywhere and to everything.

Practically every situation can be perceived in multiple ways, all of which may be true. A situation may be seen as an adventure, a formative experience, a chance for self-improvement, an opportunity to change something in our lives, a challenge, or a difficulty. Our attitude toward the situation informs our feelings about it. Psychiatrist **Theodore Isaac Rubin** observed, "The problem is not that there are problems. The problem is thinking that having a problem is a problem."

In this traditional Jewish folktale, a wise rabbi helps a villager change his attitude:

> A long time ago, there was a poor family that lived in a very small house in Poland that barely had space for the man, his wife, and the six children. One day they learned that the grandparents were coming to live with them. Everyone was excited when the grandparents arrived, but soon the house became crowded and noisy, with everybody getting in each other's way. There was so little space they could hardly breathe!
>
> Finally the man could not stand it any longer. He went to the rabbi and told him how miserable things were at home: "We are practically on top of each other all the time. What to do? Help us, Rabbi!"
>
> The rabbi replied, "Do you promise to do exactly as I tell you?"
>
> "I promise," the poor man said.
>
> The rabbi then asked, "Do you own any animals?"
>
> "Yes, I have one cow, one goat, and some chickens."
>
> "Good," the rabbi said. "Bring them one by one into the house."
>
> The poor man was astonished to hear such advice, but he had promised to do exactly what the rabbi said. So he went home and brought the chickens into the tiny house. The next day he brought the goat into the house and, finally, the cow.
>
> The next day the poor man ran back to see the rabbi.

"What have you done to me, Rabbi?" he cried. "It's awful. I did what you told me, and the animals are all over the house! The chickens are laying eggs everywhere, the goat is eating everything in sight, and the cow smashes up all the furniture! Rabbi, help us!"

The rabbi listened and said calmly, "Now go home and take the animals back outside."

The next day the man came running back to the rabbi. "Oh Rabbi," he said with a big smile on his face, "we have such a good life now. The house is so quiet, and we've got room to spare! What a joy!"

And so, the man was much happier in the same circumstances he was initially complaining about.

Our perception of reality determines our level of contentment and happiness. Just like the man in the above tale and the people visited by a happiness vendor, we can transform our lives and increase our feelings of happiness by learning to alter our attitude and control our focus.

PUT IT INTO PRACTICE

It is a given that most anything can be viewed as good, bad, or a combination of both, depending on our attitude. To be happier, we need to notice the good in everything. The poor villager from the folktale had to go through some physical changes to reconsider his perception of his life. We will practice mental exercises to achieve the same result:

- Focus on the positive.

Rebbe Nachman of Breslov instructed, "Always look for the

good in the other. Always look for the good in yourself. Focus on what is good, highlight it, and turn even depression into joy."[168]

Choose your focus in the same way a photographer chooses a focus when looking through the camera lens. Bring out your creativity by finding something positive in everything.

❖ Focus on feeling grateful: if someone offers unwanted advice, instead of getting annoyed, be thankful that they care; if you get in a car accident, instead of getting upset about it and the repair costs, be grateful that you have no major injuries or that you are alive.

❖ Focus on solutions, not the problems: if you get into an argument with a friend, instead of fretting over it, think about how you can reconcile.

❖ Focus on your unlimited potential and self-worth: if you realize you've made a mistake, congratulate yourself on noticing it and resolve to do better next time.

❖ Focus on what you have, not on what others have more of.

❖ Focus on the benefits of any situation: instead of viewing waiting as an annoying waste of your time, consider it bonus free time to read a book, meditate, or just enjoy life.[169]

❖ For every negative thought you have about anything, come up with at least two positive statements about the situation and two positive statements about life in general. For example, when you think, "I hate shoveling snow!" also remind yourself that you are lucky to have a house to shovel in front of and that you are fit enough to do it. And on a general note, get excited about being alive and sending time outside.

- Reframe the situation.

Every time you find yourself having a problem, try to look at the situation from a different angle. Give it a different description that will make you more content or even grateful and excited.

You got fired? Think of it as is a chance to get a better job with a bigger salary, as an opportunity to switch careers and try something new, or even as a long-deserved vacation.

- Do not take things personally.

There is usually more than one contributing factor to any situation. Faced with someone acting in an unpleasant way, do not immediately assume this has to do with you. Think of other possible explanations. Doing so will change your attitude and your mood. For example, if your coworker from across the hall did not return your greeting, instead of getting hurt or affronted and assuming he or she intentionally disregarded you, consider that he or she is likely distracted by an approaching deadline, is deep in thought, or just can't see you without glasses.

CHAPTER 29

EXPECTATIONS

"There is more happiness upon receiving a gift than receiving a wage."

—Rabbi **Yosef Yitzchak Schneersohn** [170]

Another form of perception that affects our happiness is our expectations. Do you notice that an unexpected day off due to snow makes children much happier than a regular Saturday and Sunday? Adults react the same way. Getting paid back for a debt we forgot about is a bigger thrill than getting paid back when we are expecting it. The more we feel entitled to have something, the more we take it for granted, and the less joy we experience because of it.

Expectations cause unnecessary disappointment and unhappiness when they do not come true. Not getting an annual raise at work feels very different depending on whether we were expecting it or not. We may blame others and become angry or blame ourselves and feel guilty. Fewer expectations result in more happiness, as illustrated by the two rabbis in the following tale.

The town of Hanipol had a rabbi who had a congregation

and ruled on matters of Jewish religious law. He was rich and had a good salary, but he was always angry, always bitter. In the same town resided Rebbe Zusya. He did not have a congregation, but people did come to him for help and advice. Rebbe Zusya had much trouble all his life, but he was always full of joy.

One day the rabbi simply couldn't stand himself anymore. He discreetly came to Rebbe Zusya and asked, "Why are you always happy, and why am I always angry?"

Rebbe Zusya replied, "Zusya will explain it to you. Take the wedding of a rich man's daughter last week. He invited you, but you saw that your name was sixteenth on the list of guests. You thought, 'What chutzpah![171] I am the rabbi! I am the one performing the wedding! I am supposed to be number one!'

"So you came to the wedding three hours late to show them how important you are. But they found someone else to officiate the wedding and were already enjoying the meal. Finally, the rich man saw you and said, 'Oh, our rabbi! We waited for you. But we couldn't wait any longer. Please come to the head table.' But the head table was already filled, so they put your chair behind somebody else. When the waiter brought the food, he didn't see you. So you weren't served. You were so angry! You cursed the bride and groom; you were cursing God. Finally, the rich man saw that you had nothing to eat. He said, 'Oh, Rabbi, please forgive me. I am so sorry you didn't get food!' He went into kitchen and collected some of the leftovers. When he brought them to you, you were even more angry. 'What chutzpah! I am the rabbi of the city, and they bring me leftovers!' On top of it, the rich man called someone else and not you to recite a wedding blessing after the Grace. You went home, cursing your wife, cursing your children, cursing the bride, cursing the groom, cursing God. You were angry!"

Zusya continued, "But see what happened with Zusya. The rich man invited him to the wedding. Zusya said to himself, 'Zusya's never done anything good to him. Why should Zusya have the privilege to be invited? And if he is such a good friend to Zusya, Zusya wants to be a good friend to him.'

"So Zusya went three hours early, to help them set up everything. When you were late, they asked Zusya to perform the wedding. Zusya sat at the head table. Zusya was asked to recite a wedding blessing and the Grace After Meals. Finally Zusya went home and was loving to his wife and his children.

"So you see, *you expect everything, and whatever you receive is too little, so you're angry. Zusya expects nothing, so he's always happy no matter what happens.*"[172]

PUT IT INTO PRACTICE

Appreciate everything you have, and you will feel happier. Make a habit of it with the help of the following easy tips.

- Anticipate less.

If you notice that you are often disappointed by something or someone, rethink your expectations. When you stop anticipating that things will happen in the way you think they should, you will be less upset when they don't and, alternatively, more joyful when they do.

- Do not take life for granted.

From time to time, remind yourself that each day, hour, and minute is not promised to you. Consider that life is a gift. Feel grateful and happy to get it.

- Appreciate everything you have.

To enjoy what you have more, imagine for a minute not having these things. Imagine living without your clothes, your morning cup of tea, running water or electricity, your health, or the ability to walk. You will immediately appreciate everything you have and feel much happier.

- Remember to be grateful.[173]

Even when you get things you really deserve, such as a meal you are paying for at a restaurant or a hug from your child when you pick him or her up from school, be thankful for them.

FOCUS ON THE GOOD

CHAPTER 30

LIFE IS BEAUTIFUL

"L'Chaim!"

(To life!)

—Traditional Jewish toast

"I love living. I have some problems with my life, but living is the best thing they've come up with so far."

—Neil Simon

There is a Jewish saying that life is the biggest bargain because we get it for nothing.[174] And what a great life it is! Full of wonder, excitement, goodness, and beauty.

"Light is sweet, and it pleases the eyes to see the sun. However many years anyone may live, let them enjoy them all," urges the Torah.[175] Celebrating the beauty of life boosts our happiness in any circumstances.

"I am so happy I woke up today!" exclaimed Alice Herz-Sommer, the oldest living Holocaust survivor at the time when she said it at the age of 107.[176] She had lived through several wars, a concentration camp, a cancer diagnosis, and the death of her only son. Still she proclaimed, "Life is beautiful. . . . Isn't it wonderful? . . . We can sit together and talk. We are alive."[177] Even her advanced age, which brought fragile health, pains, and limited mobility, did not deter Alice from enjoying life: "[Old age] is not so terrible. And I am older than you. Rather than dwell on problems, why not look for life's gifts? Every day is a present. Beautiful."[178]

Arthur Rubinstein, a great pianist of the twentieth century, concurs: "I'm passionately involved in life: I love its change, its color, its movement. To be alive, to be able to see, to walk, to have houses, music, paintings—it's all a miracle. I have adopted the technique of living life miracle to miracle." He continues, "Even when I'm sick and depressed, I love life."

It is true that life is not perfect. But sages teach that life is great particularly because it is not perfect.[179] If everything were perfect and there were no spiritual, mental, or physical work for us to do, that would be uninteresting, boring. In the world as it is, there is so much to look forward to! Amazing surprises await us every day and every hour. Life provides us with endless opportunities for creativity, for acquiring new knowledge, for positive emotions and meaning.

Jewish wisdom insists that all the world and everything in it is alive with godliness.[180] It promotes sanctification, acknowledging holiness in all actions and events. Rebbe Nachman of Breslov urged his followers to seek the remarkable within the commonplace.[181] Today, the science of positive psychology finds that, even for those who don't believe in God, imbuing aspects of life with sacred or divine qualities provides motivation, meaning, and satisfaction. Thinking that the body is holy, marriage is sacred, children are blessings, and work is a calling instills our daily lives with a spiritual dimension and a sense of awe, making us more invested in them.[182]

The more beauty we see in life, the happier we are.

PUT IT INTO PRACTICE

If you find it difficult to see the beauty of life, you do not have to seek a different life. You just have to retrain your eyes and your brain to see the life you have differently.

- Affirm

Kabbalah assigns enormous power to the spoken word. By saying positive statements, we condition our minds to develop a positive perception of ourselves and our environment and foster our happiness.

Use these affirmations or write your own:

- ❖ Life is utterly miraculous and beautiful.
- ❖ My life is great!
- ❖ I am so lucky to be alive!

Repeat these or your own statements with genuine feeling several times a day. Put a note containing them in the wallet and repeat them out loud or in your mind every time you see them. Pay full attention to the words you are saying.

- Practice mindfulness.[183]

Be on the lookout for the ways in which your life is awesome, wonderful, amazing, or simply nice. Do not let them go unacknowledged. Notice and enjoy the green leaves and flowers. Love the way the sun warms you up. Notice when your spouse looks nice, say it out loud, and smile.

Acknowledge moments of joy, insight, and spiritual relevance. Pay attention to the good things, and let them grow in your eyes.

Keep two cups on your desk—one with pebbles in it and one that starts out empty. Every time you think a positive thought, transfer a pebble from the full cup to the empty one until that cup is full. Then start transferring pebbles back to the other cup. In time, increase the number of times you move the pebbles form one cup to another, or get bigger cups.

Stay focused on every nice experience for at least twenty to thirty seconds instead of getting distracted by something else. When taken in with a bit more awareness, even mild pleasures become richer feelings and leave stronger memories.[184]

- Find the remarkable in the ordinary.

See meaning/holiness/spirituality/grace/value/blessing in everyday things, both beautiful and plain, routine or random: a meal, a laugh, or snowfall.

- Enjoy what you have not enjoyed before.

We can intentionally enhance our joy by associating (or "anchoring") things, gestures, smells, music, and events with positive emotions. If we tie an emotion to a trigger, we will be able to access that emotion by a sheer power of association.

Remember your strongest positive driving memory every time you get into a car, and after a while, you will automatically associate a car ride with a pleasant experience.

Anticipate hearing good news every time the phone rings. Soon every time you hear a ring, your spirits will lift.

Every time you relax, curl and uncurl your hands as if you are physically releasing your stress as you would an object. With repetition, this movement will become associated with relaxation, and every time you do it you will feel calmer.

- Set out to have a great life.

As you wake up, look forward to the day ahead. Even if you are facing unpleasant situations, resolve to have a good attitude. Every day ahead of you holds a promise of wonderful possibilities and pleasant surprises.

CHAPTER 31

PUT ON ROSE-COLORED GLASSES

"Look for the good, not the evil, in the conduct of members of the family."

—Yiddish proverb

The tendency to see the best in everything, or optimism,[185] is a straight path to everlasting happiness. Optimism comes easier when the sun is shining, when everything turns out the way we want, and when everyone around is genuinely nice. How do we stay happy when it rains and snows, when dreams take an unexpectedly long time to come true, and when people around us are too busy with their lives to properly shower us with affection?

Putting on rose-colored glasses helps us realize that whatever the unpleasant situation is, it is not so bad, and besides, it is only a part of our reality. There is always something to be happy about, and that is what we have to focus on. You may get fired but have beautiful healthy kids; maybe you had a fight with your spouse, but the sun is shining; perhaps your flight gets delayed, but you like the book you are reading. And the ultimate argument to counter the gloom is that we are alive, and we always have an opportunity to do something different tomorrow or even right away!

Alice Herz-Sommer experienced much difficulty and tragedy, including the Holocaust, the greatest degradation of the human spirit the Western world has ever known. And yet she found lasting happiness. "My optimism has helped me through my darkest days," she said. "It helps me now."[186]

If we look for the good, we can find it in any person and any situation. Rabbi **Mordechai Neschizer** always looked for the good in everyone. Once a stranger reputed to be a consistent sinner called on him, and the rabbi spent some time with him. Afterward, a **gabbai** asked how the rabbi could give so much time to such a person. "My visitors must have some good qualities, and it is my duty to see them and nothing else," replied the Neschizer.[187]

Is it possible to stay positive and happy in a situation in which there is seemingly nothing to be joyful about? It turns out it is, as the following story illustrates:

> Once in the early spring, somewhere on the outskirts of **Chelm**, a scruffy-looking man was walking in the mud. His shirt was old and torn in some places, his pants were greasy and had patches, his hat was of an indeterminate shape and color, and he had only one boot on. He was walking with a spring in his step, whistling a tune through a missing tooth, and he smiled broadly at another man who happened to walk toward him.
>
> *"Oy vey,"* the other man said, concerned by what he saw, "what happened? You are dirty, you look like you slept in a

field somewhere, and your clothes are all muddy and torn! Why on earth are you so happy? What is there to smile about? Look, you've lost one boot!"

The man smiled even more broadly. "Oh no, I've found one boot!"

PUT IT INTO PRACTICE:

Every time you catch yourself being displeased with something, practice optimism. Imagine putting on rose-colored glasses, and find the good in the present situation and in your life.

CHAPTER 32

BE GRATEFUL

"Gratitude is essential for happiness."

—Alice Herz-Sommer[188]

"Making a blessing over life is the best way of turning life into a blessing."

—Rabbi **Jonathan Sacks**[189]

Gratitude is a very powerful antidote to negative emotions and taking things for granted. It underscores all the good that is happening to us all the time. Giving thanks is absolutely free and takes very little time, but studies confirm that a grateful attitude makes us healthier and much happier.[190]

All of us have experienced moments of feeling very grateful for something in our lives. But these peaks of happiness do not last. Scientists now confirm what Jews have long expressed in the saying "Time is the best healer."[191] However strongly we feel happiness or sadness in response to a specific event, over time most of us revert to the baseline state. We might have been heartbroken over an unrequited high school crush or elated to get a new car at one time, but eventually these emotions level out and our sights become trained on something else. This phenomenon is called the "hedonic treadmill," and it has been blamed for preventing us from achieving a permanent gain in happiness.

Gratitude is the way to counteract the hedonic treadmill and stay happier longer.[192] We do not get as indifferent to the good stuff if we constantly pause to notice and express our appreciation for it.

Jewish tradition also emphasizes the connection between gratitude and happiness. "A Jew who walks around and is not suffused with happiness . . . is simply being ungrateful to God," said Rabbi **Aharon of Karlin**.

The Jewish tradition is imbued with gratitude. Even the word "Jew" (or *Yehudi* in Hebrew) derives from the Hebrew word for "to thank."[193] Focusing on the good, showing appreciation and gratefulness is a commandment in Judaism: "And you shall rejoice in all the good that God your God has given you and your family."[194] As Jews, we practice this commandment daily by saying blessings (i.e., giving thanks) for all the events of our lives, including surviving illness, eating, using the bathroom and having the organs working properly, and seeing a rainbow. The Talmud encourages saying at least a hundred blessings every day,[195] starting with *Modeh Ani*—which loosely translates as "Thank God I'm alive!"—the blessing that is recited every morning upon waking. Through formal blessings and daily prayers, Judaism lists for us the many reasons to rejoice throughout each day, teaches us to acknowledge what we have, be grateful for it, and by extension, be happy.

Kabbalah teaches that there are no accidents or injustices, since everything occurs by God's providence and is done for the ultimate good, even when we do not understand it. Therefore, observant Jews express gratitude not only for the good events in life, but for the sad ones too.

In the poem **Joseph Brodsky** wrote for this fortieth birthday, he makes a similar point. He lists the many hardships he has encountered. Still, he is invigoratingly grateful for his life: "Until brown clay has been rammed down my larynx, / only gratitude will be gushing from it."[196]

Our lives are full of things to be thankful for, some more obvious than others. Jewish wisdom teaches that we should appreciate both the good fortune and the blessings in disguise we encounter on our path.

GRATITUDE FOR THE GOOD

"Be grateful for everything," says Alice Herz-Sommer, "to see the sun, to see a smile, for a kind word. Everything is a present. Everything. . . . This I learned—to be thankful for everything."[197]

Sometimes we forsake feeling gratitude, focusing on little annoyances instead, just like the woman in this joke:

A mom was walking with a baby alone on the beach. Suddenly, a large wave swept the baby into the ocean. The mom became frantic, praying to God to return the baby. Another large wave came and gently deposited the baby completely unharmed into the mother's arms. She looked the baby over, frowned and yelled at the sky, "He had a cap on!"

When we fail to appreciate what we have, we lose the opportunity to feel happy. Often we realize how good we had it only when something is over. Let's not wait to notice our blessings until it's too late to fully enjoy them. Do not let the good pass unnoticed. Appreciate everything you have, the big and the little things our lives consist of, even the things you have for a long time: eyesight, possessions, the people around us, every breath.

RECOGNIZING THE GOOD

The literal translation for the Hebrew term for gratitude, *hakarat hatov*, is "recognizing the good." It means that we should feel grateful not only when we get something good but also in recognition of the good that is already ours.[198] No matter how much we lack, no matter what difficult times we are passing through, every one of us can find a myriad of things to be grateful for. When the energy bill is huge, be thankful for being warm enough. When cleaning up a mess after a party, appreciate having been surrounded by friends.

And remember, when we are dealing with something difficult, we should also recognize the many other good things we have to feel grateful for. If we've lost our job but still have our health, we can be grateful. If we can't move our legs but can move our arms, we can be grateful.

The Talmud also teaches us to think about the many people we may never even meet who improve our lives: the people who design and build our houses, research new medications, and invent the things that we use. If not for these people, it reminds us in one example, we would have to labor much more to obtain a piece of clothing to wear: we would need to shear a sheep, wash the wool, comb it, spin it, weave it, cut it, and sow the garment.[199] Having such things done for us is something to be grateful for.

If you are still having trouble feeling grateful, consider the following Yiddish proverb: "If you cannot be grateful for what you have received, then be thankful for what you have been spared." Another Yiddish proverb illustrates the wisdom of this with a graphic example: "I felt sorry for myself because I had no shoes—until I met a man who had no feet."

GRATITUDE FOR BLESSINGS IN DISGUISE

We should be grateful for all the good things that happen to us. But life is full of unpleasant and painful challenges that put us in a corner and force us to reinvent ourselves, to act in a way we would not otherwise act, or to find strengths we never thought we had. Jewish sages teach us to be thankful for challenges, because they give us an opportunity to grow spiritually, and with the difficulties and pain they bring also comes self-discovery and self-improvement. [200]

Gratefulness also helps us focus on the positive parts of difficult situations. Alice Herz-Sommer demonstrated this in the way she faced the sudden death of her only son. One day he felt ill after playing a concert. He went into emergency surgery for an iliac aneurysm and never woke up. Even in her grief, Herz-Sommer found something to be grateful for. "I am thankful that he had not suffered," she said. "He had a beautiful last day. I am thankful that his last memories are of the music. I am thankful he did not know he was going to die so that he did not have to be afraid." She accepted what she could not change with love and dignity.[201]

The Talmud tells about a man called Nachum Ish Gamzu, which means "comforted is the person who says 'this too.'" To any terrible thing that happened, he responded in the same way: *"Gam zu le'tovah."*[202] This too is for the good. Due to such an unyielding sense of gratitude, he never despaired and stayed optimistic. We too should practice feeling grateful in any situation.

PUT IT INTO PRACTICE

The following exercises will help boost your level of happiness by emphasizing and practicing genuine gratitude:

- Recognize the good.

Feeling gratitude for everything good can fill us with so much appreciation we will not have the space for unhappiness. Cultivate such gratefulness by recognizing and appreciating the most basic abilities you have, such as your sight and hearing, and enjoying both the intangible things in your life, such as your family, friends, achievements, and the sun in the sky, and the tangible ones, such as clothes, books, and computers.

- Write it down.

A study on the effects of gratefulness found that participants who wrote down five things they were grateful for each day were a full 25 percent happier than the ones who didn't.[203] Keep a journal and every day write down five new things for which you are grateful. Read the journal every once in a while, and you will be reminded of all the good that otherwise would be forgotten.

- Realize how loved you are.

Every time we receive a favor or a gift, we should be grateful not only for the gift itself but also for the fact that we are cared for by the person who gave it to us. Realizing that we are loved and cared for may be an even greater source of happiness than the gift itself.[204]

If you believe in God, rejoice in having all the gifts He grants you with and the knowledge that God loves you.

• Connect through gratefulness.

Sometimes we may feel that expressing gratitude for help means we are less self-sufficient. However, we are all interdependent, and the majority of things in our lives are provided by others. When we allow ourselves to receive and be grateful for the help of others, we become more open to connecting with the world.

Even a rather simple pleasure such as eating a cookie can provide a moment of introspection, as Rabbi **Moshe Miller** demonstrates in this "guided imagery":

> Envision a farmer plowing his field from morning till night. He rises the next day at sunrise and plants seeds of wheat in neat rows. He returns each day to remove the weeds and to irrigate the field. After a few months, tall, green stalks sway back and forth in the soft breeze.
>
> The farmer then harvests his field and binds the stalks into sheaves. The sheaves are delivered to a mill where they are pounded to remove the wheat kernels, and separate the chaff. Next, the wheat kernels are ground into flour. The flour is poured into sacks, loaded into a truck, and delivered to a bakery. The baker then measures the flour into a big mixing bowl and adds eggs, sugar, cocoa, and water. He forms the dough into balls and places them on baking trays. Next he slides the baking trays into a pre-

heated oven. After 15 minutes he removes the trays of fresh baked cookies and places them on cooling racks.

Soon another worker arranges the cookies in boxes and loads them onto a truck. The driver delivers the cookies to the market, in which you purchased the cookie that you are now holding in your hand. [205]

Look at the cookie in your hand. Appreciate how many people were involved in making it and delivering it to you. Grasp the wonders of the universe that allow for the miracle of life. Be thankful to be a part of it.

You can guide yourself through similar imagery for anything else.

- Find the positive in every negative.

Every time you face anything that feels negative, immediately formulate a positive and grateful thought about the same situation:

❖ I am thankful for a lawn that needs mowing, windows that need cleaning, and gutters that need fixing, because it means I have a home.

❖ I am thankful for the alarm that goes off in the early morning hour, because it means that I have another day in front of me.

❖ I am thankful for the things I've learned from my difficulties.

And of course do not forget to appreciate that most problems in our life are temporary:

❖ I am thankful that it is over.

CHAPTER 33

SMILE

"The greatest Jewish tradition is to laugh."

—Jerry Seinfeld

"Laughter is wonderful. It makes you and everyone else feel happy."

—Alice Herz-Sommer[206]

A rabbi walked into a bar and saw Stan from shul. "Stan, do you want to go to heaven?" he asked.

The man said, "I do, Rabbi."

The rabbi said, "Then go stand over there against the wall."

Then the rabbi asked another man he recognized, "Do you want to go to heaven?"

"Certainly, Rabbi," was the man's reply.

"Go stand over there against the wall," said the rabbi.

Then the rabbi walked up to Chaim Yankel Rabbinowitz and said, "Do you want to go to heaven?"

Chaim Yankel said, "No, I don't, Rabbi."

The rabbi was in disbelief. "You mean to tell me that when you die you don't want to go to heaven?"

Chaim Yankel said, "Oh, when I die, yes. I thought you were getting a group together to go right now."[207]

If you smiled just now, you made yourself happier in that moment, because smiling not only signals our emotions, but creates them too. Smiling and other facial expressions actually affect how we feel! For example, people whose ability to frown is compromised by cosmetic Botox injections are happier, on average, than people who can frown.[208] And smiling, even when it is fake, is found to reduce stress levels and boost mood-enhancing hormones such as endorphins.[209] Thus, both genuine and intentional smiling profoundly benefits our happiness.

We can increase our smiling and our happiness by finding humor in our lives and adding silliness. Jews are famous for seeing humor in any situation. For centuries the Jews of Eastern Europe invited professional jesters and merrymakers called **badhanim** to entertain them at already-joyous occasions such as weddings.[210] Jewish tradition considers cheering others an important act of kindness,[211] and the Talmud indicates that *badhanim* deserve a place in the world-to-come.[212] Such affinity for humor continues in Jewish culture today. It has been estimated that about 80 percent of America's leading humorists over the past forty years have been Jewish.[213]

Jokes and laughter expand our consciousness, helping us to perceive new knowledge and see things in a new light. The Talmud encourages rabbis to have a sense of humor and make a joke before a session of Torah study, as it broadens the pupils' minds.[214]

Taking life too seriously emphasizes its difficulties and can prevent us from fully enjoying the moment. A sense of humor lightens our hearts in adversity and helps us cope with stress. We need to be able to laugh at the situation or at ourselves when we face hardships. Trouble seems less ominous when we can laugh about it, as the wife in the following joke who is able to find humor in an unpleasant medical condition:

> After watching a TV commercial, which proclaimed that six out of ten people suffer from hemorrhoids, Sarah turns to her husband: "You hear, Chaim? Four out of ten people enjoy them!"

"As soap is to the body, so laughter is to the soul," says a Jewish proverb. Humor cleanses us by helping us release negative emotions, dissipate tension, reduce anger and anxiety, increase energy, and feel more in control. It provides a different vantage point from which to see our problems and everyday hassles.[215] With a sense of humor, we can smile even about the most serious problems. For example, a lady in the following joke found something positive even in the Arab-Israeli conflict and racial stereotyping:

> Rachel walked down the street and saw her old friend Rebecca sitting on a bench reading a newspaper. She was incredulous: "What do my eyes see? Are you reading an Arab newspaper?"
>
> "Yes, I used to read Israeli papers, but they gave me depression: inflation, bribes, political machinations, and other *tzuris*![216] The Arab news is different. Did you know that Jews own all the major world banks, form a secret

government, and control the Western world? Now, isn't that nice?"

Humor helps us maintain a more positive, upbeat, optimistic outlook on life and prevents us from getting overly upset or depressed. When Alice Herz-Sommer, who was a lifelong pianist, had to play piano using only four fingers instead of all five because of arthritis pain, instead of getting dispirited about it, she only laughed and said that she had progressed backward.[217]

Humor has the power to lift our spirits and help us cope with even the most difficult situations, as the story below demonstrates:

> A certain Jew fell into the swift current of the surging river in Danzig. Another moment and he would drown. Everyone on the shore panicked, and they were all crying out in terror: "Save him! Save him!" Only Rabbi Simcha Bunim who was there as well, cried out to the drowning man: "Give my regards to Leviathan"—the legendary giant fish! The drowning man, who had lost hope of fighting the current, heard him and suddenly began to struggle again to save himself. Eventually he was able to get back to shore. He went straight to Rabbi Bunim and fell on his neck saying: "If it wasn't for your clever words, I would have died because of my despair and the confusion I was in because of everyone's screams. But your joke aroused my will to live; because of you, I'm alive!"[218]

Humor is an antidote to despair. Seeing humor in her situation helped **Gilda Radner**, a Jewish comedienne and actress, keep her spirits up during her battle with cancer: "Cancer is probably the most unfunny thing in the world, but I'm a comedian, and even cancer couldn't stop me from seeing the humor in what I went through." Even in death camps, humor helped people deal with their horrible situation. "Laughter was our only medicine," Alice Herz-Sommer recalls about her time in the Theresienstadt concentration camp.[219]

In addition, smiling is contagious. Research has shown that people mimic emotional expressions. Smiling at others inspires them to mimic your behavior and smile back at you. Thus, our smiles will not only make us feel happier, but will spark happiness in others too.

PUT IT INTO PRACTICE

- Smile.

Get into the habit of smiling. Find a reason to smile within you or outside in the world, and sometimes smile even if you don't have a reason, just because you can.

Every time you see a mirror, smile. It's nice to see the reflection smile back. Besides, you look good with a smile.

Rebbe Nachman of Breslov instructed his disciples, "If you don't feel happy, pretend to be. Even if you are downright depressed, put on a smile. Act happy. Genuine joy will follow."[220]

It is always better to smile genuinely. But when you don't feel like smiling, you can fake it. In this case "fake it till you make it" is a reasonable strategy, because smiling involves muscle work that sends "joy" signals into our brain. And sometimes fake smiling is even more fun just because it is so silly. Speaking of which...

- Get the sillies.

Find silliness in frustrating or unpleasant situations. It can help you endure them with a smile.

Take a couple of minutes to see a problem in a "silly" way instead of a responsible, adult-appropriate way. If nothing else, it will make you smile.

Find positive in every situation, and take things lightly: Something fell on you? Fantastic! Gravity is still working, so you are still attached to the earth! Your wallet got stolen? Great, now you give **tzedakah** without even trying to!

CHAPTER 34

THE POWER OF MUSIC

"Music is bliss. Music brings us an island of peace."

—**Rafael Sommer**[221]

"**O**Music! miraculous art! A blast of thy trumpet, and millions rush forward to die; a peal of thy organ, and uncounted nations sink down to pray," marveled **Benjamin Disraeli**. Music is often considered the universal "language of emotions," because it is capable of producing some of the strongest emotional reactions in us, including calm and joy.

Studies prove that the musical sound waves affect us on a physical level, altering the brain's functioning and changing our mood.[222] This effect music has on us is even used in healthcare to improve physical and mental health through a treatment modality called music therapy. The famous Jewish sage and physician Maimonides knew about this hundreds of years ago. To people who were sad, he advised, "Listen to music."[223]

"Music washes away from the soul the dust of everyday life," said **Berthold Auerbach**. And the more conscious we are of music, the more it affects us. If it is just a background noise, it doesn't do much. But when we pay attention to music and listen to it with an intention to change our mood, slow and meditative music calms us, while joyful and upbeat music makes us excited and happy.[224]

Similarly to smiling, music makes a good situation even better and helps us transcend difficult ones. Alice Herz-Sommer recalls how music helped her and other prisoners at the Theresienstadt concentration camp: "While performing the prisoners could nearly forget their hunger and their surroundings. Music provided comfort and hope to the performers and their audience."[225]

Jewish culture places a major emphasis of music. The book of **Psalms** clearly instructs, "Serve God with joy; approach Him with joyful song."[226] Kabbalists hold that the world is saturated with melody, and the most direct means for attaching ourselves to God from this material world is through music and song.[227] Hasidic Jews use music to feel the connection to one another and God, singing cheerful and soul-stirring melodies at informal gatherings called *farbrengen*.

Klezmer is a specifically Jewish musical genre that translates the emotions of joy and exuberant happiness into music. It makes the listeners tap their feet and clap their hands to the lively tunes that reverberate throughout Jewish communities and are one of the key elements of Jewish weddings.

Music lifts our spirits whether we listen to it, make it, sing it, or dance to it. It works when we are alone and when we share it with others. Apply the power of music to your days, and observe how it changes your mood.

PUT IT INTO PRACTICE

Music has such a powerful ability to conjure up feelings. Use it to conjure up happiness. Infuse your days with music in all of the following ways:

• Listen.

If you feel down or depressed, fast, upbeat music can lift your spirits. If you feel overstimulated, anxious, and overwhelmed, you may benefit from listening to music with slow tempos.

• Sing.

"Get into the habit of singing a tune. It will give you new life and fill you with joy," taught Rebbe Nachman of Breslov.[228] He urged everyone, "Even when you can't sing well, sing. Sing to yourself. Sing in the privacy of your own home. But sing."[229]

Whether you are in a good mood or not, sing. Sing along with the radio, when you are in the shower, or with your family and friends.

• Dance.

Joyous, ecstatic dancing has always been the way of the Hasidim.[230] They regard it as a form of prayer, a way of getting close to God and reveling in the resulting feeling of happiness.

Dance while you are at leisure or while you clean. Dance at home or at parties. Take lessons, or dance any way you like.

• Make music.

Alice Herz-Sommer summed up her feelings about playing piano in one sentence: "Making music always made me happy."[231]

Make music whenever you can. Play musical instruments you know, or just hum or whistle a fun tune.

CHAPTER 35

CHOOSE YOUR
INFLUENCES

"Stay away from a bad neighbor."

—*Pirkei Avot* 1:7

Even though happiness is generated inside of us, we are still very affected by outside circumstances. As skillful as we may be at adjusting our perspective and mastering our reaction to whatever happens in life, we are continuously bombarded and influenced by things from the external environment. A lot of it is out of our hands. We cannot choose the weather, children's behavior, traffic conditions, and many other things. But we can choose a lot of outside influences that matter to our emotional state: we can choose what news to listen to, what books to read, and what people to befriend.

Humans are open systems; everything and everyone we are surrounded with has an effect on us. Therefore, when given a choice, we should consciously choose to surround ourselves with people, situations, and objects that encourage positivity. Since these influences come from outside of us, they will not sustain our happiness forever, but they still can give our spirits a nice boost.

Our way of thinking and our mood is greatly influenced by the people we communicate with and, according to some major studies, even by people we do not know personally.[232] Our relatives, neighbors, and coworkers are present in our lives regardless of our preferences, but we can pick whom we befriend. We learn from everyone we meet, and other people's attitudes often rub off on us. Spending time with someone who is cheerful and optimistic will likely lift our mood.

The same idea applies to the way we choose to spend our free time. Do you ever have an enjoyable experience and wonder, "Why don't I do this more often?" Well, we can choose how to spend our free time, so why not do something we really like? We can dedicate our leisure specifically to activities that we find generate positive emotions for us, such as getting together with friends, going for a walk, or scrapbooking.

Another way to fill our environment with positivity is through picking objects and media messages that inspire joy. Art, music, and entertainment can also evoke a whole range of emotions. If we choose to surround ourselves with light and joyous pictures, paintings, and sculptures, to listen to upbeat music, and to watch comedy instead of the nightly news, we will be influenced by the positive messages these things contain and be more cheery.

Be conscious of your ability to control your situation, and pick things that will influence you in a positive way.

PUT IT INTO PRACTICE

- Choose uplifting media sources.

Read books, blogs, and magazines that make you feel good, that make you appreciate life, and that make you smile.

Limit your time watching or listening to the news. It often generates negative emotions such as anger, fear, sadness, or hatred, although it rarely affects our lives directly. Unless a facet of your life depends on following the news, it is most likely not worth the aggravation it can cause.

Surround yourself with art that evokes happy feelings in you, such as sunny landscapes and photographs of smiling people.

Listen to inspiring podcasts or radio shows, and watch positive TV shows and movies about subjects that interest you. If watching beautiful vistas and animals relaxes you, pick nature shows. If you love getting creative ideas for later use, turn on programs about cooking, design, or home improvement If you enjoy instrumental music, tune into a classical radio station.

- Befriend happy and cheerful people.

"In choosing a friend, go up a step," teaches a Jewish proverb. Surround yourself with people with lighter mindsets. Spend more of your time with the people who lift you up and make you feel good and motivated.

If you can think of someone who has a big negative impact on you, consider spending less time with that person.

- Designate time for things that make you feel good.

Put yourself in situations that improve your mood. Create art, take pictures, learn a craft you enjoy, or spend time gardening or playing sports. Go to a party or a concert. Choose to fill your free time with activities and hobbies that make you happy.

CHAPTER 36

ENJOY, NOT ENDURE

"If you are going to do it anyway, do it with joy."

—Rabbi **Chaim Friedlander** of Ponevezh Yeshivah[233]

During the course of our lives, there are rather a lot of things we may not like but have to do anyway. Some people dislike chores such as cleaning the house or grocery shopping; others count the hours until the workday is over. Still others grouch at family obligations, be they holiday dinners or checking the children's homework at night. When we feel unhappy about the things we have to do, we endure life instead of enjoying it.

On top of everything everybody has to take care of in life, Jews have additional 613 mitzvot (or commandments), which some might view as chores. However, Judaism holds that when mitzvot are done mindfully, they connect us with the higher power, elevate us spiritually, and create great joy and happiness.

If our participation in an activity is inevitable, then the choice that is left up to us is how we feel during the entire time we are busy with it: resentful, spiteful, and miserable or accomplished, skillful, and cheerful. Learning to enjoy the things we do significantly increases our happiness.

The difference between a dreadful chore or waste of time and a nice pastime or proud achievement is in our attitude. We can use our mental energy by fuming or daydreaming to block out the drudgery, or we can use it by seeking happiness.

In discussing different paths to the same goal, Simcha Bunim of Pshis'cha once said, "If one can reach God by eating or by not eating, why not eat?"[234] Let's apply the same logic to unpleasant but unavoidable chores: if we can do them unhappily or happily, why not be happy? Practice enjoying, not enduring, and happiness will follow.

PUT IT INTO PRACTICE

To start enjoying everything you do, practice changing your focus from the upsetting parts to the nice parts. Here are some tips that will help you:

- Change your attitude toward your chores:

  - ❖ Find meaning in everything you do. For example, you get to improve the world a little by doing it; you help others; you attain your life goals or priorities; you promote health, peace, and love; and so on. And the faster you do it right, the sooner you will be finished with it.

  - ❖ Approach the chores as life's learning exercises. Alice Herz-Sommer said, "Enjoy even menial tasks, they help to overcome life's greater challenges."[235]

  - ❖ "Whatever is in your power to do, do with all your might," teaches Ecclesiastes.[236] Get into the habit of giving every job your best effort and your full attention. You will finish the task faster and enjoy it more than if you slack off or try to postpone it.

❖ It is said that when a task is done joyfully, it is more likely to be a success. So if you wish to achieve an excellent result, think of that as an incentive to enjoy the task more.

❖ Instead of suffering through the chore and constantly reminding yourself how unpleasant it is, allow yourself to become captivated and fascinated by what you do. You may find that you get into it and even like it. You just have to let yourself get carried away by it.

❖ Remind yourself constantly that this is supposed to be fun. Whether you find yourself running errands with your kids, doing your job, or cleaning a toilet, repeat this mantra to yourself: "Lighten us. This is supposed to be fun." The only reason it can't be fun is that you won't allow it.

❖ Be grateful: every time you feel upset about having to do something, realize how lucky you are to have the kids to cook for, to have the clothes to wash, to have the job to go to, or to have access to the doctor you have to wait for.

❖ Put on a heart rate monitor and see how many calories you can burn as you clean or do any other physical chore. Add jumping jacks between tasks to get your number higher.

❖ Sing your favorite Broadway tune while cleaning.

❖ Remember that complaining and anger do not achieve anything except spoiling your day.

• Allow the task to soothe you.

Repetitive tasks that do not require a lot of mental concentration can be very relaxing. When you can, transform the experience from stressful to soothing, using following tips and adding your own.

❖ Dim the lights, burn some incense, and turn on some slow music.

❖ Fold the laundry when it is fresh from the dryer, and enjoy the warmth of the clothes.

❖ When you are done with a chore, pause to savor the fruits of your labor: enjoy how good the house looks, how great the meal smells, or how beautiful the lawn is.

• Adjust the way you do chores.

❖ When you're cleaning up:

❖ put on a cute apron and dish washing gloves, a funny headband or another accessory to give yourself a smile.

❖ use cleaners that are gentle on your skin and have the most appealing scent.

❖ let your dishes or stained clothes soak. They'll be easier to clean.

❖ During family time:

   ❖ read aloud the books that you actually like.

   ❖ assume a foreign accent or pretend that you are a tutor to royal heirs when helping your kids with homework, and observe how your attitude changes.

   ❖ if you find that getting homework done is stressful due to lack of time, or that family gatherings like meals are strained in the hurry to get to the next playdate or class, simplify your family schedule by planning fewer activities. If you don't rush, both you and your children will relax and enjoy family time.

   ❖ lower your expectations. Remember how old your kids are and allow for imperfection. You will not get as disappointed or frustrated, your kids will enjoy you more, and you will enjoy being a parent more.

   ❖ remember that being a happy parent is the greatest gift you can give your family. You will enjoy life more and teach your kids the invaluable lesson of practicing happiness.

❖ At family gatherings:

   ❖ remember what you are looking forward to every year—building traditions, Mom's **gefilte fish**, grandfather's war stories, or seeing your favorite cousin.

❖ At work:

> ❖ look for opportunities to apply yourself in ways that spark your interest and produce great results. Ask yourself, what's interesting here, and how can I make this more fun? Rabbi Zelig Pliskin shares an account of toll booth attendants who found ways to enjoy a job that is usually considered tedious and boring. One attendant loved throwing parties for himself by playing music and dancing. Another enjoyed the challenge of finding something kind or pleasant to say to each person he interacted with.[237]

❖ When you're doing mitzvot:

> ❖ Acknowledge the spirituality fostered through mitzvot and express gratitude for every opportunity to perform a mitzvah.

• Listen to joyful music while you work.

A study demonstrates that listening to happy or sad music affects how we interpret a face irrespective of facial expressions.[238] We can apply this effect to other areas of our lives too. Listen to happy music when you are doing an unpleasant chore or have to wait. Let it positively affect your emotions.

Play lively music and dance a few steps. It'll keep you moving along while having fun.

• Improve your technique.

> ❖ Each time you do the same task, work on perfecting the routine until it requires little or no effort.

❖ Use the right tools for the job to make it easier. For example, clean windows with a squeegee.

❖ Limit the scope of the work. If you're getting organized, work on one drawer per session and don't overdo it.

❖ Limit the time you have to finish your chore, and make sure that during that time you have no distractions. For example, give yourself ten minutes to clean up a room. You'll be amazed how much you can do in ten minutes if you put your mind to it!

• Get additional help.

❖ Recruit your family members to help you. As you work, chat and sing together, any chore will seem more fun and will be done quicker.

❖ Divide up the chores with your household members according to what each enjoys doing. If everyone detests the same chore, figure out a schedule to take turns doing it, or tackle it together.

❖ If feasible, assign or hire someone else to do the task you can't figure out how to enjoy.

• Use a reward to motivate yourself.

Give yourself something to look forward to. The biggest reward is the sense of pride in giving your best effort and getting the job done well. However, there are other ways to reward yourself:

❖ Indulge in some rich chocolate or fresh juice in between chores to keep your morale up, or make your favorite dessert right after you finish.

❖ Look forward to a long, relaxing soak after a stressful day at work.

❖ When you do chores with family, start a tradition of a group hug, a cheer, or a dance routine after each successful project.

❖ Feel free to enjoy the fruits of your labor, and praise yourself even for small achievements.

WHEN BAD THINGS HAPPEN

CHAPTER 37

INTRODUCTION TO THE SECTION

So far we've discussed several aspects of the path to happiness: the need to recognize what happiness is and how it feels, the clarity that comes with formulating our priorities, the great power we have over our happiness, the value of mindfulness, and the influence of a positive attitude. We've learned to apply gratitude, humor, and optimism; surround ourselves with joyful music; and choose good influences.

The more we practice these things, the more of our personality will change and our baseline of happiness will rise, and we will feel happier in our everyday life.

Now we've come to the part of the book where we consider life's trials and tribulations. There are different ways to handle adversity. At times it may seem that escaping negative feelings makes us happier, and so some try to numb themselves with alcohol and drugs or by withdrawing emotionally, escaping from reality. Such choices will not bring us genuine, lasting happiness. Instead, in the chapters that follow, we will learn to deal with hard times in ways that fosters positive emotions.

CHAPTER 38

MAKE ROOM FOR NEGATIVE EMOTIONS

"Ma shelo horeg mekhashel."
(What doesn't kill, strengthens.)

—Hebrew saying

"There is no education like adversity."

—Benjamin Disraeli

*"What was the chief means of transportation in
ancient times? Fear."*

—**Mel Brooks**, *The 2,000-Year-Old Man*

We should always apply our best efforts to accentuate the
positive in our lives. But contrary to what the popular
song says, humans should not completely eliminate the negative.
Psychologist Jerry Duvinsky notes that we are conditioned to
think that emotions such as grief, anger, despair, helplessness,
and loneliness are inherently evil, dangerous, and wrong, so we

feel the need to suppress or disregard them.[239] Granted, they are unpleasant, powerful, and at times rather inconvenient. However, discomfort, both physical and mental, serves an important purpose. In fact, scientists say that negative emotions have protected us and helped us survive as a species.

Negative emotions signal that something in our environment is wrong and thus enable us to deal with it. Fear propels us to escape danger. To have no fear at all can be detrimental to our health and well-being. Pain also lets us know when we are in harm's way and prompts us to act on this knowledge. People with very high pain thresholds (such as diabetics) may not notice getting a cut or a burn and consequently not tend to it, increasing their risk of developing infections. Tiredness signals we need to rest and replenish our energy so that we don't collapse, and so on.

Additionally, pain and failures teach us about the world and ourselves. We learn not to do a lot of harmful things thanks to negative reinforcement. We know not to stick a finger in a fire because it hurts. We get into the habit of washing our hands to avoid getting sick. We learn to be polite because we want to avoid a reprimand. We learn not to eat dirt because it feels gross.

Discomfort and discontent also motivate us to improve ourselves and our conditions. Stress spurs us on. Most often growth and progress occur not in spite of unpleasant experiences but because of them. Not liking our present circumstances makes us work toward something better, something more acceptable, something more comfortable.

Not least important, the negative serves to highlight the positive for us. We would not enjoy pleasures as much if we didn't know suffering.[240] It is difficult to appreciate a meal if we've never felt hungry, to understand the blessing of joy if we've never been sad, or to treasure love if we've never felt loss.

Finally, sometimes displaying negative emotions is a part of sound mental health. Emotions, unpleasant and pleasant, allow us to distinguish the good from the bad in our lives and to adjust our behavior accordingly, therefore, we should not ignore them.

Of course, we have to apply moderation and match the negative reaction to the scale of the adverse event. We should distinguish between real tragedies and nuisances in our lives. If we get a traffic ticket, a bad performance appraisal, or a cold, strong negative emotions would be an overreaction that could throw us out of balance. But when appropriate, negative emotions are a necessary and beneficial part of our reality.

PUT IT INTO PRACTICE

Below are some suggestions that will help you recognize and accept your negative emotions for what they are—clues to disturbances in either your environment or your attitude. When we learn to be mindful of negative emotions, we will be better able to react in ways that bring contentment and happiness.

- Do not discriminate against emotions.

When an unpleasant emotion arises, do not resent it or, worse yet, yourself for feeling it. Recognize that it is just a symptom of something else that is happening. Do not label fear, anxiety, or stress as negative. They are just your reactions to the surroundings. If they protect you from harm or help you deal with the situation, they are not negative but useful.

- Learn to differentiate.

When you feel an unpleasant emotion, examine the reason for it. Determine which emotions alert us to valid problems that need solving and which are overreactions that indicate we need an attitude adjustment.

- Focus on the cause.

Once you've decided that there is a valid underlying reason for an unpleasant emotion, do not suppress it. Instead, deal with the cause. For instance, it is not the pain that is your problem but the nail you've stepped on. You can suppress the pain by taking pills or reframing your attitude toward pain, but you would be much better off removing the nail. This is an extreme example, of course, but this principle works in many situations: instead of being overwhelmed by an emotion or suppressing it, act to resolve its cause.

CHAPTER 39

EMOTIONAL RESILIENCE

"Every day is a miracle. No matter how bad my circumstances, I have the freedom to choose my attitude to life, even to find joy. Evil is not new. It is up to us how we deal with both good and bad. No one can take this power away from us."

—Alice Herz-Sommer, Holocaust survivor[241]

"God gave burdens, also shoulders."

—Yiddish proverb

There are times when negative emotions protect us from danger. These are the times when we should listen to them and run away. But there are plenty of situations that do not pose a direct threat to our lives or wellbeing and still trigger stress, depression, anxiety, anger, and other feelings that interfere with our contentment and happiness.

Difficulties are an intrinsic part of life, and we cannot avoid them. But the extent of our suffering depends on our reaction to them. Suffering comes from the thoughts in our minds, and we can counteract it with thoughts as well.

Emotional resilience is the ability to deal with whatever life throws at us and to maintain good spirits in the face of difficulty and stress. Resilience grants us with the ability to bend without breaking and bounce back from adversity. The better resilience skills we have, the happier we will be in the long run.

The life of Alice Herz-Sommer is an illustration of resilience and how positively it can affect our lives. Herz-Sommer had more than a fair share of problems and tragedies. Her family was killed in concentration camps, where she was also imprisoned; her promising career as international pianist was crushed by World War II; several times she had to start her life over and build it from the ground up; she survived breast cancer; and she faced the death of her only son. But despite these blows, she continued to proclaim herself a happy person, grateful for her life.[242]

Psychologists observe that resilience is not something that we are either born with or without. It can be learned and developed over our life-span.[243] Resilience skills develop as we grow up and gain more knowledge and greater ability to manage our thoughts, behaviors, and actions.

PUT IT INTO PRACTICE

- Understand.

> *"If you don't know, the thing to do is not to get scared,*
> *but to learn."*
>
> —Ayn Rand, *Atlas Shrugged*
>
> *"Contemplation alone reduces bad thoughts,*
> *anxiety and distress."*
>
> —Maimonides, *Regimen of Health*[244]

Sometimes, ignorance is bliss. Other times, when we find ourselves scared or overwhelmed by a situation, or when somebody offends us or behaves in an unexpected way, knowledge is power. Often the reaction that keeps our heart pounding in anger or fear stems from uncertainty and lack of understanding. Baruch Spinoza instructed, "Do not weep. Do not wax indignant. Understand." In other words, instead of crying, complaining, or feeling indignant, we should make an effort to understand exactly what has happened and what has caused it.

Understanding takes knowledge about a situation, and we must realize that assumptions do not add to our knowledge. In fact, assumptions often lead to negative thoughts. When we do not know something, the best thing to do is acknowledge this instead of thinking up explanations that fit our world view.

The more we learn about a situation, the more in control we are, and the better we can cope. Understanding the underlying causes of a scary event or someone's difficult behavior can be very calming. Thunder and lightning, for example, are much easier to deal with when we know that they are caused by atmospheric changes and not by God's wrath. Dad's harsh remark will not cause as much resentment if we understand that it is intended to benefit and not offend us. And illness may be less overwhelming when knowledge of the causes helps us understand the available treatment options.

In an unfamiliar and stressful situation, before giving in to depression, fear, or anger, we should first try to figure out what is really happening and why. Even if we do not like the reality or agree with another person's point of view, understanding it makes us less vulnerable and more resilient. Understanding is a fundamental pillar of peace in our minds and hearts.

- Distinguish between tragedy and nuisance.

Jews know the difference between disasters and annoyances. This wisdom is passed down in apt proverbs such as "If you can make trouble go away with money, it's not trouble; it's an expense," "When there is a way out, there is no need for fear,"[245] and "When there's a remedy for an ailment, it's only half an ailment."[246]

Author Robert Fulghum recalls a moment that made him rethink his reactions to problems forever. In his youth, he once made a scene over being forced to eat wieners and sauerkraut for a whole week at his job (which he also didn't like!). Sigmund Wollman, a German-born Jew and an Auschwitz survivor, happened to witness the angry outburst. He said, "If you break your neck, if you have nothing to eat, if your house is on fire—then you got a problem. Everything else is inconvenience. Life is inconvenient. Life is lumpy. Learn to separate the inconveniences from the real problems. You will live longer." Since then, in times of stress and strain, Fulghum always pauses and asks himself, "Problem or inconvenience?" He calls this the Wollman Test of Reality.[247]

If an event is minor or temporary, if it does not affect your entire life, or if there is a way to deal with it, consider it just a bump in the road and move on with a lighter heart.

- Put it in perspective.

Events and words by themselves have no defined meaning. We are the ones who infuse every situation with meaning and emotions. A situation becomes a problem only when we think it's a problem. If we learn to think differently, suddenly, it's not a problem anymore.

The first step is updating your vocabulary. "Words are powerful," teaches **Lori Palatnik**, "as soon as you reframe from 'problem' to 'opportunity,' you pull down the covers, get out of bed, pull up your boot straps and rise to the occasion. No one wants problems, but who doesn't want opportunities?"[248]

We can achieve a similar effect by replacing the word "failure" with "acquired experience and knowledge." We need this knowledge in order to succeed. In describing his earlier attempts at inventing the light bulb, Thomas Edison said that he did not fail; he just found a thousand ways a light bulb did not work, which ultimately led him to the right design.

Reframing helps even in the most difficult situations, as a story I once heard demonstrates:

> One time a man came to see the Lubavitcher Rebbe. The man was so desolate after the death of his son, he did not want to go on living.

The Rebbe asked, "What if your son went far away and would be safe, but would not communicate with you? Would you be happy?"

"Yes," the man replied.

"And if you could send gifts to him that would uplift him, even if he wouldn't say thank you, would you be happy?"

"Yes!"

"Your situation is the same. Your son is safe, and you can make uplifting gifts to him by doing mitzvot in his honor."

The above story illustrates how shifting perspective can help in a tragedy. In our everyday lives, we can change our perspective by realizing that not many things in life are truly very important. We probably won't even remember most of our present problems in a couple of years. Such issues do not deserve to be taken to heart.

Often we feel impatience and annoyance with life's small inconveniences—getting stuck in traffic due to a motor vehicle accident ahead, being jolted by a jarring wail of an ambulance siren, being trapped in an airplane near a baby who cries for the whole flight, and so on. Rabbi **Zalman Schachter-Shalomi** suggests that whenever we are inconvenienced by other people's problems or unhappiness, we should empathize and wish for a speedy and good resolution of the situation for the strangers who find themselves in difficulty. So we should pray for the car accident to be without injuries, for the ambulance to get to its destination in time, and for the baby to feel better. By accustoming ourselves to empathizing with other people and sending good wishes to them, even if they are strangers, instead of getting annoyed, we will feel better ourselves and more connected to our neighbors and maybe even somehow help them through our positive energy and prayer.[249]

Besides, with a little bit of creativity, we can even find ways to benefit from any situation. We can learn from it, forge new friendships or reinforce old ones, or use it as inspiration to change something in our lives for the better.

It's also useful to compare your situation with that of people who have it worse. Your air conditioner broke in the middle of a heat wave? Some don't even have a home. If we make such comparisons instead of complaining, they will provide us with appreciation for what we have.

Finally, to get some perspective on a negative situation, imagine temporarily removing yourself from it and seeing it from a distance. How would you console a friend in a similar situation? What would you advise? See if you can apply your advice to yourself.

- Remember reasons to overcome.

With both small and big problems, give yourself a reason to overcome and bounce back. It can be a trip to look forward to, wanting to set an example for your kids, or the good memories associated with the things that are bothering you now, such as your family or job.

Alfred Dreyfus was a French army officer who was convicted of treason and sentenced to life imprisonment in 1894. It is believed that he was a victim of anti-Semitic sentiment. He later recounted that throughout the whole affair his biggest motivation to overcome any hardships was his desire to prove his innocence. In 1906 an appeals court reexamined the case and Dreyfus was exonerated.[250]

In his case, the importance of clearing his name kept Dreyfus strong, resilient, and able to deal with a grave injustice. Whatever your reason is, it will energize you to cope with the present stress.

- Get inspired.

Look around for inspiring examples of resilience. They can come from anywhere. We can draw inspiration from nature, observing how trees that appear dead in the winter sprout new leaves every spring. We can draw inspiration from history or fiction, from movies and quotes that remind us that even in the worst circumstances people have rebounded.

We can observe resilience in other people and learn from their example: from friends or strangers, from our parents or our kids. Think of wise and happy people you know and admire. Think of spiritual leaders. Ask yourself, "What would that person do?"

And we can get inspired by ourselves and our own past experiences. Remembering situations when we successfully coped with adversity in the past can help us realize in the present that we are strong and courageous and that we have what it takes to live life happily despite hardships.

- Act.

"There is nothing in the world that can't be fixed."

—Arkady and Boris Strugatsky, *Roadside Picnic* [251]

Every time a problem arises, to counter depression or discouragement, immediately thinking of a potential solution or way to improve the situation. Taking control and doing something about the situation provides a powerful boost of positive energy, and it should not be delayed, as the professor in the following story graphically illustrates.

At the beginning of class, a professor pointed to a glass with water and asked his students, "How much do you think this glass weighs?"

"Six ounces! Eight! Ten!" shouted the students.

"Frankly, I am not sure myself," confessed the professor, "but this is not important. What will happen if I will hold it in my outstretched hand for two minutes?"

"Nothing, Professor."

"Indeed, you are right. What if I hold it for two hours?"

"Your arm will hurt!"

"What if I hold it in the outstretched hand for a day?"

"Probably your arm will go numb or your muscles will seize."

"Do you think the weight of the glass will change from me holding it all day?"

"No, it will not change," responded the students with surprise.

"Where are the pain and the muscle spasm coming from, then? And what do I need to do to alleviate the pain?"

"Just put the glass down! Let it go!" the students suggested.

"You are right!" replied the professor. "Remember to do the same with life's difficulties and failures. The more we hold on to them, the heavier they feel. The more we think about our problems, the more they weigh us down and cause us pain until we are paralyzed. The best way to cope with problems is by acting! Even a simple but timely action is better than endless speculation. Solve your problems or set them aside. Let them go. Otherwise they will take over your life."[252]

However, if you cannot think of any ways to resolve or improve a situation, if it is out of your control, then the solution is to change your attitude toward it.

- Make lemonade.

Sigmund Freud wrote that instead of suppressing our negative feelings, it is extremely important to sublimate them into constructive pursuits. What this means is that rather than wallowing in negative feelings and thoughts, we can divert that energy into something positive.

Zelig Pliskin teaches that we should do this by transforming problems into goals. Instead of saying, "I have a problem," say "I have a goal." Turn "I don't have a good job" into "My goal is to have a good job." Sometimes, a goal can be simply coping with the problem gracefully. While problems cause stress and anxiety, goals energize and motivate us, elevating our emotional status.[253]

Not only can we redirect negative energy to resolve a problem, but with a little creative thinking, we can try to benefit from it! For example, after getting fired comedic actress **Annabelle Gurwitch** wrote a book about it and became a best-selling author. Her book includes comeback stories by other celebrities who were fired at some point, including **Andy Borowitz**, **Jeff Garlin**, **Judd Apatow**, **Robert Reich**, and **Sarah Silverman**.

• Learn and grow.

"I asked for strength. God gave me difficulties to make me strong. I asked for wisdom. God gave me problems to solve."

—Anonymous, "I Offered a Prayer to God"[254]

"There are no problems, only opportunities for growth."

—Rebbetzin **Dena Weinberg**

Judaism holds that the meaning of life is in self-improvement, and every regression is a *yeridah tzorech aliyah*, a descent for the sake of ascent. Adversity is a powerful teacher, and sometimes the downs are necessary precursors to the ups. As **Bernard M. Baruch** said, "The art of living lies less in eliminating our troubles than in growing with them."

Rabbi Akiva noted that suffering can be precious.[255] Problems create opportunities to improve; to forgive; to be courageous; to see the big picture; to practice humility, patience, spirituality, or independence; and to strengthen our feelings of contentment, calmness, and appreciation for life. Hardships and mistakes are the price for developing our character and becoming wiser at any age. **Wendy Mogel**, clinical psychologist and author of a best-selling book on raising children, explains that when a parent complains to her about a child's awful teacher, her usual reply is, "Great! He'll learn a whole new set of coping skills dealing with her, skills he'll need on the job and in marriage."[256]

Abraham Maslow, the famed humanistic psychologist, studied self-actualizers, people at the peak of mental wellness. He noted that adversity is required for psychological growth: "The most important learning lessons . . . were tragedies, deaths, and trauma . . . which forced change in the life-outlook of the person and consequently in everything that he did."[257] In Judaism, the process of spiritual growth through difficulties is called *nesayon*, which means "test." We don't know our potential until we are tested by life's trials.

Maimonides cites a story of a distinguished person who was asked to describe the most joyous day of his life. "It was a day I was on a ship," he replied. "There were people who mocked and jeered at me. They even threw garbage on me. My joy was that I was able to transcend this and create my own inner joy." The day of most joy for this man was the day he realized that his happiness was independent of external circumstances and only dependent on his own mind.[258]

Appreciating a negative experience for the chance it provides to grow can change our perception of a situation dramatically. For example, some cancer patients confess to being grateful for getting the disease because it triggered a personal change that lead them to happiness.[259]

If you make a mistake, consider it a very useful diagnostic opportunity. Mistakes show which areas in our thinking and behavior need attention. Forgive yourself and resolve to do better next time. Instead of saying, "I'm so bad at this," say, "Knowing what I know now, I will do better next time."

Recognize and appreciate all opportunities for self-improvement. Moreover, feel joy in every action that develops your character, as this helps to fulfill our purpose in life.

• Adapt.

"Better to be bent over than to be broken down."

—Yiddish proverb[260]

Some problems are actually not so much problems as indicators of change in our life. The suffering comes when we resist the change. At times, we hold on to our situation, as bad as it may be, for fear of the new and unknown. At other times, we are just being stubborn, trying to maintain the status quo even when it is no longer relevant. On the other hand, sometimes we want to instigate change when the circumstances aren't right and keep trying to force it at any price.

The art of adaptation is a major survival trait in nature. It is also a major tool for emotional resilience. "If you can't go over, go under," teaches Yiddish wisdom.[261] Be persistent, but know how to adapt to a situation and be flexible, like the Jews in the following joke.

A Spaniard, an Italian, and a Jew are discussing climate change and what would happen if the ocean flooded all the land.

The Spaniard and Italian muse, "There is nothing we can do about it. What would you do?"

"Our answer is a foregone conclusion," replied the Jew. "We Jews would learn to live under water."[262]

- Accept.

"Of course there is no formula for success, except perhaps an unconditional acceptance of life, and what it brings."

—Arthur Rubinstein

There are times when the only feasible coping strategy is acceptance. If we can't influence the situation, obsessing over it only makes us miserable. "If despite all your determined efforts you cannot seem to reach your goal, be patient. Between acceptance and anxiety, choose acceptance," teaches Rebbe Nachman of Breslov.[263]

Sometimes we have to deal with tragedies and great loss. The book of Job tells a story of a man called **Job**. When he lost everything—his money, children, house, and cattle—he cried and tore his hair at first. But then he said, "Naked I emerged from my mother's womb, and naked I will return there. God has given and God has taken; blessed be the name of God."[264] When we consider that we start life with nothing and we leave it with nothing, we realize that everything we gain during it is like a loan and will be taken back from us one day. Some things are recalled earlier, others later. But if we know it can happen, we can be more accepting and thus more peaceful and content when it happens.

Recognize and accept that certain things and events are just beyond your control. That does not mean that they are bad; it means that they are the way they are. Do not get caught up in thinking, "If only he would do that differently," or "I should have . . ." or "Why didn't she . . . ?" Give up judgment, regrets, blame, and any other negativity you feel about what you cannot change, and gracefully let go of it.

- Stay optimistic.

  "Tracht gut, vet zein gut."
  (Think good, and it will be good.)

  —Yiddish proverb

Believe that everything is going to work out without expecting things to happen exactly the way you envision. Optimism can help us stay positive in any situation:

> A doctor is making rounds in a hospital, and he tells three of his patients that their condition took a turn to the worse. When he leaves, the patients discuss their options.
>
> "I am going to get my finances in order," heavily sighs one.
>
> "I am going to see a priest and make a confession," says another with distress.
>
> "And I am going to see another doctor," concludes Frenkel.[265]

Because the doctor's announcement implies the bad outcome, two patients jump to the worst conclusions. But Frenkel's choice to stay optimistic encourages him to search for other possible solutions and stay in good spirits.

- Ask for help; accept support.

"Sometimes you may want to unburden yourself and talk about your problems Sometimes just saying it out loud makes us feel much better."

—Rebbe Nachman of Breslov[266]

In difficult times, we can find emotional and practical support in our connections to other people. They provide love, encouragement, care, and reassurance to support our resilience as well as words of advice or help with solving the problem. Sometimes just the knowledge that we are not alone renews our strength.

Communicate your problem. Just talking about it may add clarity to the issue and lead to a solution. Seek help and resources. Ask for and accept the support of people who care for you or people you do not know. Bonding over a problem can strengthen existing relationships and create new friendships.

It also helps to pray for divine assistance. Rebbe Nachman of Breslov urged, "Express your innermost thoughts and feelings before God each day in the language you are most comfortable with. Even if all you have to say to God is 'Help!' it is still very good. Repeat this over and over again, until God opens your lips and the words begin to flow from your heart."[267]

- Put faith in God.

"Blessed is the man who trusts in God; God will be his reassurance."

—Jeremiah 17:7

"Nothing bad comes down from Above."

—**Midrash**, Bereshit Rabah

In Judaism, bitachon, or trust in God, is the faith that everything that God does, everything that occurs, is good. Shneur Zalman of Liady writes in the *Tanya*, "Only good comes from God. It is only that there are two types of good: revealed good, which we experience as such; and hidden good, which comes from a place so lofty that our finite faculties are incapable of assimilating it, so that we experience it as pain and suffering."[268] Everything happens by God's will and is good for us, even if we do not feel this way at the time. That is why religious Jews answer *"Baruch HaShem"* (praise God) when asked about their welfare.

When we put our faith in God and trust that He knows what is best for us, we can find meaning and happiness in any circumstances: in traumatic events and in ordinary life. For example, **Mendel Futerfas** was incarcerated for fourteen years in Siberian Gulags for operating clandestine Jewish schools in the USSR. But instead of feeling depressed or resentful, his complete faith in God kept him cheerful. He believed that whatever happened to him was what was supposed to happen by the will of God. His part was to be a good person and a good Jew in any situation he found himself in. He explained, "I was a Jew out there, and I was doing what I was supposed to do; and I am a Jew here and doing what I am supposed [by God's will] to do."[269]

Besides, if we trust that everything comes from God in the way it is supposed to, we can let go of blame, jealousy, resentment, or anger toward other people involved in our problems. Realizing that whatever others say or do they are only passing along the message that is meant for us by the Creator brings reconciliation and tranquility.

Sages also teach that when God places obstacles in our way, He himself is "hidden" in them. Thus, if we don't shy away from our difficulties but instead take a closer look at them, we may uncover God within.[270]

And let's not forget that Jews believe in partnership between people and God. We are involved in creating the present with our attitude and behavior, and our conviction that God will make things good actually draws down blessings. **Menachem Mendel Schneersohn**, the third Lubavitcher Rebbe, taught that positive thinking not only is a way to weather negative occurrences but also actually produces positive results.[271]

- Accept that it is for the best.

"When things get 'hard' it reminds me that this too is for the best and I need to reorient my thinking to this realization."

—Rabbi **Yitz Greenman**

On Passover, the holiday of liberation from slavery, Jews eat a sandwich made of bitter herbs that symbolize the bitter fate Jews had in Egypt and **matzah** that symbolizes freedom. Jewish sages explain this tradition as a reminder to reassess the difficulties we experience and recognize that problems are valuable motivators to lead us to better and happier things.[272]

We feel much happier when we see an advantage in a disadvantage and believe that whatever seemingly negative thing we experience is a blessing in disguise.

That is how Golda Meir thought about the fact that she was not a conventional beauty: "Not being beautiful was the true blessing. Not being beautiful forced me to develop my inner resources. The pretty girl has a handicap to overcome."

There is a famous fable about a fox who loved grapes. One day she saw beautiful looking grapes, but they were hanging too high, and she could not reach them no matter how hard she tried. She walked away upset, telling herself that the grapes must have been sour anyway. Rabbi Zelig Pliskin provides an excellent example of contemplating the big picture by adding some possible future developments to the story:

> A tall bear came along later that day and was able to reach the grapes. He had to spit them out because of how sour they were.
>
> Another fox came along but also could not reach the grapes. This fox decided to pile rocks to climb up. As he was about to reach the grapes, he fell down and injured himself.
>
> A bear came along and reached the grapes. They were the best grapes he had ever eaten. He ate so many of them that he got sick.
>
> A few moments after the fox left the scene some fox hunters came along. They ate some grapes, but missed out on shooting the fox, who unbeknown to her had a very narrow escape. If she were to have lingered to eat the grapes, she would have become a fur coat.

The grapes were really good. But our friend the fox found another vine that she could reach and enjoyed herself more than she would have with the original grapes. The grapes she did find were tastier than any on the other vine.

The fox couldn't reach the grapes. "I accept my Creator's will," she said. And this was the beginning of the fox's path to spiritual enlightenment. In the future, she was grateful to the Creator for the grapes she did eat and accepted with serenity anything that did not work out the way she preferred."[273]

The moral is not to despair if your original plan for life does not work out. What you planned could not have been as enjoyable as you thought, or it could have caused problems you had not anticipated. Your failure could make other plans and opportunities possible that could be better in the long run.

When we accept that everything happens for the best, we become more content in the face of setbacks and more optimistic and happier in general.

- Accept that this is life.

"Try to respect life not only for its charms, but also for its difficulties."

—Joseph Brodsky

In life, bad things happen. They just do. In response to the tragedy of 9/11, Alice Herz-Sommer said, "Good and evil have been around since prehistoric times. It is how we handle it, how we respond, that is important."[274]

Az men lebt, erleybt men, says a Yiddish proverb: when one lives, one experiences. Life is a journey: one day we visit the best places and taste the best food, and the next we find ourselves some-where completely different. Life does not have to be easy to be enjoyable. It is an unpredictable adventure, and as long as we continue traveling, it can lead us anywhere.

The Talmud teaches us to "eat the inside of the pomegranate and throw away the peel."[275] In the following story, a mother uses another fruit to show that in life good is intermingled with bad, but this shouldn't preclude us from appreciating how great life is and taking pleasure in it.

> When her daughter was complaining about life being dif-ficult, Sarah asked her, "Do you like cherries?"
>
> "Yes, I do."
>
> "But darling, every cherry has a pit. One can chip a tooth or choke on them. Doesn't that prevent you from enjoying the cherries?"
>
> "Not at all, Mom! You know I just spit them out."
>
> "Same with life, dear. It is great. You just need to learn to spit the pits out."

Mistakes, failures and losses are inevitable. They are part of life just as success, pleasures, and love are. We cannot completely prevent them; therefore, we shouldn't get too upset over them. Love your life instead, and maybe you will find the same correlation as Arthur Rubinstein did when he said, "I have found that if you love life, life will love you back."

- Know that it will get better.

"Anyone who doesn't believe in miracles is not a realist."

—David Ben-Gurion

Nothing is permanent in our lives. Things can—and do—change. Even grief diminishes or changes into something else with time.

Rebbe Nachman of Breslov taught, "Remember: things can go from the very worst to the very best . . . in just the blink of an eye."[276]

Whatever the situation seems to be right now, it can always change and become better. Not getting something we want or encountering a difficulty can lead to better things. For example, **Michael Bloomberg** was fired from his position at Salomon Brothers, so he founded his own billion-dollar company and went on to become a mayor of New York City.

Anything is possible. Miracles happen every day. People spontaneously heal from cancer,[277] unexpectedly find themselves in the right place at the right time, or find soul mates through extraordinary circumstances.

Whenever you encounter a difficulty, know that things will get better.

- Do not dwell on problems.

*"Never think of pain or danger or enemies a moment longer than
is necessary to fight them."*

—Ayn Rand, *Atlas Shrugged*

Finally, after you've dealt with a problem using the resilience
methods discussed above, there is one more thing to do—let
go of it the moment it is resolved. Maimonides wrote, "[Many]
thoughts that cause distress, sorrow, sadness or grief, occur
[when] one thinks of the past like the loss of money or a beloved
one. Yet it is known through rational observation that thinking
about the past is of no benefit at all . . . There is no difference
between a person who grieves over lost money and the like, and
someone who grieves because he is human and not an angel, or a
star, or similar thoughts which are impossibilities."[278]

Once something is in the past, it is gone forever. Don't stay
stuck thinking about the details of a past distress. Be grateful for
the lesson and move on. Consider the example of Alice Herz-
Sommer. Once she was freed from Theresienstadt concentration
camp, she never looked back, never attended a reunion or a me-
morial ceremony held for survivors. She left her horrible past
behind and drew her strength from living in the present.[279] That
is where the happiness is.

Distract yourself from dwelling on the negative by staying busy.
Meet with friends, go to museums, read books, take walks outside, run, or exercise.

Concentrate on the good things in your life—your health, family,
and friends; an interesting book; the sun rising in the morning;
or just being alive.

And remember that every morning can be a fresh start. If you weren't happy with yesterday, try something different today. Establish new goals and keep moving forward.

CHAPTER 40

EVERY CLOUD HAS A SILVER LINING

"Got helft dem oreman: er farhit im fun tayere aveyres."
(God helps the poor man: he protects him from expensive sins.)

—Yiddish proverb

Good and bad, positive and negative, light and shadow—these opposites coexist in everything in our lives. There is nothing that is completely good or completely bad. Jewish sages teach that every problem and trouble we face is packaged with a silver lining. [280] Therefore, when faced with a difficult situation, a good way to stay content and happy is to look for the positive in it. [281]

Sometimes, the silver linings are rather obvious and generally accepted. Pregnancy may be uncomfortable, but it is necessary in order to have a child. Getting a college degree may be expensive and difficult, but it is the way to get good education. A colonoscopy may be anxiety producing, but it helps prevent the development of illness.

Other times, we need to think a little harder to recognize the good, but if we squint, we can see it. "If you have no linen, you save on laundry," and "Cheap borsch is a blessing for the toothless" Yiddish folk wisdom tells us. It is possible to find something positive in more difficult situations as well. For example, Joseph Brodsky found a benefit even to exile: "If there is anything good about exile, it is that it teaches one humility. . . . Exile brings you overnight where it would normally take a lifetime to go."

There are many well-known examples of hardships having a positive "side effect." Irving Berlin was born Israel Baline in 1888 in a cantor's family living near the Siberian border. In 1893 the family experienced a terrible pogrom. That experience brought them to New York, where Berlin went on to become one of the most famous American composers.[282]

The breakup of the legendary comedy duo of **Jerry Lewis** and Dean Martin in 1956 felt like the end of an era, but it was the beginning of a brilliant and diverse solo career for Lewis.[283]

There is some intrinsic good in virtually every situation. The silver lining in having an argument with your husband or kids is the fact that you have a husband or kids. The good in your knee hurting is that you have a knee and can walk. If you are extremely nervous about an upcoming public speech, the positive angle is that people are coming to listen to you. When we grieve the loss of something, it means we had something to love. When we face death, it means that we were granted the gift of life.

Sometimes, the silver lining in a difficult situation is the realization that it could be much worse. As a Yiddish proverb teaches, it is better to break off an engagement than a marriage.[284]

And as the following joke demonstrates, there is always room for humor, which itself is a type of silver lining:

> The Titanic is sinking, and Louis and his wife find themselves in the same life raft. Unfortunately, the raft was damaged during the panic, and it is slowly sinking. To make matters worse, the water around them is ice cold; there are sharks; they have no food or drink; nor is there any kind of weapon or emergency flare on board.
>
> After a few minutes of silence, Louis turns to his wife and says, "I suppose we shouldn't be too ungrateful, Naomi. Things could have been much worse."
>
> "What on earth do you mean—things could have been much worse?" replies Naomi. "Are you *meshugga* or something? How could it be any worse?"
>
> "Well," replies Louis, "we could have paid full price for return tickets!"[285]

Sometimes we have to apply creative thinking to finding the silver lining, but it is present in all situations. When we make the effort to become mindful of it, we become more content.

PUT IT INTO PRACTICE

These two simple steps will help you find the silver lining and feel better about any negative situation.

- Get used to finding the silver lining in any situation.

Do not underestimate the difficulties, but do not turn a blind eye to good possibilities either. What does the situation teach you? How does it makes you stronger, better? What good can come out of it?

Think about the way in which this situation will have the most positive impact on your life.

- Express gratitude for the little bit of good you have discovered.

CHAPTER 41

ENEMIES OF HAPPINESS

When we find ourselves in trouble, it is easy to understand why we are not at our happiest. But why are we sometimes not happy when nothing bad is happening? There are four major enemies of happiness and contentment in quiet and pleasant times: worry, cynicism, habit, and boredom.

WORRY

One evening my daughter said to me, "Imagine you are in a tank with hungry sharks with no way to escape. What should you do?" There are sharks and no way to escape? That thought, though highly hypothetical, caused me some anxiety and fear before I gave up and asked for the right answer. It turned to be simple: "Stop imagining." That is a great advice for every single time we find ourselves worrying.

The extent of our worries depends on our attitude toward the unknown future. Here is how Ayn Rand regarded the future: "I do not think that tragedy is our natural fate and I do not live in chronic dread of disaster. It is not happiness, but suffering that I consider unnatural. It is not success, but calamity that I regard as the abnormal exception in Human Life."[286] If you agree with Rand, there is no reason to doubt and fret about the future.

However, when we lack such confidence that things will be good in the future even when nothing is wrong at present, we tend to spoil our happiness with worrying.

Anxiety, fear, doubt, and other forms of worry are our fantasies about possible bad outcomes. Worry is so powerful it can give us high blood pressure, depression, or an ulcer. However, it is pretty useless when it comes to affecting actual outcomes. "Any anxiety that results from thoughts about what may happen in the future are pointless because every possible thing lies in the realm of possibility: maybe it will happen and maybe it will not," Maimonides wrote on the uselessness of worrying.[287] While constructive thinking about and planning for the future are helpful, worry just detracts from our happiness without a practical benefit.

Even if the things we feared actually happen, we are not better off because we worried. But a lot of times we worry absolutely in vain, as we worry about things that never happen, or if they do, they do not transpire or feel the way we imagined. Meanwhile, as we worry about the possibility of being unhappy in the future, we make ourselves unhappy in the present.

The Tanakh instructs, "A worry in a person's heart—cast it away."[288] Here are some tips to help you follow this advice:

- Ask yourself how worrying will make the situation any better or will help you deal with it.

- Hope may be as useless in actually affecting the future as worrying, but it makes us feel happier. Therefore, instead of imagining bad outcomes, imagine good ones. You won't know the real outcomes until they happen, so why needlessly stress over them? Gloomy predictions are no more real than optimistic ones. Use your imagination to create happy endings. While not all of them will come true (just as with worrying), at least you will feel happier.[289] An added bonus: by practicing this technique, you automatically become an optimist!

- Focus on the present moment instead. Is there anything wrong right this second and right where you are? When you catch yourself worrying, keep reminding yourself: "I am here and now".

CYNICISM

Cynicism is the attitude that kills happiness. When we encounter goodness and happiness, cynicism makes us doubt that it is genuine or justified. When someone is content and happy, a cynic thinks he must not know what is going on or, worse yet, be off his rocker. If someone pays us a complement, cynicism will make us think he or she must want to get into our good graces. Cynicism is a nagging voice that won't let us just enjoy life.

When you have a cynical thought, stop to ask yourself:

- Do you know it's true?

Many times we do not know why someone looks happy or why he or she is paying us a complement. It could be for variety of reasons, and we just don't know which one it is. Remember that assumptions cause negative feelings.

- Is it helpful?

If we belittle another's or our own positive feelings or actions, will anyone benefit from this? Most of the time, the answer is no.

- Is it kind?

If we do not know that our cynical thoughts are true or even helpful, consider whether they are at least kind.

"No" on all accounts? Then let life be what it is and enjoy yourself.

HABIT

Humans get used to anything positive and with time feel less happy about it. As we learned earlier, this is known as the "hedonic treadmill."[290] The third piece of candy is not as tasty as the first, the fifth year of marriage feels less exciting and more prosaic (even if no less meaningful) than the honeymoon, and several months after hitting the jackpot, the lucky winner comes down from the high and reverts back to viewing life in his or her usual way. Hedonic treadmill is the reason we don't live "happily ever after..." when something remarkably joyous happens to us.

When we get into habits, we stop appreciating good circumstances as much as we did on the first day, and that takes away from our happiness just as much as worry and cynicism do.

Rabbi **Bahya ben Joseph ibn Paquda**, a Jewish philosopher who lived in eleventh-century Spain, describes with a parable how it is the human nature to take things for granted:

> Once upon a time a kindhearted individual found an infant in a desert. The benevolent man took the baby, brought him up, fed him, clothed him, and provided him generously with all that was good. The child grew up into an adult capable of understanding the many benefits he received. The same benefactor once rescued a man from captivity

and brought him to his home for a meal. The kindness that he showed this man was a fraction of the kindness he showed the child. Which one do you think appreciated it more?[291]

For some practical tips on how to avoid falling into the habit of not appreciating things, reread the chapters "Expectations" and "Be Grateful."

BOREDOM

Boredom is a melancholy state in which we simultaneously are not interested in lifting a finger and at suffer from our lack of activity. It occurs when we have too much free time.

Joseph Brodsky was fascinated by boredom because, as he put it, "It represents pure, undiluted time in all its repetitive, redundant, monotonous splendor. . . . Boredom is your window on the properties of time that one tends to ignore to the likely peril of one's mental equilibrium. It is your window on time's infinity."[292]

Whatever the case may be, for most of us, feeling bored puts a damper on happiness. There are several ways to get back into higher spirits.

• Appreciate your good luck

"Patsh zikh in tuchis und schrei 'hooray!'"[293] (Slap your backside and yell "hooray!"), Jewish moms say to children who complain about having nothing to do. That is what we should do too when we find ourselves bored.

Being bored means freedom. Jews were not always free. Until we were liberated from slavery in ancient Egypt, we were forced to work to exhaustion. Since then, this freedom has been celebrated every year on Passover. So every time you feel bored, immediately appreciate your freedom, and instead of feeling frustration for not knowing what to do with extra time, feel gratitude for being able to choose how to spend it.

- Find ways to reframe "boring" as "interesting."

"All work is creative work if done by a thinking mind," declared Ayn Rand.[294] When you find certain activities boring, switch on your "thinking mind" and turn them into stimulating and uplifting by adding meaning to them. Think about how you are improving the world with your action. Envision the people who benefit from your work.

Add challenges: run races against yourself. Set a timer to go off every ten minutes, and see in which ten-minute interval you can get the most work done.[295]

Keep it fresh: Even when we do the same activity repeatedly, we can find something interesting and new about them every time. Famous pianist Arthur Rubinstein always felt excited about playing the same musical pieces. He said it's like making love: "The act is always the same, but each time it's different."[296]

Which brings us to my final suggestion for livening up boring activities: add music. Dance while vacuuming, sing while doing dishes, or listen to music while waiting for an appointment.

CHAPTER 42

RELEASE YOUR EMOTIONS

"If emotional stress is maintained for a long period, one will definitely become ill."

—Maimonides, *Regimen of Health*[297]

"I know that pain is to be fought and thrown aside, not to be accepted as part of one's soul and as a permanent scar across one's view of existence."

—Ayn Rand, *Atlas Shrugged*

A range of emotions well up in us in response to our various thoughts and circumstances. Negative emotions signal trouble and can be dealt with by practicing emotional resilience, as we discussed in previous chapters. Positive emotions highlight pleasures. As situations change, so should our emotional states. But sometimes we cling to emotions, not letting them pass with the passage of events. Holding on to emotional baggage from the past may prevent happiness in the present.

Being a happy person does not mean feeling positive and joyous all the time. It requires the ability to feel different emotions and then release them completely.

At times, we do not let go of negative emotions. Either we suffer from them, unable to get rid of old fear or anger, or we revel in feelings such as self-pity and sadness long after the cause for them is gone. In doing so, we force ourselves to relive the unpleasant situations. When we hold on to hurt, we make ourselves suffer the insults that caused it over and over again. When we complain, we just perpetuate the problem. When we bear grudges, we constantly strain under the weight of the hatred and spite we originally felt.

Surprisingly, the same thing can happen with positive emotions. When happiness is tied to the past, it turns into nostalgia, which keeps us focused on a memory of former joy as opposed to the possibility of actual happiness in the present.

Every spring in preparation for Passover, Jews must clean their homes of all *chametz*, or leavened food. This requires a thorough house cleaning that involves moving furniture, scrubbing every shelf and every corner, and hunting for every last crumb. Sages assign a spiritual meaning to this tradition. It is an opportunity to clean out stale thoughts and get unstuck from the past state of mind. Releasing past emotions is necessary for a fresh start in the journey to self-improvement, spiritual liberty, and happiness.

Emotions move through us similarly to how water flows through pipes. Healthy emotions should flow in and out so that nothing from the past is carried over into the present. Stagnation indicates a problem in the process and should be cleared up as soon as possible. Therefore, we should not hold on to emotions, positive or negative, for too long. When we let go, we are able to fully experience each new moment and cultivate happiness.

PUT IT INTO PRACTICE

Release stress and tension in a healthy way by following these guidelines:

- Establish a time limit.

When you experience negative emotions such as anger, annoyance, or frustration, know that it's okay to feel them, but start letting them go in thirty seconds or a minute. Do not hold on to them.

- Forgive.

Jewish law expects us to forgive. The Hebrew Bible contains a commandment "not to bear a grudge."[298] Holding on to resentment and anger can be compared to holding hot coals with the intention to throw them at someone else: you are the one getting burned. Withholding forgiveness steeps bitterness within us and prevents our happiness. Forgive for your own sake, even when you are hurt or dislike the other person. It will restore your own well-being.

Zelig Pliskin recommends getting into the habit of forgiving others nightly before you go to sleep, whether or not they've asked for forgiveness. Never wait too long to forgive. Your happiness is too precious.[299]

And do not forget to forgive yourself for any mistakes you might have made.

- Purge past emotions.[300]

Make a list of the most emotional moments from your past as far back as you can remember, both positive and negative. When you are finished, look over the list and remember the events as fully as you are able to. (Warning: tissues may be necessary.) Then, when you are ready, have your own fire ceremony and burn the list. In doing so, mentally release any suppressed emotions left over from those events.

- Look into available resources.

If you feel that you need more guidance in dealing with your emotions, seek professional help. There are several techniques and professionals that specialize in emotional release:

Emotional Freedom Technique (EFT) helps release emotions through tapping certain body parts.

Cognitive behavioral therapy (CBT) is a kind of psychotherapy that helps you recognize and release undesired emotional reactions and the underlying thoughts.

Enroll in stress-management classes, see a qualified psychotherapist or an energy healer, or try hypnosis to help you release emotions that you can or cannot consciously remember.

EXPAND YOUR HAPPINESS ARSENAL

CHAPTER 43

INTRODUCTION TO THE SECTION

We have now covered the skills that are essential to achieving happiness: recognizing happiness in ourselves, setting priorities and goals, loving, believing in and caring for ourselves, focusing on the positive, and dealing with the negative.

In this section we will learn additional skills that will add to our feeling of happiness: connecting with something bigger than ourselves, imbuing life with meaning, practicing kindness, increasing joy by verbalizing it, developing an undying sense of curiosity, and, when life becomes too serious, acting out happiness.

CHAPTER 44

CULTIVATE CONNECTION

"Acquire yourself a friend."

—Pirkei Avot 1:6

Judaism and the modern science both assert that humans flourish when we feel connected with something outside of ourselves. Such connection with someone or something is not defined by proximity or relationship but rather by our perception of a deep bond. We may feel such a connection even with an eighteen-century author we have never met. Feeling this type of connection benefits our happiness, well-being, and some researchers say even our health.

Among the most significant and strongest connections we develop are the bonds we feel to other people, whether through love, parenthood, friendship, ancestry, work, hobbies, or shared ideas. Research shows that this feeling of deep connection affects our inner state regardless of the number of friends we have or even whether the people we feel connections with are our personal friends or not.[301]

While modern culture praises individualism and independence,

Jewish wisdom emphasizes the importance of being connected to a community. The openness to others that comes with community enriches our encounters and experiences and makes us see more beauty and wonder in the world and the people around us.

Reaching out to others can even turn Hell into Heaven, as the following story illustrates:

> As a reward for her benevolent life, Ariella, a lamed-vavnik (one of the thirty-six people in the world who are completely good) was taken to see Hell and Heaven while she was still alive. In Hell she saw a magnificent palace with an opulent dining hall. The tables were filled with the most delicious food: fragrant soups, creamy cheeses, fresh vegetables, juicy fruits, and exquisite cakes. But the people in the room all looked thin, hungry, and unhappy. When Ariella looked carefully, she realized why the people did not eat the scrumptious food: they all had splints strapped to their arms so they could not bend their elbows. They could pick up the food, but they had no way of getting it into their mouths. She was sad that they sat amid plenty but starved.
>
> Next, the lamed-vavnik went to visit Heaven. She found herself in a beautiful palace once again. The dining hall was also laden with all kinds of fragrant and delicious dishes. And the people at the table all looked healthy and well fed. They were happy and chatted with each other as they settled down to eat the wonderful meal laid out before them. But to her surprise, Ariella noticed that everybody in Haven had exactly the same splints on their arms as the people in Hell.

"Same palace, same meal, same splints, same everything," she murmured to herself. "The same challenges and opportunities exist in Heaven as in Hell. What is different?" And then Ariella saw that although the people in Heaven could not bend their arms to feed themselves, they were stretching their arms to feed each other. No one was angry, and everyone was getting enough to eat.

Ariella understood the difference between Heaven and Hell. She returned home and told others about her visit and the lessons she had learned. "Heaven and Hell are not just places that you go to after you die," she would tell the children who sat at her feet. "They are also part of how each of us looks at the world every day. And people who reach out to others are already halfway to Heaven."[302]

Another powerful connection that brings tremendous joy to many people is the spiritual bond that can be felt with God, the divine, or the universe. In Judaism, being connected to God is the purpose of practicing the laws of the Torah, as well as the true path to happiness.[303] A relationship with God is a powerful comfort during difficult times because it gives us the feeling that we are loved and cared for. It is a source of hope, peace, calm, gratitude, love, awe, joy, and even ecstasy, all of which increase our happiness.

We can feel such bond when we attend religious services. But there are different ways to experience moments filled with spirituality. Regular activities such as mediating, gardening, running, or dancing can generate a similar connection to *something* larger than ourselves that can results in joy and happiness.

Other important and very gratifying connections in our lives are to nature, to pets, to our professional calling, to sports and hobbies, to art and music, or even to abstract ideas.

Being a part of something bigger—a community, an idea, a friendship, or even a mental connection with someone— recharges our batteries, boosting our energy and happiness.

PUT IT INTO PRACTICE

Below are some concrete ways to boost your happiness by strengthening your feeling of connection with the outside world.

- Boost your connection with other people.

  ❖ An arm around a shoulder, a friendly pat on the back, a hug, or another form of human contact is an easy and very effective way to strengthen a bond. Scientists believe that such contact, especially hugging, releases oxytocin, a hormone that makes us feel happier.

  ❖ Sara Yoheved Rigler teaches that when you find yourself arguing the people you're closest to (a spouse, parents, or children), look at the situation through a "connection/disconnection" lens. When you look at things this way, the goal is not to prove that you are right at any cost but to stay connected with the other person. When you consciously choose to cultivate connection over estrangement, it will be easier to argue without anger and to solve disagreements in friendly and respectful ways.[304]

  ❖ Create more friendships and bonds. Find like-minded people. Buddy up for activities such as exercise, going to museums, or anything else. Volunteer for a community organization. Join sport teams or enroll in classes that interest you. Become a mentor.

- Strengthen your connection with a higher power.

  ❖ Go on nature walks. Connect with the uniqueness and the preciousness of the present moment by cultivating a sense of awe at the vastness of the universe, the beauty of a starry sky, or the limitlessness of the horizon.

  ❖ Add one spiritual activity to your daily routine. Join a temple or start meditating. Read spiritually themed or religious books.

  ❖ Communicate with the divine through prayer. This will reinforce your sense that you are not alone, that there is a loving being that listens to you and cares for you.

- Develop other types of bonds.

  ❖ Get a pet.

  ❖ Explore an idea or a cause you feel very strongly about. This can give you a feeling of being a part of a philosophical system or a movement.

CHAPTER 45

FIND MEANING

—Do you have a dream, Sarah?
—Yes, to lose weight.
—So why don't you?
—And live without a dream?

—Anonymous

Positive psychology has discovered that the pursuit of meaning and engagement makes us happier than the pursuit of pleasure.[305] Such findings coincide with the Jewish teaching that man is a purposeful being.[306] We feel fulfilled and happy when our lives have meaning. Ayn Rand compared a meaningful life to a train because we are happy when we are in motion toward a purpose.[307]

Dreams and goals are important for leading a meaningful and enjoyable life. They excite and inspire us; they give us a zest for life that keeps us young. "A man is not old until his regrets take the place of dreams," notes a Yiddish proverb. Dreams also connect us with like-minded people.

We can fulfill our need for purpose through grand projects or through small daily activities. The scale of our goals is not as important as our perspective on what is meaningful. Martin

Seligman illustrates this pointing out that a physician who views the job simply as a way to make a good income may find less meaning in her work than a hospital cleaner who sees himself critical in maintaining the germ-free environment that helps save lives.[308]

Moreover, Judaism insists that there is never a moment in life that is devoid of meaning and purpose, even when we are doing mundane or unexciting things. Rabbis interpret the biblical verse "God establishes the steps of man"[309] as meaning that nothing in our life is random, that every step, every circumstances is directed by God. Therefore, any activity we are engaged in at that moment constitutes the purpose of our existence.[310]

PUT IT INTO PRACTICE

Here are some ways to increase your happiness by setting meaningful life goals and recognizing that there is meaning in everything you do.

- Reflect on what makes your life meaningful.

Take a moment to ask yourself: What gets you out of bed in the morning? What are you looking forward to? What projects excite you? What have you always wanted to do with your life?

- Be mindful.

If at times you feel that life is meaningless, think again. You may already be involved in something worthwhile but be taking it for granted.

- Enjoy the process.

Do not tie your happiness only to the moment you reach a goal while neglecting to enjoy working toward it before you get there and forgetting to take pleasure in the accomplishment soon after. Relish the process of contemplating your goals and fulfilling your dreams. Enjoy even the smallest progress along the way, one day at a time. This way no task will seem too overwhelming, and life will become full of meaning and happiness regardless of outcomes.

After you have achieved a desired result, you may set your eyes on another dream, but you should not stop feeling happy and proud about your past achievements.

- Get organized.

Review your life's to-do list. Do you see any items that do not spark your enthusiasm? Delete them or complete them as soon as you can, and then cross them out. You will feel better.

Next, add anything you can think that makes your insides flutter in anticipation. Include self-improvement, work, hobbies, and time with family and friends in your planning. Do not forget about taking some time just for yourself.

Remember, plans are the blueprints of your life. Include the things you love. Make them interesting, exciting, and meaningful.

Remember to check the list against the list of priorities that I suggested you make earlier in this book. This will help you make sure you are moving in the right direction.

- Dream big but be realistic.

Psychiatrist and rabbi **Abraham J. Twerski** teaches that being aware of our limitations as well as our potential is very important for our self-fulfillment and happiness.[311] If we are looking to achieve something that is beyond our present abilities due to circumstances, health, age, or other factors, we may be setting ourselves up for failure and disappointment, not for joy.

Set goals that you can achieve and enjoy, and be mindful of your present circumstances and abilities.

That said, do not despair even when you cannot achieve your goals. Remember to appreciate the present and enjoy the process.

- Keep things in balance.

Some goals inspire us to spend all our free time and efforts on them. Be mindful of the golden mean. Balance achievement of worthy goals with other important parts of your life, such as family, friends, and hobbies.

CHAPTER 46

PRACTICE KINDNESS

Rock is strong, but iron breaks it.
Iron is strong, but fire melts it.
Fire is strong, but water extinguishes it.
Water is strong, but the clouds carry it.
Clouds are strong, but the wind carries them.
Wind is strong, but man withstands it.
Man is strong, but fear weakens him.
Fear is strong, but wine removes it.
Wine is strong, but sleep overcomes it.
Sleep is strong, but death stands over it.
But more powerful than all ten
are sweet acts of charity and loving kindness.

—Judah Bar Ilai

"Be kind. Kindness is free. It costs you nothing, and the rewards
are great for everyone."

—Alice Herz-Sommer[312]

Jewish tradition holds that the world stands on acts of kindness as much as it does on the Torah.[313] It teaches that even a simple act of kindness, such as a good wish or a blessing, can change the world, as illustrated by the following story:

> Once a prominent rabbi lamented the development of railroad system in the Russian Empire. When asked why he did not approve of such great convenience, he explained that when people went to seek his blessing, it used to take them weeks of travel. Every night they would stay in a different village on the way to his residence. Every night the locals asked the travelers for the reason for their trip, and after listening to their story, the local residents would extend their good wishes for the best resolution of their problem. By the time people came to the rabbi, half of the work had already been done by all the good wishes. Now, however, the people took a train and arrived in a day or two. Thus, the rabbi concluded, he had to do all the spiritual work to improve their situation by himself.[314]

As we can see, kindness can change the world. It also makes us happy. Modern science has proved that acts of kindness toward others increase the happiness not just of the recipient but of the giver as well. In other words, when we act kindly to others, we become happier ourselves.

Practicing kindness can yield surprising benefits. For example, volunteering is associated with a "helper's high"—decreased depression and enhanced feelings of self-worth, mastery, and happiness.[315] A study by Harvard Business School demonstrates that, contrary to the prevalent logic, spending money on others makes us happier than spending it on ourselves.[316] Also unexpected, doing kind things benefits us regardless of the response of the intended recipient or an acknowledgement from others.[317] As it turns out, we do not even have to consider ourselves especially kind to enjoy the benefits of practicing kindness: one study showed that engaging in a random act of kindness improved the happiness level of participants even when they only did so because a researcher told them to.[318]

Abraham Joshua Heschel, one of the leading Jewish theologians and philosophers of the twentieth century, once reflected, "When I was young, I admired clever people. Now that I am old, I admire kind people." Jews believe that God himself admires kind people, as evidenced by this tale about the creation of the Holy Temple in Jerusalem:

> There were two brothers. One was married with kids, the other was single and lived alone, and each had a farm. The childless brother thought, "My brother has many mouths to feed. I have only myself and my wife. I will help him." So, in the dark of the night, he would take a large bundle of grain and deposit it near his brother's house.
>
> The other brother reckoned, "I am blessed with many children, and my brother has none. He and his wife have no one else to look out for them. I want to help him." So, in the dark of the night, he would take a large bundle of grain and deposit it near his brother's house. Neither knew where the gifts of grain were coming from.
>
> One night the two brothers happened to meet, and they discovered the secret of the gifts. They embraced and cried on each other's shoulders. God looked down and decided to build the Holy Temple in this exact spot.[319]

OLGA GILBURD

The book of Genesis makes an even stronger point about the magnitude of kindness. When God appears to Abraham, He has to wait while Abraham tends to some strangers. By doing so, Abraham demonstrates that a kind deed is even greater than a divine experience. And God lingers patiently, demonstrating that for Him, our acts of kindness are well worth waiting for.

However, rabbis teach that even the practice of kindness requires moderation. The commandment to "love your neighbor as yourself,"[320] which according to Hillel is the essence of Judaism, implies that we have to love ourselves first, work to be happy ourselves first, and be kind to ourselves first. Judaism teaches that compassion does not entail a sacrifice of our interests. Therefore, though Jews are commanded to give tzedakah (charity), the rabbis of the Talmud passed an ordinance that no one should give away more than 20 percent of his income[321] so that he would not become impoverished and end up needing help from others.[322]

Similarly, Ayn Rand urged people to distinguish between acts of kindness, which can make us happy, and act of self-sacrifice, which can result in self-destruction.[323] She strongly believed that valuing self, not sacrificing your own dreams for somebody else's sake, is one of the conditions of true happiness.

Additionally, kindness is not always defined by giving. It is also kind to graciously receive from others—to accept sincere complements, gifts, offers of help, and tokens of love. Accepting acts of kindness with grace and gratitude strengthens connections and increases happiness for everyone involved.

PUT IT INTO PRACTICE

Practice kindness more by using the tips below. You will be happier for it.

- Recognize kindness.

Acts of kindness come in many shapes and sizes. An act of kindness may be a monetary donation or a kind word, offering to do a favor to someone or just spending time with loved ones. It may be large-scale, like an entire community getting together to help victims of a hurricane, or small-scale, like giving your seat to a pregnant woman. Notice opportunities for all types of kind deeds you can do for others, and recognize when others act kindly toward you.

- Cultivate kindness and compassion through meditation.

Meditating on loving kindness has been shown to increase positive emotions and our level of life satisfaction.[324] Sit quietly and comfortably, close your eyes, and simply direct well-wishes toward other people, silently repeating a phrase like "May you be happy." Start by meditating on yourself and your loved ones, then gradually expand to all the people you know, and finally, include the entire population of earth.

- Be kind to yourself.

Be gentle and loving to yourself in thoughts and in acts.

Appreciate yourself: avoid self-scorn and work on self-esteem.

Treat yourself: make plans with a friend, draw yourself a bath, go dancing, or watch a video that makes you laugh. Do something every day to improve yourself and your life, such as working out or practicing happiness skills.

- Practice kindness by giving.

Dr. **Alfred Adler**, a pioneer in psychoanalysis, used the "kindness" method to help his clients with depression. Adler instructed them to go out of their way to perform major acts of kindness for people who could use them. Having their actions improve the lives of others made his clients feel great about themselves, even when the acts of kindness went unnoticed. And if they received gratitude and appreciation for their efforts, that created an additional emotional lift.[325]

Perform at least one act of kindness for another person each day, whether the kindness is known or unknown to the recipient. Even small acts, such as a word of appreciation, a smile, a thoughtful gesture, or listening to somebody's story, can make others happy. And that, in turn, can make you happy too.

- Practice kindness by receiving.

Allow others the chance to be happy by doing acts of kindness for you. Recognize the kindness the other person wants to offer. Learn to gracefully accept love, help, and other forms of kindness.

CHAPTER 47

VERBALIZE YOUR HAPPINESS

"Death and life are in the power of the tongue."

—Proverbs 18:21

From the creation of the world, which was accomplished through God's utterances,[326] to our daily lives, Judaism ascribes amazing power to words. Since speaking requires action, words are more potent than thoughts, and they affect our lives more. **Chofetz Chaim** asserted that speech shapes the destiny of the Jewish people.[327] The **Vilna Gaon** said that proper speech is the single biggest factor in determining one's portion in the world to come.[328]

Jewish sages have always taught that we should mind what we say. In the following story, Rabbi Simcha Bunim makes just this point:

> Once a Jew invited a group of Hassidim to a meal with him. The Hassidim bombarded him with questions on whether the Jewish dietary laws were upheld in every

detail. Upon hearing all this, Rabbi Simcha Bunim said: "It's encouraging that we are so careful about what enters our mouths—but it is necessary that we be equally careful about what comes out of our mouths."[329]

Words are important because they enrich and reinforce our experiences, highlight and amplify our emotions. When we talk about sad or painful things, we may start crying. When we talk about our joys, it raises our happiness. Rabbi Sholom Dovber Schneersohn wrote:

> When a person pours his feeling of love into words, the act of speaking these words fuels and intensifies the love. Through speaking about it, the emotional energy radiates with more passion, and the persona is aroused with more love and fondness for the object of his love. . . . The same applies to all emotions. When they are not expressed through speech, they are reduced until they completely dissipate. When they are expressed verbally, they augment and grow considerably.[330]

When we speak, we usually follow our habitual patterns, even though in the English language we can choose from over a million words to get our thoughts across. Diversifying our vocabulary and using more positively charged words to describe feelings gives those emotions greater depth and meaning. When you are enjoying yourself, consider the difference between "This is okay" and "This is great." The former takes away from the joy; the latter enhances it.

Our words inspire and uplift or depress and hurt not only those around, but ourselves as well. If we know how to use them, they can boost our happiness. Let's pick the right vocabulary to help us make life happier.

PUT IT INTO PRACTICE

- Be mindful of what you say.

"A bird that you set free may be caught again, but a word that escapes your lips will not return," teaches a Yiddish proverb. Be conscious of you vocabulary and self-expression. Use positive words to express your thoughts. For example, replace "I don't want to be miserable" with "I want to be happy" and "I am still sick" with "I am getting better."

- Be mindful of how you say it.

The tone of voice we use can create different emotions. Saying "everything is great" in a sad or a sarcastic tone changes the meaning of the phrase and the mood as well. Put a little energy into your words by talking genially or enthusiastically, and it will lift your spirits.

- Don't be stingy with positive words.

"Let your ears hear what your mouth says," another Yiddish proverb advises. When we express our emotions verbally, they flourish and grow. Do not keep good feelings inside. Verbalize them. When you hear yourself enthusiastically describe your joy, you'll feel even more enthusiastic about it.

Instead of saying that something is "good," consider describing it as "brilliant," "magnificent," "terrific," "beautiful," or "thrilling."

- Talk about the good in your life.

By talking about the blessings in your life, you foster happy emotions. Reinforce all the good in your life by describing it out loud:

"I have a steady job; I have healthy children; today is a good day!"

- Say it with *kavanah*.

Jewish tradition prescribes that we should pray with *kavanah*—sincere concentration and intention, where the words come from our heart and soul, not just from our lips. Without *kavanah*, reciting prayers can be boring and meaningless. Apply the same principal to verbalizing your happiness. Be sincere in expressing the positive side of things. It will shift your focus and make you feel joyous.

CHAPTER 48

STAY INTERESTED IN LIFE

"A man should go on living—if only to satisfy his curiosity."

—Yiddish proverb

"None of them knew for sure what is happiness or the meaning of life. So they accepted a working hypothesis that happiness lies in the continuous exploration of the unknown, as does the meaning of life."

—Arkady and Boris Strugatsky, *Monday Begins on Saturday*

A sense of curiosity is a trait consistently associated with happiness in psychological studies.[331] Alice Herz-Sommer embodied this connection. "I am . . . never too old so long as I breathe to wonder," she said in an interview about enjoying life that she gave at 107 years old. She was always ready for something new: a new thought, a new book, a new idea, and new people. She took university courses until the age of 103. She was interested in fashion. She welcomed nearly everything innovative. Herz-Sommer attributed her ability to take pleasure in life until the end to her curiosity and interest in others.[332]

Judaism encourages taking an interest in life, as evidenced by this story related by **Samson Raphael Hirsch**:

> Once a rabbi told his congregation that he was planning a trip to Switzerland.
>
> "Why Switzerland?" they asked him. "There is hardly any Jewish community there. What reason do you have for travelling so far?"
>
> The rabbi replied, "I don't want to meet my maker and have Him say to me, 'What? You never saw my Alps?'"[333]

Curiosity transforms everyday tasks into interesting and enjoyable experiences, adding wonder and intrigue to almost any situation or interaction. It prompts us to embrace opportunities, makes us feel engaged and passionate about life, and, as a result, increases our happiness.

PUT IT INTO PRACTICE

There's a Yiddish proverb that says, "To a worm in horseradish, the whole world is horseradish." Perhaps the worm just wasn't curious enough to peek outside. If it had, it would have discovered a whole world beyond its home. We, however, can expand our horizons, explore the magnificent and awesome world filled with interesting and beautiful things and people, and increase our happiness by cultivating our curiosity. Here's how:

- Change things up.

Do something you have never done before. Take a different route to work. Go into an unfamiliar café or a high-end store. Take a guided tour of your city. Explore and discover the unknown.

- Stay curious about familiar.

Our world and the people in it are constantly changing and evolving, especially in small, subtle ways. Put aside assumptions about people you know or seemingly familiar activities and events, and approach them with an attitude of curiosity. Be on the lookout for even the tiniest thing that is different, special, or notable. Find the unfamiliar in the familiar.

Make it a goal to learn something new about the people you know. Ask questions about their lives, interests, families, or jobs. Consider every conversation an opportunity to discover something truly interesting and thought provoking.

- Experiment.

In a study, researches asked participants to do something they disliked and find novel features in it. An eighteen-year-old male body builder scoffed at crocheting, so he was asked to do it for ninety minutes. He reported being surprised by discovering that crocheting is more challenging than he had thought; that it is nonetheless meditative, as "time flew by"; and that he could make his own flip-flops. This small exercise altered the way he felt about the activity.[334]

Apply this experiment to any low-interest or unpleasant activity in your typical day by searching for novel or unexpected things about it. For example, if you dislike eating broccoli, give it another try and aim to discover some interesting, new-to-you things about it, such as a pleasant crunchy texture when it is raw or a sweeter taste when it is roasted. Try this experiment for other items on your "that's not for me" list.[335]

- Explore the unknown.

Pick up a magazine on a topic you don't regularly read about. Choose a book from a section at the library you don't normally visit. Listen to a different radio station. Embrace the diversity of the world and the possibility of finding the next interesting thing in unexpected places.

CHAPTER 49

ACT IT OUT

"If the only way to make yourself happy is by doing something silly, do it."

—Rebbe Nachman of Breslov[336]

When we start taking life too seriously and lose our sense of humor and sense of joy in the bustles and the troubles of our lives, or when we get so caught up in our habits and routines that we find it difficult to act differently even when we want to, it is time to playact. Adding a little playfulness back into our days can make us a lot more relaxed and happy.

There are two ways to playact that actually increase our happiness: viewing life events as games to play and acting out emotions we want to feel.

The first strategy—looking at our experiences as though they are games—allows us to have fun with life even when we are working hard and trying to do our best. The playful approach often makes situations feel lighter, easier, and more enjoyable. It gives us a different perspective, takes away stress, and can even change how we actually feel about a situation or experience.

The second strategy is to bring about desired emotions through our actions. Actions and feelings always go together, impacting one another. We act a certain way because of how we feel and vice versa—our feeling change because of what we do. By acting as if we feel a certain way, we induce that emotion in ourselves.

Judaism teaches that going through the motions of happiness can trigger feelings of happiness. In 1740, Rabbi **Luzzatto** wrote, "Act with enthusiastic joy and you will actually experience it."[337] Along the same lines, Menachem Mendel Schneerson, the Lubavitcher Rebbe, instructed, "At times, assume a demeanor and mannerisms as if your heart were full of joy; even if at the moment this is far from the case. Such behavior will eventually lead you to truly feel happy, because behaviors and actions impact the heart."[338]

Today science supports these teachings. The "fake it till you make it" approach has a surprisingly strong impact on our emotions even when we don't believe that it is going to work. Researchers say that acting positive is the quickest way to get into a positive mind-set. For example, in one study, students were asked to act like extroverts for fifteen minutes in a group discussion, even if they didn't feel like it. The more assertive and energetic the students acted, the happier they were.[339]

Talmudic sages teach that even when we do good with an ulterior motive, good comes for its own sake.[340] Start acting happy and you will get happy.

PUT IT INTO PRACTICE

• Stop stopping yourself.

Zelig Pliskin notes that our self-perception often stands in the way of our acting differently.[341] We want to be a certain way but think that that's just not us. Do not limit yourself only to your habitual behavior. Make it your intention to embody a trait in order to become better and happier. Start speaking and acting in ways consistent with your ideal self, even if you're only playacting. It can be fun just to imitate your imagined self, to pretend. When you see you can act the ideal behavior out, even as make-believe, you will realize that you really can think, speak, and act that way. Once you start pretending, you will gradually become that person.

• Think of your life as a theater play.

Give yourself the part of a happy person in the theater of life. Act the way you want to feel. If you feel shy, act friendly. If you feel irritated, act loving. Pay attention to the words you are saying and the intonation you are saying them with. See how much this affects your true feelings.

• Think of your life as a self-improvement workshop.

Rabbi Pliskin suggests approaching everything that happens to you as an experiment designed to teach you something. This will allow you to see difficult situations as fun exercises and challenges that enrich you and benefit you. The people around you can be your teammates, and you can think of everything they say or do as part of the exercise designed to develop your character. And just like a self-improvement workshop, any situation is temporary. Develop a sense of humor and enjoy the experience.[342]

- Think of your life as a challenge.

See how many happiness points you can "score" in any situation. Give yourself a point every time you see humor in a situation, use a situation to improve a skill, acquire a new friend, and so on. Challenge yourself to score more points every month.

- Pretend to be a happiness specialist.

Imagine you are a life coach, and it is your job to counsel people in difficult situations. If someone presented you with the circumstances you presently struggle with, how would you spin them for that person?

Imagine you are an incorrigible optimist. What would you say about your situation?

- Add silliness and playfulness.

When doing a chore, start dancing or singing. Make up lyrics about what you are doing, and sing or rap them to yourself: "I am frying a fish. It's such a tasty dish!"

RELAX

CHAPTER 50

INTRODUCTION TO THE SECTION

Relaxing is a very important happiness skill. On the physical level, it rests and renews our bodies. On the mental level, it refreshes our brains and counteracts nervousness, fear, and anger. And on the spiritual level, it helps us to enjoy our lives and be content and happy with what we have.

Menuha, or rest, is an important concept in Jewish tradition. According to Jewish sages, the universe is incomplete without it. Rest was created by God along with earth, water, and life. *Menuha* is a source of tranquility, serenity, peace, and happiness.

Relaxing can mean several things—pausing from the work we do and concentrating on rest, living life with ease, feeling content with what we have and not chasing after bigger and better possessions, or practicing patience in the face of the inevitable.

The following chapters will offer suggestions on how to relax and help you find your own golden mean in balancing activity with pauses and an energetic mindset with a relaxed attitude that makes you feel the happiest.

CHAPTER 51

TAKE IT EASY

The storytelling master the Baal Shem Tov recounted a time he was driving a coach with three horses. For some reason the horses were not neighing, and he could not figure out why. A passing peasant saw the horses and shouted at the Baal Shem Tov to loosen the reins. The moment he did so, the horses began to neigh. With this allegory the founder of Hasidism taught that, while we should "rein" ourselves in, with too much rigidity and control, we suppress joy and don't let the soul sing.[343]

Several things can get in the way of taking it easy. One such obstacle is expecting perfection from ourselves and others. We can wear ourselves out in our attempt to get to all the items on our to-do list, to always look and behave a certain way, or to keep a perfect household and still not be satisfied because of inevitable flaws. When we expect everything to be just so, a minor imperfection can cause major irritation. The inability to relax and enjoy things as they are only causes stress and precludes joie de vivre.

This relates to another obstacle we must overcome in order to relax and enjoy ourselves—stressing out. Stress often results when we attach too much meaning and importance to objects and events. When we take things very seriously, we become overly affected by them or behave in a way that only worsens the situation. The more intensely we cherish a car, the more upset we are when it gets scratched. The more we are invested in a sport, the more heartbroken we are when our team loses. The more necessary we think it is to us to make a good impression, the more likely we are to behave nervously or arrogantly, minimizing our chances of success.

Often when we feel stress, fear, or lack of control, we try to force things to happen the way we want. Frequently this produces the opposite effect and leaves us feeling defeated or angry. The more we prompt our loved ones to do what is best for them, the more they rebel. The more we clutch a bicycle handlebar and concentrate on staying upright and balanced, the less we enjoy the ride. The more we struggle, the faster we sink. Sometimes, by forcibly fighting the circumstances, we create extra obstacles to our happiness, as demonstrated by this parable about a thirsty knight:

> Once a knight went through a desert. He traveled for a long time and lost his horse and all his armor except for his sword on the way. He was tired, hungry, and thirsty. Suddenly, he saw a lake in the distance. He gathered his remaining strength and went to it. As the knight approached the water, he saw a dragon lying on the shore. The knight drew his sword and with his last strength began to fight the monster. He fought for one day and for another. Finally he managed to wound the beast, and the dragon fell down. The exhausted knight fell nearby.
>
> Weakly turning its head, the dragon asked, "What did you want, knight?"
>
> "A drink of water," the knight wheezed out.
>
> "You could have just said so . . ."

Even when we do not face major problems, we can still make our lives difficult by taking everything too seriously, expecting perfection, stressing over small things, or fighting the circumstances instead of harmonizing with them. When we take it easy, seemingly difficult things become simpler and we become happier.

PUT IT INTO PRACTICE

Lighten up with the techniques below:

- Breathe.

Take slow, deep breaths. It is the easiest way to relax.

- Laugh.

Laughter is a powerful way to beat stress and relax. It helps us loosen up and enjoy the humor in a situation. Laugh at your mishaps. Keep a book of jokes handy, or watch a funny video for a quick de-stressing session.

- Easy come, easy go.

Zelig Pliskin points out that we all are born with nothing. Anything we have in life is an added privilege. Thinking of our status and possessions as extra bonuses makes it easier to deal with their loss. Such perspective makes us more joyous and happy.[344] For example, when you go through a divorce, appreciate that you had the good fortune to know love and to get married in the first place.

- Embrace imperfection.

Relax your demands on yourself and the world. As Rabbi Abraham J. Twerski reminds us, "When trying to achieve perfection, we are holding ourselves to the standards of an angel or such rather than a human."[345] Let go a little, and be content with small imperfections.

- Put it in perspective.

Everything is temporary and shall eventually pass. If you will not remember the current stressful situation in a year, it is probably not big or important enough to let it ruin your mood and interfere with your happiness. See it for what it is—a small thing—and react accordingly.

CHAPTER 52

BE PATIENT

*"A patient man is better than a warrior, and he who rules his
temper, than he who takes a city."*

—Proverbs 16:32

Life does not always go the way we want it to—we get stuck
in the slowest checkout line, have to repeat something for
the twentieth time, or do not see results from our work or self-
improvement efforts as soon as we would like to. We do not
always get to make the choice of whether to wait for something
or not. But we can choose how to wait—we can get impatient,
annoyed, and angry (although such unhappiness rarely leads to
anything beneficial), or we can choose to stay content. Staying
relaxed in face of delayed gratification lets us enjoy the process
while we continue to work on achieving our goals. When we
are able to stay calm in the face of a delay or adversity, we are
more likely to be happy, as patience is linked to increased well-
being.[346]

Impatience is an aspect of our attitude. It emerges when we focus on the perceived delay and the seemingly too-long distance to

our goals. If we stay in line without thinking that we are wasting time, we do not need patience. But when we focus on the long wait, when we get twitchy and nervous because of it, we need to learn to exercise patience in order to counteract that annoyance.

Scholars have noticed with alarm that today's world lacks stillness. Technology increased the tempo of our lives, accustoming us to instant responses and constant entertainment and compromising skills that require patience and the ability to focus on one subject for a long time, such as deep thinking.[347] Our day is still the same twenty-four hours it was a century ago, but we often find ourselves getting upset because of a thirty-minute wait in a doctor's office or a ten-minute wait for a bus. We dash across a hall to get into a closing elevator to avoid the two-minute wait for the next one. We can't stand the extra seconds it takes a slow computer to load. This type of attitude can be counteracted by emphasizing patience, relaxation, and contentment.

Judaism encourages patience by teaching that everything in our lives has an intended purpose. We are always where we are supposed to be in terms of our mission in life. To illustrate this, sages cite the life of **Joseph** described in Genesis. Joseph spent years in Egypt enslaved and imprisoned before he rose to power, became an advisor to the pharaoh, and was able to help his people in a famine.[348] When we find ourselves in a frustrating situation, we can remind ourselves that we are where we are supposed to be and, instead of becoming annoyed, be patient and look for the situation's purpose.

Besides, when we practice patience, we are rewarded with better results. When we keep at something, we are more likely to achieve it. "With patience you can even bore through granite," observes a Yiddish proverb.[349] Patience helps not just with grand projects, but with moments of passion as well. When we experience strong emotions, it is good to be able to delay an impulsive decision, response, or action for a few moments. This ability may help us avoid mistakes and regrets.

Whether we practice patience because we do not have any choice but to wait or simply because it is the practical thing to do, it helps us put things in perspective and relax, leading to a happier state of mind even when we do not get the quick gratification we desire.

PUT IT INTO PRACTICE

Practicing patience is an exercise in contentment, changing perspective, and adapting to circumstances. Even when you cannot change a situation, you can still control it in choosing your reaction to it by deciding that it is okay to wait your turn, by staying peaceful and happy.

- Step back.

When you cannot change a situation, consciously choose not to get upset but instead to just stay with it and be content. If you feel you are so busy you simply cannot afford to be patient even in situations you can't rush, then maybe you are too busy to be happy, and it's time to relax.

- Be kind.

Counteract your annoyance at others slowing you down with kindness. When children or family members are too slow with something, remember that you love them and focus on this instead.

- Be patient with yourself.

When you're working to achieve personal goals, allow for gradual improvement and occasional mistakes.

- Consider the meaning of the delay.

We are where we are supposed to be in terms of our mission in life. **Levi Yitzchak of Berditchev** taught that when we find ourselves in an annoying situation, before we react we should ask ourselves, "Why am I here? For what purpose I was brought here?" It is certainly not for naught.[350]

- Find the positive in the wait.

When you have to pause in life, learn to enjoy the scenery as much as the destination.

- Savor each experience.

When you are involved in a project, reflect upon it and relish it. Do not rush. You may never get to do this again. Though this may seem sad, remembering this can calm you down and remind you to relax.

CHAPTER 53

PAUSE

It is written in the Tanakh that God created the world in six days and rested on the seventh.[351] If the world was created in six days, why are there seven days in the week? Rabbis explain that an extra day was needed because work is not complete without rest.[352] Besides, physical and mental relaxation is extremely important for health and well-being. Stopping to enjoy life, to savor its precious moments, has an enormous impact on our happiness level.

God paused after creating the world. We, on the other hand, are so absorbed in the hustle and bustle of our lives that too often we forget to relax, can't spare the time for it, or even if we try, can't manage to sit still. Nowadays we tend to stay in a near-constant state of stress not only at school and work but also during our leisure time. Our idea of resting rarely means just "being." We "relax" by staying up late, sitting at our computers for hours playing games or checking status updates, watching TV, or going out to party.

Often we get so caught up in our busy lives that we forget to truly enjoy the simple fact of being. We hurry from one activity to another, trying to achieve the things that we think will finally make us happy and successful. We are in such a rush to get to the weekend, to vacation, or to retirement that we fail to notice that we are rushing life itself without pausing to relish the experience fully.

We forget about the transient nature of this world. We do not often stop to admire the sunset or appreciate fragrant flowers. While our modern lives may seem especially rushed, this was true even for people two hundred years ago, as the following story illustrates:

> From his window facing the marketplace Rebbe Nachman of Breslov spotted one of his followers rushing by.
>
> "Have you looked up at the sky this morning?" the Rebbe asked.
>
> "No, Rebbe, I haven't had the time."
>
> "Believe me, in fifty years everything you see here today will be gone. There will be another fair, with other horses, other wagons, different people. I won't be here then and neither will you. So what's so important that you don't have time to look at the sky?!"[353]

The inability to put aside what we are doing turns us into slaves to that activity. The Jewish tradition of stopping on Shabbat celebrates the fact that we are masters of our own life, not its victims or slaves, teaches Rabbi David Aaron.[354] It celebrates being, not doing. We can leave behind the business of the workweek, take a pause from the media, relax, and rejuvenate. Shabbat is the time to have a nice meal with family and friends, sing songs, reflect on ourselves, feel gratitude for our blessings, and reaffirm that we are happy.

Judaism requires that we pause, stop complaining, and count our blessings not only every seventh day but also on Rosh Hodesh, or the beginning of the month; Rosh Hashanah, the Jewish new year; and the many Jewish holidays. It is a good idea to practice such occasional pausing even if you are not Jewish or observant.

Pausing also helps in unpleasant situations. It provides us with the time to be mindful, to stop and think about what we are doing and why we are doing it, and to calm down and prevent an unwanted eruption of negative emotions that we may regret later.

Pausing is a big part of several important happiness skills: remembering our life priorities, being mindful, and realizing that life is beautiful. Taking a moment to pause in the middle of our hectic day allows us to find our center, reassess our situation, rest a little, restore our selves, enjoy the moment, and be happy.

PUT IT INTO PRACTICE

- Enjoy inactivity.

Sometimes we get so used to the fast pace of life that a pause in activity feels like a waste of time. We feel like we're not doing anything when we could be doing something useful or at least doing *something*. Pausing won't benefit your happiness if you continue to think this way. Change your attitude toward it. Remember that switching gears is also a necessary thing to do. Look forward to it, relax into it, and enjoy it.

- Schedule breaks.

Remember that pausing is extremely valuable, and schedule it in your week as you do with other activities.

- Keep track of time.

Set the timer on your cell phone to chime every sixty minutes (or choose another time interval). When it goes off, pause for a minute or two. If you can, step away from you are doing, stretch a bit, talk with your coworkers, or just relax.

- Rest your mind.

When you get too busy with life or your thoughts start racing, step back, quiet your mind, and just observe. As you do so, find a deep sensation of calm and peace in your body and emotions.

- Get distracted by the beauty of life.

Next time you are outside running errands, pause to notice how blue the sky is, how magnificent the clouds are, how beautiful the trees are. It only takes a few moments to notice that the world is awe-inspiring.

- Collect yourself.

Before agreeing with or arguing about something, pause to collect your thoughts and understand. If you get upset about something, take a little time to reflect on your life priorities.[355] This can change your attitude toward the current situation as well as your emotional state.

- Separate day from night.

Before going to bed, sit down and breathe in through your nose and out through your mouth for a four count, ten times. Then reflect upon all of the great things that happened that day.

CHAPTER 54

DO NOT CLUTTER YOUR LIFE

"Too much of anything is undesirable."

—A Yiddish proverb [356]

"A table, a chair, a bowl of fruit and a violin; what else does a man need to be happy?"

—Albert Einstein

How much do we need to feel happy?

Sometimes it seems that we need rather a lot. The more things and experiences become available, the more we want to have. Gerald Epstein notes a common trend when he writes, "We believe that accumulating a lot of material goods makes us special. Our entire sense of self-worth is tied up with our possessions and level of our importance in the society."[357] The cornucopia of available choices may seem like a blessing, but in fact, it may cause discontentment with the things we already have as we pine for something better, bigger, and newer.

In addition to the anxiety and itch of dissatisfaction that comes with wanting more than we already have, excess is a cause of illness. The rate of obesity, diabetes, and heart diseases grows with increased consumption of sugary and fatty junk food. Excess in mental stimuli result in stress, anxiety, and lack of sleep.

When there is no moderation, having or wanting too much of everything prevents us from finding deep meaning or fully enjoying any single thing. Differentiating between needing and wanting something, feeling content with what we already have, and even getting rid of unnecessary things, worries, and stress in our lives will make us happier.

PUT IT INTO PRACTICE

"Too much is superfluous," teaches Jewish wisdom.[358] Implement the following tips to let go of unnecessary things that take up the space in your home and your head.

- Do not clutter your space.

Throw away all the things you do not use, do not love, or are not inspired by. Look at it this way: if you have less, there's less to clean and maintain. Enjoy the space that opens up.

Remind yourself that you do not have to have the best of everything to be happy. Possessions do not control your happiness; you control your happiness.

- Do not clutter your time.

Let go of unnecessary wastes of time, such as checking endless status updates and committing to unwanted and unneeded activities.

- Do not clutter your brain.

Our brains can only contain so much. Do not waste your precious mental energy by exposing yourself to all available mental stimuli. Limit the number of TV shows you watch in one day. Let go of worrying. Relax.

LET'S DO IT

CHAPTER 55

INTRODUCTION TO THE SECTION

"The essential thing is not study, but deed."

—*Pirkei Avot* 1:17

One morning after a heavy snowfall the inhabitants of a small shtetl had to wade waist-deep through the snow to come to shul for the daily service.

The rabbi asked them, "What should we do about the snow?"

Someone shrugged. "What can we do except to wait for a warmer weather?"

Another person suggested, "We should pray for the snow to thaw."

A third person said thoughtfully, "This is a valuable opportunity for us to learn something."

The rabbi then said, "And now listen to what I tell you."

Everyone stilled and prepared to listen to great wisdom.

The rabbi looked at the congregants, sighed, and said, "Grab your shovels and let's go!"[359]

When something needs to happen, we have to act to get it done! Now that we've learned about happiness and the skills that reinforce it, it is time to apply those lessons.

Susan Levit, a distinguished doctor, a community leader, and a very wise woman, once said that time passes inevitably and at the same rate regardless of what we fill it with. We can complain or appreciate what we have, act kindly or angrily, practice our happiness skills or not; no matter what, the day will pass away. As days pass, so do our lives.

Sometimes years pass without our consciously trying to change our behavior to boost our happiness. We may get jolted into wanting to do so only when faced with misfortunes (which may have resulted from us not feeling happy for a long time) such as a divorce or an illness. Do not wait for something to happen or until you become older to start increasing your level of happiness. Do not waste even one day. Start practicing and be happy now!

Remember that skills, including happiness skills, do not descend on us suddenly. We have to practice daily to build them over time.

CHAPTER 56

SETTLE BUT STRUGGLE

Jewish wisdom and science both teach that a relaxed attitude leads to happiness, but also that we should not be inactive. The way to happiness is a delicate balance that can be found somewhere on the *kav ha-emtza*, the middle path. This balance is different for each of us, and there is no right or wrong approach. For example, the two people in the parable below have different life goals and different understandings of happiness. Both their views are valid and can result in a joyous life. Or perhaps both of them abandoned moderation and took their attitudes to the extreme. What do you think?

> Once upon a time a man was lying under a tree munching on an apple. Another man approached.
>
> "Where did you get the apple from?"
>
> "Plucked it from a tree."
>
> "Well, you know, you could pick a few apples and sell them."
>
> "What for?"
>
> "With that money you could hire someone to help you pick more apples and sell them too."

"What for?"

"In time, you'd be able to hire more people to pick apples and maybe berries and mushrooms for you, sell them, and make a lot of money."

"What for?"

"Well, then you would be able to lie under a tree, enjoy life, and do nothing!"

"But I already do!"[360]

On the one hand, having an easygoing and unconcerned attitude is a powerful shortcut to a happier life. It is liberating to realize that we do not need much to be happy, that being happy means being content with life at all times and all junctures. If we never settle for anything but instead always pine and fight for more, we risk ending up miserable, emotionally wrecked, and exhausted.

But while accepting life as it is and enjoying it brings content-ment, this should not to be confused with complacency and inac-tivity. In our efforts to settle for enough and feel happy with what we have, we do not have to give up our dreams and ambitions. Overcoming challenges to achieve meaningful goals generates a sense of progress and personal growth. Struggles keep us mov-ing forward and make us happy when we are working for things that are important to us: our priorities, values, and loved ones.

Even those who leave fate up to God or the workings of the uni-verse have to work to overcome challenges, as this well-known joke illustrates:

An old man got trapped in his house during a flood. As the water level rose, his neighbors offered to drive him away in his car. Then a rescue squad arrived in a powerboat, and finally, the National Guard sent a helicopter to get him out of the house. But he refused all offers to help because he had great faith that God would save him. Eventually, the man drowned. When he appeared before the Almighty, he asked why God hadn't helped him. God replied: "I sent a car, a boat, and a helicopter. You had to get in yourself."

We have to know when to settle for things as they are and when to continue struggling. It is even better to find the golden mean and combine the two by appreciating and enjoying what we have while still working on achieving our goals.

PUT IT INTO PRACTICE

- Recognize when it's okay to settle.

Review your priorities, and let go of nonessential goals and ambitions.[361]

Sometimes we spend years unsuccessfully trying to change something that is out of our control. Recognize what you cannot change, such as other people or the past, and stop exerting yourself over these things. Feel the relief of not having to fight for everything.

- Recognize when it's best to work for something.

Review your priorities again. Pick a meaningful goal and work toward it.

Acknowledge the important things that you can control, such as your personality and your happiness. Put effort into self-improvement. Pick a happiness skill and practice it daily. Feel proud of making the difference in your own life.

CHAPTER 57

CHANGE YOUR BEHAVIOR

Most of the time we react to things in our everyday lives out of a sheer habit. Years of similar behavior create neural pathways in our brains that become patterns we follow automatically. Albert Einstein very wisely noted that it is insanity to keep doing the same thing over and over again and expect different results. For our purposes this means that if we do not feel consistently happy reacting to life in the ways we always do, we need to start doing something differently. Specifically, we need to start practicing happiness skills.

Producing any emotion takes mental energy. Whether we make ourselves worried or excited, gloomy or loving, miserable or happy, we have to put some effort into it. So to become happy, we don't have to exert more energy than we would being unhappy. We just have to stop repeatedly reacting in ways that do not make us happy and redirect that energy into positive reactions. In other words, we have to change our behavior.

Jewish sages insist that we can transform our habits. "Don't make the same mistake as all those people who give up trying to change because they feel stuck in their habits. If you truly want to, and are willing to work hard enough, you can overcome them," insists Rebbe Nachman of Breslov.[362]

Modern science confirms that our brains are capable of amazing plasticity and can form new pathways and new habits. We can use this ability of our minds and choose to form habits that nourish our happiness.

Gerald Epstein notes that breaking one habit and forming another requires an act of our intentional will.[363] Thus, we need to find a strong incentive to start practicing different behavior. An old Jewish tale demonstrates the importance of a strong motivation:

> Once upon a time, a king's daughter set out to travel to another kingdom to get married. Before they departed, the king gifted her a small but heavy chest and instructed her to carry it to her new home herself. The princess complied, but soon she became sweaty and achy under the weight of the chest. She complained to the king, and he instructed the princess to look inside it. She opened the chest and saw that it was full with the most precious stones and valuable possessions. Once the princess saw the treasures she was carrying, she greatly rejoiced and was happy to carry the chest herself the rest of the way.

Just as the princess in the story was motivated and even happy to carry her treasure chest once she realized that her efforts would be rewarded with a great prize, so should we be motivated and enthusiastic about mastering happiness skills, as they bring us great rewards. The obvious motivation is the good life that comes with a happy attitude.

Another reward for practicing such self-improvement is the fulfillment of our life's purpose. As we have learned, according to Jewish wisdom, the purpose of human life is to improve one's character.[364] "If you are not a better person tomorrow than you are today, what need have you for a tomorrow?" inquires Rebbe Nachman. Becoming a better person is a strong motivation for putting in the effort to hone new skills.

Having a strong motivation is a first step on the way to change. But what should be done when we just don't have positive feelings toward someone or something in our lives? Abraham Twerski teaches that we can change our feelings through behavior. He gives the example of carrying a grudge against someone and, while knowing that it's best to let go, not being able to do so. In this case, he recommends doing something nice for the person we have a grudge against (keeping in mind that we are doing this not for that person's sake but for our own peace of mind and happiness). The more we are nice to the person, the less significant our grudge will be. The change in behavior will improve our character and lead us to become more spiritual and happier people.[365]

This concept of changing your attitude through action has worked for thousands of years. On Mount Sinai, when Jews received the Torah (which is considered the source of happiness in Judaism), they resolved, "We will do and then we will understand."[366] Later Maimonides described a model of change called *teshuvah*, which is wildly used in Jewish tradition. He taught that to change a habit we have to consciously stop the undesired behavior and practice the new behavior over and over again. Even if the new habit is not caused by a genuine shift in attitude, just committing to practicing it can gradually result in an enduring change.[367]

Today cognitive psychology adds that when we work at something and invest ourselves in it, we understand it better and appreciate it more. Through practicing happiness skills, we gain an experiential understanding of how amazing it feels and how beneficial it is for us to let go of frustrations and be content and joyous.

Creating and reinforcing a new habit is usually not an instant process. Our current habits and attitudes toward life did not form instantaneously. It took us years to arrive here. It is only reasonable that it will take some time to make adjustments. There are different ideas about how long it takes to form a new habit. Some experts say that twenty-one day of continuous practice of a desired trait is enough to reinforce a new neural pathway, while others say it takes at least sixty-six days. So it is important to accept that the change will be gradual and never be disappointed at not getting quick results. Rebbe Nachman of Breslov cautions, "Too often we want to improve ourselves and our relationships so quickly that we make ourselves frustrated and confused."[368]

A change in your behavior will take time, but it will change your life. Start now!

PUT IT INTO PRACTICE

- Get motivated.

You are your biggest motivation. Ask yourself if you are willing to waste time in your precious life on inconsequential arguments, anxieties, or resentments. If you focus on those things a minute longer, you will have lost sixty seconds of happiness.

And consider your future self. Suppose you do not start practicing happiness skills. How do you imagine your life will be in several years? Now think about what your life will be like if you practice consistently.

Do not doubt that you can become happier. You do not have to continue being the same way. You do not have to keep on doing what you have always done. You can choose a new way to think, to talk, and to act every time you are presented with a choice. Think about how you want to be and act to make it happen. It is not that difficult.

- Start small.

If you try to change all your undesirable traits at once, you are may get frustrated and quit. Trying to change too much in our thinking and acting may feel overwhelming. But the good news is you do not have to implement all the changes right away.

The Midrash teaches us to approach any big task gradually, as this passage illustrates:

> Who is a fool? One who says, "Who can possibly cut down [this] entire field?" The wise person says, "I will cut two basketfuls today and two tomorrow, until I've completed the whole task." A foolish student will say, "Who can possibly learn the whole Torah? . . ." A wise student will say, "I will learn two laws today, and two tomorrow, until I have mastered the whole Torah."[369]

Start with something easy and slowly progress to more difficult skills. Pick one skill and practice it consistently. If you find that you fall back on your old pattern of behavior, get back on track the next time a similar situation comes up. Each time, it will become easier. As the sages assure us, "A good deed leads to another good deed."[370]

Once you have changed one habit, pick another. You will be more confident about your ability for self-improvement and find that it becomes easier each time.

- Be consistent.

Consistency is the key to forming new habits. Do not skip practice, because even one act is important. As the Mishnah teaches, "He who repeats what he has learned one hundred times cannot be compared to one who repeats it a hundred and one times."[371]

A great example of how consistency works is a project called A Complaint Free World. For this project millions of people around the globe resolved to go twenty-one days without negative thoughts. At the start, they put on a purple bracelet, and every time they said or thought something negative, they had to move the bracelet to the other wrist until they managed to wear it on one wrist for twenty-one days straight. Participants reported that for the first couple of weeks they had to move the bracelet ten to twenty times per day. After a couple of months, it would stay on one wrist for about a week. On average, it took people three to six month to go twenty-one days without having a negative thought. Their patience and consistency paid off handsomely in the end. Many participants reported that they felt as if a veil was lifted from their eyes—they started noticing how many positive things there are in the world and how great their lives were.[372]

Review this book periodically to remind yourself of the happiness skills you've learned. Practice consistently, even when you fall back into old patterns.

- Don't stress out.

Sometimes you will slip back into your old ways, in the same way that at an intersection you'll sometimes take the turn for an old route out of habit. This can happen especially when you do not pay attention to your thoughts, words, and behavior. When it does happen, do what you would do on the road: back up or turn around, go back to the intersection, and take the new way instead.

Aim to simply do your best, not to be perfect. If you were able to stay positive several times in a row when faced with a potential irritant but reacted negatively another time, that does not take away from the progress you have made. Evaluate your success in terms of adherence to the process, not the immediate results. Focus on and celebrate the smallest successes. Be content and happy even with the smallest change in your attitude.

CHAPTER 58

DO IT NOW!

"How wonderful it is that no one need wait a single moment to start to improve the world."

—Anne Frank

"If not now, when?"

—*Pirkei Avot* 1:14

See if you recognize yourself in this description: You know what lifestyle is good for you. You've read some self-improvement books, watched some videos, or listened to some talks. You are inspired and have resolved to act on this knowledge—to eat healthy food, to quit smoking, or to take up exercising. Only not right away, maybe starting next Monday, next month, or right after you are done with the current projects.

Also, you really want to be more content and generally happier. But right now you are going through some stressful times. So you've decided to work on changing your attitude after your family situation gets better, or your health gets better, or whatever else bothers you gets better. The problem is that there is always another stressful situation that follows the current one, so you end up delaying your happiness further and further.

Or, conversely, you expect happiness to descend upon you when something big happens in life, like when you finally attain that difficult goal, find out that your true love is reciprocal, or witness the births of your kids or grandkids. So, you wait. But happiness is not just for momentous occasions. In fact, lasting happiness is mostly made up of our responses to routine moments like the one right now.

Judaism is a faith that is practiced through action. It brings concepts and ideas to life through behavior. It indicates that simply "believing" is not enough. It encourages and requires "doing" such as engaging with the mitzvot, most of which are fulfilled through action.[373] And it insists that the time for action is now. *Pirkei Avot* teaches, "Do not say 'I will study when I have the time,' for perhaps you will never have time."[374]

That said, it is never too late to start. Rabbi **Joseph Telushkin** relates a story about a shoemaker who worked late into the night by a flickering candle. When someone reminded him that it was too late to work, he replied, "As long as the candle is burning, it is still possible to mend." Rabbi Telushkin then paraphrases these words to teach that as long as there is life, we can change and improve.[375]

Let's take the example of Rabbi **Israel Meir Kagan**, who was known to be a great *tzaddik*, an elevated and righteous person. How did he become who he was? According to Zelig Pliskin, Rabbi Kagan always applied all that he learned.[376] So don't wait for happiness to overcome you. Start improving yourself and, by extension, your life and happiness by doing what you've learned!

PUT IT INTO PRACTICE

- Do it right this moment

Pause right now and just appreciate for a moment that life is good, and you are happy.

- Start now

Regina Spektor reminds us in her song "Small Time Moon" that "today we're younger than we ever gonna be."

Do not put off till tomorrow what you can do today! Start the rest of your life right now!

AFTERWORD

Believing that you can be happier and choosing to do so are two of the most important decisions you can make in life. These decisions will affect you tremendously, and they will also affect your family, your children, and the world.

Your circumstances may need to change in order for you to have a better lifestyle. That may be a goal you want to work toward. But the secret to happiness is realizing that your circumstances do not need to change in order for you to be happy. As soon as you understand the difference between pursing a better lifestyle and pursuing happiness, you will not need to wait for anything to enjoy your life.

Ideal circumstances are not a mandatory condition for happiness. Rather, we achieve happiness by choosing to focus on all the good that is happening in our lives. And there is so much good happening at any given moment! When we pay attention to that, when we are grateful for it and content, we are truly happy.

The happiness skills listed in this book will help you notice and appreciate how great life is. Every time you practice them, your "happiness muscle" will become stronger. Gradually, you will change from a happiness amateur to a master, in the same way you become an expert in any field. Everyone starts small and progresses with experience, and so will you.

My closing wish for you is that you will enjoy this lifelong journey!

Yours in happiness,

Olga Gilburd

AUTHOR'S NOTE

If you enjoyed this book, please consider writing a review on Amazon (goo.gl/IgTxVC). It really does make a difference. Thank you!

If you find a mistake or have a suggestion, please contact the author at www.olgagilburd.com

###

Want to know about the release of my next book and to be informed about related news? Sign up for my mailing list at www. olgagilburd.com

GLOSSARY OF JEWISH PERSONALITIES AND TERMS LISTED IN THE BOOK

After each name or term, the chapters in which they appear are listed in parenthesis.

Aaron, David (Master of Your Happiness; Pause), born in 1957, is a rabbi, author, and founder of the Isralight Institute.

Abraham (Self-Esteem) is the first of the three biblical patriarchs described in Genesis. He established the *brit*, the covenant between God and the Jewish people.

Adler, Alfred (Practice Kindness), 1870–1937, born in Austria, was a medical doctor, a world renowned philosopher, and a psychiatrist. Adler was the founder of the school of individual psychology.

Aharon of Karlin (Be Grateful), 1738–1771, known as Rabbi Aharon the Great, was one of the pioneers of Hasidism in Lithuania.

Akiva ben Joseph (How to Become Happy; Emotional Resilience), approximately 50–135 CE, known as Rabbi Akiva, was one of Judaism's greatest scholars. He was tortured to death by Roman authorities.

Apatow, Judd (Emotional Resilience), born in 1967 in New York City, is a film producer, director, comedian, actor, and screenwriter. His work has won numerous awards, and he was ranked number one on *Entertainment Weekly*'s "The 50 Smartest People in Hollywood" list.

Auerbach, Berthold (The Power of Music), 1812–1882, born in Germany as Moses Baruch Auerbach, was a poet and an author. He originated "tendency novel", in which fiction is used as a means of influencing public opinion various social and moral questions.

The **Baal Shem Tov** (The Good, the Great, and the Awesome; Self-Esteem; Take It Easy), 1698–1760, born in Ukraine as Israel ben Eliezer, also called Besht, was a rabbi and the founder of the Hasidic movement, which emphasizes joy.

Badhanim (Smile), from the Hebrew for "entertainer," are merrymakers, rhymesters, or professional jesters who entertain guests with drollery, riddles, and anecdotes, especially at Jewish weddings.

Bahya ben Joseph ibn Paquda (Enemies of Happiness), born in the eleventh-century Spain, was a philosopher and rabbi whose book *The Duties of the Heart* is a guide for spiritual growth and one of the first Jewish systems of ethics.

Bar Ilai, Judah (Contentment and Moderation, Practice Kindness), born in the second century CE in the Galilee, is the most frequently mentioned sage in the Mishnah.

Baruch, Bernard (Emotional Resilience), 1870–1965, was an American financier, philanthropist, and adviser to US presidents.

Ben-Gurion, David (Emotional Resilience), 1886–1973, one of the most important Zionist leaders of the twentieth century, was the first prime minister of the state of Israel and is considered its founding father.

Ben-Shahar, Tal (Jewish Thinkers on Happiness), born in 1970, holds a PhD in Organization Behavior. Ben-Shahar is a noted author and lecturer on positive psychology. His books include best sellers *Happier* and *Being Happy*.

Berlin, Irving (Our Happiness Delusions; Attitude Is Everything; Every Cloud Has a Silver Lining), 1888–1989, born in Russia as Israel Baline, became an American composer and lyricist. He wrote some of the most enduring songs of the twentieth century, including "God Bless America," "White Christmas," and "Easter Parade."

Bloomberg, Michael (Emotional Resilience), born in 1942, is an entrepreneur and philanthropist who served as the 108th mayor of New York City for three consecutive terms.

Borowitz, Andy (Emotional Resilience), born in 1958 in Ohio, is a best-selling writer, actor, and award-winning comedian.

Brodsky, Joseph (Be Grateful; Emotional Resilience; Every Cloud Has a Silver Lining; Enemies of Happiness), 1940–1996, was a Russian-born poet, winner of the Nobel Prize in Literature, and United States Poet Laureate.

Brooks, Mel (Make Room for Negative Emotions), born in 1926 as Melvin James Kaminsky, is an award-winning American film director, screenwriter, actor, producer, composer, and songwriter.

Bunim, Simcha (Four Secrets of Happiness; Contentment and Moderation; Smile; Enjoy, Not Endure; Verbalize Your Happiness), 1765–1827, was a rabbi who became one of the key leaders of the Hasidic movement in Poland.

Chabad (Self-Esteem) is a Hasidic movement founded in 1755. The name "Chabad" is a Hebrew acronym for "Wisdom, Understanding, and Knowledge," a reflection of the movement's intellectual-mystical school of thought.

Chelm (Put on Rose-Colored Glasses) is a community in Poland that has earned a unique place in Jewish folklore because of the supposed naiveté of its residents—ironically referred to as the "wise men of Chelm."

Chofetz Chaim (Verbalize Your Happiness), 1839–1933, born in the Russian Empire as Israel Meir Kagan, became an influential rabbi in the Musar movement. His works continue to be widely influential.

David (The Big Picture) was Biblical king of Israel whose forty-year reign is regarded as Israel's "golden age." He is the father of Solomon.

Davidson, Richard (Mindfulness), born in 1951 in New York City, is a professor of psychology and psychiatry, Director of the Waisman Laboratory for Brain Imaging and Behavior and the Laboratory for Affective Neuroscience, and founder of the Center for Investigating Healthy Minds.

Dessler, Eliyahu Eliezer (Mindfulness), 1892–1953, was a rabbi, Talmudic scholar, and Jewish philosopher from Libau, Latvia.

Disraeli, Benjamin (The Power of Music; Make Room for Negative Emotions), 1804–1888, was a British statesman and novelist and two-term British Prime Minister.

Dreyfus, Alfred (Emotional Resilience) 1859–1935, was a French army officer, convicted of treason and sentenced to life imprisonment in 1894.

Ecclesiastes (The Big Picture; Enjoy, Not Endure) is a book of the Tanakh, the Hebrew Bible.

Einstein, Albert (Our Happiness Delusions; How to Become Happy; The Shortcut; Mindfulness; Do Not Clutter Your Life; Change Your Behavior), 1879–1955, was a German-born scientist, humanist, Zionist, and recipient of Nobel Prize for Physics. Einstein is most famous for the general theory of relativity.

Elijah (The Big Picture) is the preeminent hero and one of the most beloved prophets of Jewish folklore.

Epstein, Gerald (Four Secrets of Happiness; Master of Your Happiness; Do Not Clutter Your Life; Change Your Behavior), born in 1935, is a psychiatrist, author, and researcher. Epstein is a pioneer in the use of mental imagery for treating physical and emotional problems.

Ethics of Our Fathers (Our Happiness Delusions): see *Pirkei Avot*.

Farbrengen (The Power of Music) is a Yiddish word for "joyous gathering," an informal gathering of Hasidim characterized by singing and inspiring talk. A farbrengen is regarded as a time of great holiness.

Flanzbaum, Hilene (The Big Picture) is a poet and professor of American literature and Holocaust studies. Her books include *The Americanization of the Holocaust* and *Jewish American Literature: A Norton Anthology*.

Frank, Anne (Our Happiness Delusions; Do It Now!), 1929–1945, born in Germany, hid in Amsterdam with her family for nearly two years during World War II. She was fifteen when the family was found and sent to the camps, where she died. Her diary, in which Frank wrote about her experiences and wishes, has been the basis for several plays and films.

Frankl, Viktor (Choices That Lead to Happiness), 1905–1997, was an Austrian-born neurologist and psychiatrist and the founder of logotherapy, a form of existential analysis. His best-selling book *Man's Search for Meaning* tells of his experiences in concentration camps during World War II and discusses the importance of finding meaning in all forms of existence, even the most brutal ones, and thus, a reason to continue living.

Friedlander, Chaim (Enjoy, Not Endure) was a rabbi of Ponevezh Yeshivah and a prominent Torah scholar.

Freud, Anna (Master of Your Happiness), 1895–1982, born in Austria, was the youngest daughter of Sigmund Freud. She is considered a founder of child psychoanalysis.

Freud, Sigmund (Jewish Thought on Happiness, Self-Esteem, The Big Picture, Emotional Resilience), 1856–1939, was an Austrian neurologist and the founder of psychoanalysis. His work on the human psyche remains powerful even in fields removed from psychology.

Futerfas, Mendel (Emotional Resilience), 1906–1995, was a Chabad spiritual mentor. Futerfas spent fourteen years in Siberian gulags for operating clandestine Jewish cheders in the USSR.

A **gabbai** (Put on Rose-Colored Glasses) is a person who assists in the running of synagogue services, an assistant to a rabbi (particularly the secretary or personal assistant to a Hasidic rebbe).

Garlin, Jeff (Emotional Resilience), born in 1962, is an American writer, director, producer, stand-up comedian, and actor.

Gefilte fish (Enjoy, Not Endure), Yiddish for "stuffed fish," is a traditional Ashkenazi Jewish dish.

Gilbert, Daniel (Our Happiness Delusions), born in 1957, is a professor of psychology at Harvard University and the author of best seller *Stumbling on Happiness*.

Greenman, Yitz (Emotional Resilience) is a rabbi and the Executive Director of Aish HaTorah in New York.

Gurwitch, Annabelle (Emotional Resilience), born in 1961, is an American actress, activist, and best-selling author.

Hasidism (The Good, the Great, and the Awesome; Four Secrets of Happiness; Master of Your Happiness; Self-Esteem; The Power of Music; Take It Easy) is a branch of Orthodox Judaism that uses mysticism to attain spirituality. It was founded in eighteenth-century Eastern Europe by the Baal Shem Tov. **Hasidic** is the adjective form of Hasidism.

Hebrew Bible (The Good, the Great, and the Awesome; Cherish Your Body; Release Your Emotions): see Tanakh.

Herz-Sommer, Alice (Choices That Lead to Happiness; Life Is Beautiful; Put on Rose-Colored Glasses; Be Grateful; Smile; The Power of Music; Enjoy, Not Endure; Emotional Resilience; Practice Kindness; Stay Interested in Life), 1903–2014, born in what is now the Czech Republic, survived Theresienstadt concentration camp and lived to 110 to become world's oldest-known Holocaust survivor.

Heschel, Abraham Joshua (Practice Kindness), 1907–1972, a Polish-born rabbi and author, was one of the preeminent Jewish theologians and philosophers of the twentieth century.

Hillel (Cherish Your Body; Practice Kindness), born in the first century BCE in Babylon, was a renowned sage, scholar, and religious leader and is associated with the development of the Mishna and the Talmud.

Hirsch, Samson Raphael (Stay Interested in Life), 1808–1888, a Gernan-born rabbi, philosopher, and author, was a founder of modern orthodox Judaism.

Job (Emotional Resilience), Iyov in Hebrew, is the main character in the book of Job, one of the writings of the Tanakh.

Joseph (Be Patient) is a Biblical character whose story is told in Genesis portion of the Torah.

Kabbalah (The Good, the Great, and the Awesome; The Shortcut; Life Is Beautiful; Be Grateful), literally "receiving," is an influential school of thought within Jewish mysticism.

Kagan, Israel Meir (Do It Now!): see Chofetz Chaim.

Kissinger, Henry (Our Happiness Delusions), born in 1923 in

Germany, is an American diplomat, political scientist, and author. He served as the fifty-sixth US Secretary of State and is a recipient of the Nobel Peace Prize.

Klezmer (The Power of Music) is the traditional instrumental music of the Yiddish-speaking people of Eastern Europe.

Kramer, Chaya Sara (What Is Good and What Is Bad; Choices That Lead to Happiness), 1924–2005, was a Holocaust survivor. Her biography, *Holy Woman: The Road to Greatness of Rebbetzin Chaya Sara Kramer*, written by Sara Yoheved Rigler, became a best seller in the Jewish world.

Levi Yitzchak of Berdichev (Be Patient), 1740–1809, was a Hasidic rebbe whose commentary on the Torah, *Kedushat Levit*, is a classic popular to this day.

Levit, Susan (Let's Do It!: Introduction to the Section), born in the Soviet Union, served as a captain in the Israeli army and is now an American physician, educator, TV and radio personality, successful entrepreneur, community leader, and recipient of the Ellis Island Medal of Honor.

Lewis, Jerry (Every Cloud Has a Silver Lining), born in 1926 in New Jersey as Joseph Levitch, is a famous comedian, actor, singer, and philanthropist.

The **Lubavitcher Rebbe** (Which Theory of Happiness Is the Right One?; Are We Too Lazy to Feel Amazing?; Mindfulness; Emotional Resilience; Act It Out): see Schneerson, Menachem Mendel.

Luzzatto, Moshe Chaim (Act It Out), 1707–1746, was a prominent Italian rabbi who was also a Kabbalist and a philosopher.

Lyubomirsky, Sonja (Jewish Thought on Happiness; How to Become Happy; Practice Kindness), originally from the Soviet Union, she received a PhD in social/personality psychology and became a leading expert in positive psychology. She is the author of *The How of Happiness* and *The Myths of Happiness*.

Maimonides, Moses (The Good, the Great, and the Awesome; Contentment and Moderation; Jewish Thinkers on Happiness; Cherish Your Body; The Power of Music; Emotional Resilience; Enemies of Happiness; Release Your Emotions; Change Your Behavior), 1135–1204, also known as Moshe Ben Maimon or Rambam, was a rabbi, philosopher, author, and physician. Born in Spain, he moved to Egypt, became the leader of Jewish community there, and served as court physician to the vizier of Egypt. He is most noted for authoring the *Mishneh Torah*, an encyclopedic arrangement of Jewish law, and for his philosophical work, *Guide for the Perplexed*.

Majeski, Shloma (The Good, the Great, and the Awesome) is an American rabbi, scholar, and renowned lecturer on Chasidic philosophy. He is the author of *The Chassidic Approach to Joy* and *A Tzaddik and His Students*.

Marx, Karl (Jewish Thought on Happiness), 1818–1873, was a Prussia-born economist, journalist, sociologist, and philosopher. He published many books including *Das Kapital* and *The Communist Manifesto*, which greatly influenced the Soviet Communist Party.

Maslow, Abraham Harold (Emotional Resilience), 1908–1970, was an American professor of psychology best known for his "hierarchy of needs" and the founder of humanistic psychology. He was one of the first psychologists to focus on happy individuals and their psychological trajectory.

Matzah (Emotional Resilience) is unleavened bread traditionally eaten during Passover.

Meir, Golda (Are We Too Lazy to Feel Amazing?; Emotional Resilience), 1898–1978, born in the Russian Empire, became the fourth prime minister of Israel.

Mendelssohn, Moses (Judaism on Happiness), 1729–1786, was a noted German-Jewish philosopher.

Midrash (Emotional Resilience; Change Your Behavior) is rabbinic literature that interprets stories from the Tanakh and fills in gaps in the biblical narrative.

Miller, Moshe (Be Grateful), born in South Africa, is a rabbi, a teacher specializing in Jewish mysticism, and a prolific author. He is most well-known for his widely acclaimed translation of the Zohar.

A **mitzvah** (Which Theory of Happiness Is the Right One?; The Good, the Great, and the Awesome; Our Happiness Delusions, The Jewish Way: Introduction to the Section; What Is Good and What is Bad; Cherish Your Body; Enjoy, Not Endure; Emotional Resilience, Do It Now!) is one of God's commandments. The plural form is **mitzvot**.

Mogel, Wendy (Emotional Resilience) is a clinical psychologist, parent educator, speaker, and author of best-selling books on parenting.

Moses (Self-Esteem), according to the Hebrew Bible, led the Jews from Egyptian slavery on God's behalf. He received God's word on Mount Sinai and brought down the Ten Commandments. He is one of the most important prophets in Judaism, Christianity, and Islam.

Nachman of Breslov (Which Theory of Happiness Is the Right One?; The Jewish Way: Introduction to the Section; Judaism on Happiness; Know Your Happiness: Introduction to the Section; Get Your Priorities Straight; Choices that Lead to Happiness; Self-Esteem; Cherish Your Body; Mindfulness; Attitude Is Everything; Life Is Beautiful; Smile; The Power of Music; Emotional Resilience, Act It Out; Pause; Change Your Behavior), 1772–1810, born in Ukraine, became a Hasidic master famous for his storytelling, supreme optimism, and down-to-earth wisdom.

Naftali of Ropshitz (Our Happiness Delusions), 1760–1827, was a prominent Hasidic rabbi and spiritual leader.

Neschizer, Mordechai (Put on Rose-Colored Glasses) was a Hasidic rabbi.

Oppenheim, James (Our Happiness Delusions), 1882–1932, was an American poet, novelist, and editor.

Passover (Emotional Resilience; Enemies of Happiness; Release Your Emotions) is a seven- or eight-day festival celebrated in spring. It commemorates the liberation of the Jewish people from slavery in ancient Egypt.

Palatnik, Lori (Emotional Resilience), born in 1960 in Canada, is a writer, Jewish educator, and the founding director of The Jewish Women's Renaissance Project.

Pirkei Avot (Disclaimers; Our Happiness Delusions; Contentment and Moderation; Choose Your Influences, Cultivate Connection;

Let's Do It!: Introduction to the Section; Do It Now!), named "Ethics of our Fathers" in English, is a collection of the sages' wisdom on Jewish ethics and character development and is one of the most fundamental works of the Jewish Oral Law.

Philo Judaeus (Jewish Thinkers on Happiness), born in the first century CE, was a Hellenistic philosopher and the most important representative of Hellenistic Judaism.

Pliskin, Zelig (Self-Esteem; Mindfulness; Enjoy, Not Endure; Emotional Resilience; Act It Out, Take It Easy; Do It Now!), born in 1946, is an Orthodox rabbi, psychologist, and author of many self-improvement books, including *Gateway to Happiness*.

Psalms (The Good, the Great, and the Awesome; The Power of Music) is a section of the Hebrew Bible.

Radner, Gilda (Smile), 1946–1989, was an American comedian and actress.

Rand, Ayn (Preface; Our Happiness Delusions; Four Secrets of Happiness; The Jewish Way: Introduction to the Section; Jewish Thought on Happiness; Get Your Priorities Straight; Mindfulness; Attitude Is Everything; Emotional Resilience; Enemies of Happiness; Find Meaning; Practice Kindness), 1905–1982, born in Russia, was the author of the best-selling novels *The Fountainhead* and *Atlas Shrugged* and the founder of the philosophical system objectivism.

Reich, Robert (Emotional Resilience), born in 1946, is an American political economist, educator, former Secretary of Labor, and best-selling author.

Rigler, Sara Yoheved (What Is Good and What Is Bad; Cultivate Connection) is a best-selling author and international lecturer on the subject of Jewish spirituality.

The Rohr Jewish Learning Institute (Self-Esteem), founded in 1998, is a provider of Jewish learning that offers courses on an array of topics including Jewish ethics, Jewish mysticism and philosophy, Jewish history and culture, and Jewish belief and practice.

Rubin, Theodore Isaac (Attitude Is Everything), born in 1923, is an American psychiatrist and author.

Rubinstein, Arthur (Life Is Beautiful; Emotional Resilience; Enemies of Happiness; Act It Out), 1887–1982, born in Poland, became one of the greatest pianists of the twentieth century.

Sacks, Jonathan (Be Grateful), born in 1948, is a former Chief Rabbi of the United Kingdom, philosopher, and prolific author.

Salovey, Peter (Our Happiness Delusions), born in 1958, is an American psychologist, one of the early pioneers and leading researchers in emotional intelligence, an author, and president of Yale University.

Schachter-Shalomi, Zalman (Emotional Resilience), 1924–2014, born in Poland, was a rabbi, psychologist, writer, and influential spiritual leader.

Schneersohn, Sholom Dovber (The Good, the Great, and the Awesome; Verbalize Your Happiness), 1860–1920, born in the Russian Empire, became the fifth Lubavitcher Rebbe. He authored many volumes of Hasidic discourses and is renowned for his lucid and thorough explanations of Kabbalistic concepts.

Schneersohn, Yosef Yitzchak (Expectations), 1880–1959, born in the Russian Empire, was the sixth Lubavitcher Rebbe.

Schneersohn, Menachem Mendel (Emotional Resilience), 1789–1866, born in the Russian Empire, was the third spiritual leader of the Chabad Hasidic movement.

Schneerson, Menachem Mendel (Which Theory of Happiness Is the Right One?; Mindfulness; Act It Out), 1902–1994, born in Ukraine, the seventh and last Lubavitcher Rebbe, known as "the Rebbe," is considered one the most influential Jewish leaders of recent times.

Seinfeld, Jerry (Smile), born in 1954, is an American comedian, actor, writer, and producer.

Seligman, Martin (Our Happiness Delusions; How to Become Happy; Find Meaning), born in 1942 in New York State, is a leading authority in the field of positive psychology and the author of best-selling books including *Flourish*, *Authentic Happiness*, and *Learned Optimism*.

Silverman, Sarah (Emotional Resilience), born in 1970, is an American stand-up comedian, writer, producer, and actress.

Simchat Torah (The Good, the Great, and the Awesome), Hebrew for "rejoicing in the Torah," is a celebration in honor of the completion of one annual cycle of weekly Torah readings and the beginning of the next one.

Simon, Neil (Life Is Beautiful), born in 1927, is an American playwright and screenwriter who won a Pulitzer Prize and other awards for his work.

Solomon (The Big Picture; Verbalize Your Happiness) was a biblical Israelite king famous for his wisdom. He built the First Temple in Jerusalem and is considered a prophet.

Sommer, Rafael (The Power of Music), 1947–2001, born in Czech Republic to Alice Herz-Sommer, was one of only a handful of children to survive Theresienstadt concentration camp during World War II. He became an Israeli cellist and won many prizes for his music.

Spektor, Regina (Do It Now!), born in 1980 in the Soviet Union, is an American singer-songwriter and pianist.

Spinoza, Baruch (Jewish Thought on Happiness; Perspective: Introduction to the Section; Emotional Resilience), 1632–1677, was a Dutch philosopher.

Strugatsky, Arkady and Boris (Are We Too Lazy to Feel Amazing?; Emotional Resilience; Stay Interested in Life) were brothers and famous Soviet science fiction authors. Arkady lived 1925–1992 and Boris lived 1933–2012.

Sutro, Alfred (Introduction), 1863–1933, was an English author, dramatist, and translator.

The **Talmud** (Judaism on Happiness; Start with Yourself: Introduction to the Section; Self-Esteem; Cherish Your Body; Be Grateful; Smile; Emotional Resilience; Practice Kindness) contains the teachings and opinions of thousands of rabbis on a variety of subjects, including law, ethics, and philosophy. The name "Talmud" is derived from the Hebrew for "to study."

The **Tanakh** (The Good, the Great, and the Awesome; The Jewish Way: Introduction to the Section; How to Become Happy,

Get Your Priorities Straight; Enemies of Happiness; Pause) is the Hebrew Bible. The name is an acronym for its three sections: Torah, Nebi'im, and Ketuvim (Law, Prophets, and Writings). In the Christian tradition, the books of the Tanakh (with minor changes) are known as the Old Testament.

Tanya (Happiness Is a Skill; Self-Esteem; Emotional Resilience), written by rabbi Shneur Zalman of Liadi, is the fundamental work of Chabad Hasidism. It deals with spirituality, psychology, and theology.

Telushkin, Joseph (Do It Now!), born in 1948 and raised in New York, he is a rabbi, lecturer, and best-selling author.

The **Torah** (Our Happiness Delusions; Judaism on Happiness; Jewish Thinkers on Happiness; Start with Yourself: Introduction to the Section; Self-Esteem; Cherish Your Body; Attitude Is Everything; Life Is Beautiful; Smile; Cultivate Connection; Practice Kindness; Change Your Behavior), literally "instruction," is the name for the five books of Moses, which Judaism considers the words of God given to Moses on Mount Sinai. In its broader usage, it means the entire corpus of Jewish law that includes the Written and Oral Torah.

Twerski, Abraham J. (Find Meaning; Take It Easy; Change Your Behavior), born in 1930, is an American rabbi, psychiatrist, and noted author who has written more than fifty books on self-help and Judaism.

Tzaddik (Self-Esteem; Do It Now!) is Hebrew for an exceptionally good, righteous person.

Tzedakah (Smile; Practice Kindness) is the obligatory act of charity for those in need.

The **Vilna Gaon** (Verbalize Your Happiness), 1720–1797, also known as rabbi Eliyahu of Vilna, was named *gaon* which means "genius." He was a noted scholar and one of the most influential Jewish leaders in modern history.

Walters, Barbara (Our Happiness Delusions), born in 1929, is an award-winning American television journalist and author.

Weinberg, Dena (Emotional Resilience) is an **American** rebbetzin, a speaker on women's issues, and founder and dean of EYAHT College of Jewish Studies for Women.

Weinberg, Noah (Choices That Lead to Happiness), 1930–2009, was an American rabbi and the founder of Aish HaTorah, an influential Jewish Orthodox organization.

Winner, Moishe (Judaism on Happiness) is an American rabbi and the Director of Chabad Lubavitch of West Brighton Beach in New York City.

Zalman, Shneur (Happiness Is a Skill; Emotional Resilience), 1745–1812, born in Belorussia and known as Rabbi Zalman of Liadi or Alter Rebbe, was a mystic, philosopher, talmudist, and the founder of the Chabad school of Hasidism. **He is the author of *Tanya*, an interpretation of Kabbalah, and** *Shulchan Aruch HaRav*, a code of Jewish law.

The **Zohar** (The Good, the Great, and the Awesome; Perspective: Introduction to the Section), the foundational work of Kabbalah, is a mystical commentary on the Torah.

Zusya of Hanipol (Self-Esteem; Expectations), 1718–1800, was a Hasidic rabbi famed for his simple ways who is considered a *tzaddik*.

ACKNOWLEDGMENTS

I am deeply grateful for the people and organizations that supported me in writing this book and whose presence in my life helped me become who I am today:

My mother, Manya; father, Boris; and brother, Aleksandr, for the unconditional love, support, and belief in me.

My husband Alex for his love and moral and technical support in all my endeavors.

My daughters Rachel and Rebecca for teaching me that learning happiness is possible.

My family-in-law: Raisa, Leonid, Michael, and Zinaida for their love, kindness, and help.

The COJECO BluePrint Fellowship, UJA-Federation of New York, and Genesis Philanthropy Group for choosing to support this project, teaching me about my Jewish heritage and community, and empowering me to work on my calling.

My editor, Katie Herman, for making this book better.

Michael Langman and Anna Novak for showing me that we can look at life differently.

Yigal Kotlyar for being my mentor for this project.

Valerie Khaytina for pointing me in the right direction and supporting me throughout my work on this book.

Sabina Singer for reading and editing the first drafts, for her kindness, enthusiasm, and wisdom.

Michael Pikman for being my first fan.

Yuliya Chernova and Yury Shlionsky for reading the first draft.

Hanan Harchal (of JewishFoodForThought.com) for sharing Jewish wisdom and his personal wisdom with me and giving me and many others a lot of food for thought.

Susan Levit for being my mentor and unfailing friend.

Olga Manzano for inspiring me to always be grateful, content, and loving.

My friends and coworkers who always offered encouragement and praise.

NOTES

INTRODUCTION

1 "Relate Calls for Statutory Provision of Counselling in Schools," http://www.relate.org.uk/about-us/media-centre/press-releases/2013/12/11/relate-calls-statutory-provision-counselling-schools/.

2 Catherine Rampell, "American Jews Lead the Happiest Lives," *New York Times*, January 2011, http://economix.blogs.nytimes.com/2011/01/07/american-jews-lead-the-happiest-lives/?_r=0/.

DISCLAIMERS

3 *Pirkei Avot*, 5:23.

1. WHAT IS HAPPINESS: Introduction to the Section

4 *Online Etymology Dictionary*, http://www.etymonline.com/index.php?term=hap&allowed_in_frame=0/.

5 *Yiddish Word of the Week*, http://yiddishwordoftheweek.tumblr.com/post/315848528/naches/.

6 *Wikipedia*, http://en.wikipedia.org/wiki/Happiness/.

7 Nirvana state in Buddhism.

8 Paraphrase of Mason Cooley, *City Aphorisms, Tenth Selection*.

2. Which Theory of Happiness Is the Right One?

9   Moshe Mycoff, *The Empty Chair: Finding Hope and Joy; Timeless Wisdom from a Hasidic Master, Rebbe Nachman of Breslov*, 49.

10   Tzvi Freeman, "To Each His Path: Based on Letters and Talks of the Rebbe, Rabbi M. M. Schneerson," http://www.chabad.org/library/article_cdo/aid/58840/jewish/To-Each-His-Path.htm/.

3. The Good, the Great and the Awesome: The Benefits of Happiness

11   Shloma Majeski, *The Chassidic Approach to Joy.*

12   D. S. Berry and J. S. Hansen, "Positive Affect, Negative Affect, and Social Interaction," *Journal of Personality and Social Psychology* 71 (1996): 796–809; L. Harker and D. Keltner, "Expressions of Positive Emotions in Women's College Yearbook Pictures and Their Relationship to Personality and Life Outcomes across Adulthood," *Journal of Personality and Social Psychology* 80 (2001): 112–124.

13   See note above.

14   C. Estrada, A. M. Isen, A. M., and M. J. Young, "Positive Affect Influences Creative Problem Solving and Reported Source of Practice Satisfaction in Physicians," *Motivation and Emotion* 18, 285–299.

15   C. S. Carver et al., "How Coping Mediates the Effect of Optimism on Distress: A Study of Women with Early Stage Breast Cancer," *Journal of Personality and Social Psychology* 65

(1993): 375–390; B. L. Fredrickson and T. Joiner, "Positive Emotions Trigger Upward Spirals toward Emotional Well-Being," *Psychological Science* 13 (2002): 172–175; D. Keltner and G. A. Bonanno, "A Study of Laughter and Dissociation: Distinct Correlates of Laughter and Smiling during Bereavement," *Journal of Personality and Social Psychology* 73 (1997): 687–702.

16   E. Diener and M. E. P. Seligman, "Very Happy People," *Psychological Science* 13 (2002): 81–84.

17   Proverbs 17:22.

18   Maimonides, *Regimen of Health*, quoted in David Zulberg, "How Maimonides Dealt with Stress & Anxiety," https://www.ou.org/life/health/how-maimonides-dealt-with-stress-anxiety/.

19   Kelly A. Turner, *Radical Remission*.

20   Martin Seligman, "Positive Education and the New Prosperity," *Education Today* (August 2008): 20-21.

21   M. Csikszentmihalyi and M. M. Wong, "The Situational and Personal Correlates of Happiness: A Cross-National Comparison" (1991), in F. Strack, M. Argyle, & N. Schwarz, eds., *Subjective Well-Being: An Interdisciplinary Perspective* (Elmsford, NY: Pergamon Press), 193–212; D. Watson et al., "Affect, Personality, and Social Activity," *Journal of Personality and Social Psychology* 63 (1992): 1011–1025.

22   D. D. Danner, D. A. Snowdon, and W. V. Friesen, "Positive Emotions in Early Life and Longevity: Findings from the Nun Study," *Journal of Personality and Social Psychology* 80 (2001): 804–813; T. Maruta et al., "Optimists vs. Pessimists: Survival Rate

among Medical Patients over a 30-Year Period," *Mayo Clinic Proceedings* 75 (2000): 140–143; G. V. Ostir et al., "Emotional Well-Being Predicts Subsequent Functional Independence and Survival," *Journal of the American Geriatrics Society* 48 (2000): 473–478.

23   *Sefer Baal Shem Tov*, vol. 2, p. 202, no. 41.

24   Yitzhak Buxbaum, *Jewish Tales of Mystic Joy* (San Francisco: Jossey-Bass, 2002).

25   Zohar 2:179b.

26   As told by Rabbi Moishe Winner.

27   B. M. Staw, R. I. Sutton, and L. H. Pelled, "Employee Positive Emotion and Favorable Outcomes at the Workplace," *Organization Science 5* (1995): 51–71.

28   M. R. Cunningham et al., "Separate Processes in the Relation of Elation and Depression to Helping: Social versus Personal Concerns," *Journal of Experimental Social Psychology* 26 (1990): 13–33; S. Williams and W. T. Shiaw, "Mood and Organizational Citizenship Behavior: The Effects of Positive Affect on Employee Organizational Citizenship Behavior Intentions," *Journal of Psychology* 133 (1999): 656–668.

4. Our Happiness Delusions (or Why Happiness Does Not Make Us Happy)

29   Alan W. Watts, *The Book on the Taboo Against Knowing Who You Are.*

30   "Happiness," *Merriam-Webster Online*, http://www.merriam-webster.com/dictionary/happiness.

31   The Dalai Lama XIV, *The Way to Freedom.*

32   "Success," Thesaurus.com, http://www.thesaurus.com/browse/success?s=t.

33   "Henry A. Kissinger Quotes," http://www.brainyquote.com/quotes/quotes/h/henryakis153465.html/.

34   David Aaron, *Living a Joyous Life: The True Spirit of Jewish Practice* (Boston: Trumpeter Books, 2007), 88.

35   Wendy Mogel, *The Blessing of a Skinned Knee* (New York: Scribner, 2001), 41.

36   "Depression Rates Highest in Wealthy Countries," Jeremy White, *International Business Times,* July 2011, http://www.ibtimes.com/depression-rates-highest-wealthy-countries-818657/.

37   Suniya S. Luthar, "The Culture of Affluence: Psychological Costs of Material Wealth," *Child Development* 74, no. 6 (2003): 1581–1593.

38   *Pirkei Avot* 2:7.

39   Ayn Rand, *Atlas Shrugged.*

40   Jennifer Senior, "All Joy and No Fun: Why Parents Hate Parenting," *New York,* July 4, 2010, http://nymag.com/news/features/67024/.

41   Kate Devlin, "Marriage without Children the Key to Bliss," *Telegraph,* May 9, 2008, http://www.telegraph.co.uk/news/1941195/Marriage-without-children-the-key-to-bliss.html/.

42   "A Brief History of Emotional Intelligence," *Practical Emotional Intelligence*, http://www.emotionalintelligencecourse.com/eq-history/.

43   Yitzhak Buxbaum, *Jewish Tales of Mystic Joy* (San Francisco: Jossey-Bass, 2002) 184.

44   Unites States Declaration of Independence, 1776.

45   Martin Seligman, "Positive Education and the New Prosperity: Australia's Edge," *EducationToday*, http://www.minnisjournals.com.au/articles/ET%20Aug-Sep%20web%20pp%2020_21%20(10.9.08)-11.pdf/.

46   Yitzhak Buxbaum, *Jewish Tales of Mystic Joy* (San Francisco: Jossey-Bass, 2002).

6. Four Secrets of Happiness

47   Gerald Epstein, *Healing into Immortality* (New York: ACMI Press, 2010).

48   "Rabbi Frand on Parshas Kedoshim," Torah.org, http://www.torah.org/learning/ravfrand/5757/kedoshim.html/.

49   Kelly A. Turner, *Radical Remission*, 172.

8. Contentment and Moderation: The Building Blocks of Happiness

50 Adapted from *Hedvat HeHayim, vol. 1: Osher V'Simha*, 127, quoted in Yitzhak Buxbaum, "The Shirt of a Happy Man," *Jewish Tales of Mystic Joy* (San Francisco: Jossey-Bass, 2002), 147.

51   See chapter "Settle but Struggle."

52   Wendy Mogel, *The Blessing of a Skinned Knee* (New York: Scribner, 2001).

53   Dovid Rosenfeld, "Maimonides on Life," Torah.com, http://www.torah.org/learning/mlife/ch1law3-4a.html/.

54   Martin Buber, *Tales of the Hasidim: Later Masters*, 249-250.

55   "Mentsch: On Being a Mensch—an Upstanding Member of Society—and Leading an Ethical Life," Michael Strassfeld, My Jewish Learning, http://www.myjewishlearning.com/article/mentsch/.

56   Moshe Mycoff, *The Empty Chair: Finding Hope and Joy; Timeless Wisdom from a Hadisic Master Rebbe Nachman of Breslov*, 99.

10. Judaism on Happiness

57   Proverbs 3:18.

58   Simeon Singer, *The Standard Prayer Book: Authorized English Translation*, 9.

59   Adapted from a story told by Rabbi Moishe Winner.

60   David Aaron, *Living a Joyous Life: The True Spirit of Jewish Practice* (Boston: Trumpeter Books, 2007).

61   Yitzhak Buxbaum, *Jewish Tales of Mystic Joy* (San Francisco: Jossey-Bass, 2002), 1.

62   Abraham J. Twerski, *Let Us Make Man*, citing *Jerusalem Talmud*, Kiddushin 48b.

63   Psalms 27:11.

64   Yitzhak Buxbaum, *Jewish Tales of Mystic Joy* (San Francisco: Jossey-Bass, 2002).

65   David Aaron, *Living a Joyous Life: The True Spirit of Jewish Practice* (Boston: Trumpeter Books, 2007).

66   Leora Kaye and Hanan Harchol, "Study Guide for Jewish Food for Thought episode on Faith," http://jewishfoodforthought.com/wp-content/uploads/2014/05/Faith_StudyGuide.pdf/.

11. Jewish Thinkers on Happiness

67   "Philo of Alexandria," *Internet Encyclopedia of Philosophy*, http://www.iep.utm.edu/philo/.

68   "Philo Judaeus," *Encyclopaedia Britannica*, http://www.britannica.com/EBchecked/topic/456612/Philo-Judaeus/5688/Originality-of-his-thought/.

69   Philo Judaeus, *On Rewards and Punishments*.

70   "Jews in Philosophy," http://www.jinfo.org/Philosophy.html/.

71   "Moses Ben Maimon," *Jewish Encyclopedia*, http://www.jewishencyclopedia.com/articles/11124-moses-ben-maimon/.

72   Baruch Spinoza, *Theological-Political Treatise*.

73   Joseph Demakis, *The Ultimate Book of Quotations*.

74   Karl Marx, *Critique of Hegel's Philosophy of Right*.

75   Sigmund Freud, *Civilization and Its Discontents*.

76   "Sigmund Freud," April Bullock, California State University, Fullerton, http://hssfaculty.fullerton.edu/liberal/abullock/305/Freud%20study%20guide.htm/.

77   Ayn Rand, *Atlas Shrugged*.

78   The Rohr Jewish Learning Institute, *How Happiness Thinks*, 17.

79   "Harvard's Crowded Course to Happiness: 'Positive Psychology' Draws Students in Droves," Carey Goldberg, *Boston Globe*, http://www.boston.com/news/education/higher/articles/2006/03/10/harvards_crowded_course_to_happiness/?page=full/.

12. How to Become Happy

80   "Rabbi Akiba: A Drop of Water", Nissan Mindel, *Chabad.org*, http://www.chabad.org/library/article_cdo/aid/111924/jewish/Rabbi-Akiba-A-Drop-of-Water.htm/.

13. Happiness Is a Skill

81   Rabbi Zalman of Liadi, *Tanya*.

14. The Shortcut: If You Think You Are Happy, You Are

82   Adapted from http://www.fit4brain.com/123/.

15. KNOW YOUR HAPPINESS:
Introduction to the Section

83   Adapted from www.fit4brain.com.

84   Rebbe Nachman of Breslov, *Likutey Etzot* 54.

16. What Is Good and What Is Bad

85   "Taking Control (of What You Can)," Sara Yoheved Rigler, Aish.com, http://www.aish.com/sp/pg/Taking-Control-of-What-You-Can.html/.

86   Sara Yoheved Rigler, *Holy Woman: The Road to Greatness of Rebbetzin Chaya Sara Kramer*, quoted in Aish.com, http://www.aish.com/sp/so/48910592.html/.

17. Recognize Your Happiness

87   Yosef Yitzchak Schneersohn, *Shefer Hama'amarim*, 49.

18. Get Your Priorities Straight

88   Moshe Mycoff, *The Empty Chair: Finding Hope and Joy; Timeless Wisdom from a Hasidic Master, Rebbe Nachman of Breslov*, 17.

89   "What is the Soul?" Yanki Tauber, Chabad.org, http://www.chabad.org/library/article_cdo/aid/3194/jewish/What-is-a-Soul.htm/.

90   Genesis 1:27.

91   Efim Svirsky, *Connection*, 74.

92   Edward Glaeser, "Coercive Regulation and the Balance of Freedom," *Cato Unbound: A Journal of Debate* (May 11, 2007), http://www.cato-unbound.org/2007/05/11/edward-glaeser/coercive-regulation-balance-freedom/.

93   Proverbs 29:18.

94   "Stones and Pebbles," Yaakov Lieder, Chabad.org, http://www.chabad.org/library/article_cdo/aid/3225/jewish/Stones-and-Pebbles.htm/.

95   Adopted from Elisha Goldstein, *The Now Effect*, 3-4.

96   See chapter "Do Not Clutter Your Life."

97   See chapter "Enjoy, Not Endure."

19. Choices That Lead to Happiness

98   Moshe Mycoff, *The Empty Chair; Finding Hope and Joy; Timeless Wisdom from a Hasidic Master, Rebbe Nachman of Breslov*, 17.

99   Adapted from "The Secret of Happiness," Noah Weinberg, Aish.com, http://www.aish.com/sp/f/48968901.html/.

20. START WITH YOURSELF: Introduction to the Section

100   Adapted from Shoshana Boyd Gelfand, "The Prince Who Thought He Was a Rooster", *The Barefoot Book of Jewish Tales* (Concord, MA: Barefoot Books, 2013).

21. Master of Your Happiness

101 "And God Said No," *Jewish Magazine*, April 1999, http://www.jewishmag.com/20mag/anon/anon.htm/.

102 David Aaron, *Living a Joyous Life: The True Spirit of Jewish Practice* (Boston: Trumpeter Books, 2007), 114–115.

103 Irving Kirsch, Thomas J. Moore, Alan Scoboria, Sarah S. Nicholls, "The Emperor's New Drugs: An Analysis of Antidepressant Medication Data Submitted to the U.S. Food and Drug Administration", Prevention & Treatment 5 (Jul 2002).

104 Arjun Walia, "Consciousness Creates Reality – Physicists Admit the Universe Is Immaterial, Mental & Spiritual", http://www.collective-evolution.com/2014/11/11/consciousness-creates-reality-physicists-admit-the-universe-is-immaterial-mental-spiritual/.

105 Gerald Epstein, *Healing Into Immortality* (New York: ACMI Press, 2010), 44.

106 *Az di ken nit tantsen, zogt zi az di klezmorim kenen nit shpilen,* a Yiddish proverb.

107 The original Yiddish proverb translates, "If you don't want to do something, one excuse is as good as another."

108 For more on worrying about the future, see the chapter "Enemies of Happiness."

23. Self-Esteem: Love Yourself Just the Way You Are

109   Yitzhak Buxbaum, *Jewish Tales of Mystic Joy* (San Francisco: Jossey-Bass, 2002).

110   The Rohr Jewish Learning Institute, *How Happiness Thinks*, 34.

111   Abraham J. Twerski, *Let Us Make Man.*

112   Numbers 13:33.

113   Erik A. Kimmel, *Days of Awe: Stories for Rosh Hashanah and Yom Kippur*, 12.

114   Abraham J. Twerski, *Let Us Make Man.*

115   Genesis 28:12.

116   Yisroel Baal Shem Tov, *Keter Shem Tov*, quoted in the Rohr Jewish Learning Institute, *How Happiness Thinks*, 27.

117   S. Felix Mendelsohn, *The Merry Heart: Wit and Wisdom from Jewish Folklore.*

118   Shneur Zalman of Liadi, *Tanya*, chap. 27.

119   Aryeh Nivin, "Discover Your Life's Purpose" (webinar, Jewish Workshops).

120   Lisa Friedman, "#BlogElu 3: Bless – Inclusion Can Help Us to See Blessings in Disguise," *Jewish Special Needs Education: Removing the Stumbling Block* (blog), August 2013, http://jewishspecialneeds.blogspot.com/2013/08/blogelul-3-bless-inclusion-can-help-us.html/.

121   Zelig Pliskin, *Life is Now* (Brooklyn, NY: Me'sorah Publications, 2009), 23.

122   Zelig Pliskin, *Life is Now* (Brooklyn, NY: Me'sorah Publications, 2009), 38.

123   Menachem M. Schneerson, *Torat Menachem.*

124   For more on affirmations, see the chapter "The Shortcut."

23. Are We Too Lazy to Feel Amazing?

125   "Golda Meir Quotes," http://www.brainyquote.com/quotes/quotes/g/goldameir119635.html/.

126   For more on assuming responsibility for our own happiness, see the chapter "Master of Your Happiness."

127   Menachem M. Schneerson, "How to Beat Laziness," letter, Brooklyn, 5 January 1966, Chabad.org, http://www.chabad.org/therebbe/letters/default_cdo/aid/1878120/jewish/How-To-Beat-Laziness.htm/.

24. Cherish Your Body

128   Maimonides, *Guide for the Perplexed*, 1190 (3:8; 3:27).

129   Maimonides, *Mishneh Torah.*

130   Benjamin Blech, *The Complete Idiot's Guide to Understanding Judaism* (New York: Penguin, 2003), 21.

131   "Shmirat Haguf: Health and Wellness in Body and Mind," Amy Dorsch, United Synagogue Youth, http://www.usy.

org/wp-content/uploads/2011/07/exercise-nutrition-stress-management-Shmirat-Haguf.doc/.

132 "Caring for One's Own Health," Louis Jacobs, My Jewish Learning, http://www.myjewishlearning.com/article/caring-for-ones-own-health/.

133 Moshe Mycoff, *The Empty Chair: Finding Hope and Joy; Timeless Wisdom from a Hasidic Master, Rebbe Nachman of Breslov*, 24.

134 Proverbs 11:17.

135 *Der shlof iz der bester dokter*, a Yiddish proverb.

136 *A nacht on shlof iz di gresteh shtro*, a Yiddish proverb.

137 As told by Sara Yoheved Rigler at the "Kesher Wife Workshop."

138 "How Much Sleep Is Enough?" National Heart, Lung and Blood Institute, http://www.nhlbi.nih.gov/health/health-topics/topics/sdd/howmuch/.

139 "How Much Sleep Do We Really Need?" National Sleep Foundation, http://sleepfoundation.org/how-sleep-works/how-much-sleep-do-we-really-need/page/0%2C2/.

140 Exercise by Sara Yoheved Rigler for the "Kesher Wife Workshop."

141 Moshe Mycoff, *The Empty Chair: Finding Hope and Joy; Timeless Wisdom from a Hasidic Master, Rebbe Nachman of Breslov*, 25.

142   Elise Hancock, "A Primer on Taste," *John Hopkins Magazine*, http://pages.jh.edu/~jhumag/996web/taste.html/.

143   "Is Cleanliness Next to Godliness?" GotQuestions.org, http://www.gotquestions.org/cleanliness-next-godliness.html/.

25. PERSPECTIVE: Introduction to the Section

144   Tikunei Zohar 22.

145   Liberman, ed., "Happiness Vendor," in *Jewish Fairy Tales for Children and Adults*, translation mine.

26. The Big Picture

146   *Merov etzim lo ro'im eth ha'ya'ar.* "Hebraic Proverbs," Wikiquote, http://en.wikiquote.org/wiki/Hebraic_proverbs/.

147   "Hebraic Proverbs," Wikiquote, http://en.wikiquote.org/wiki/Hebraic_proverbs/.

148   Adapted from the parable "Life Is Like a Cup of Coffee."

149   S. Felix Mendelsohn, *Here's a Good One: Stories of Jewish Wit and Wisdom*, "Story of Solomon."

150   Adapted from "Elijah's Wisdom," Shoshana Boyd Gelfand, *The Barefoot Book of Jewish Tales* (Concord, MA: Barefoot Books, 2013).

151   See chapter "Get You Priorities Straight."

152   Hilene Flanzbaum, "The Possibility of Joy: How Breast Cancer Changed My Life," *O, The Oprah Magazine*, October 2007.

27. Mindfulness

153   Moshe Mycoff, *The Empty Chair: Finding Hope and Joy; Timeless Wisdom from a Hasidic Master, Rebbe Nachman of Breslov*, 20.

154   Claire Bates, "Is This the World's Happiest Man? Brain Scans Reveal French Monk Found to Have 'Abnormally Large Capacity' for Joy, and It Could Be Down to Meditation," *Daily Mail*, October 31, 2012, http://www.dailymail.co.uk/health/article-2225634/Is-worlds-happiest-man-Brain-scans-reveal-French-monk-abnormally-large-capacity-joy-meditation.html/.

155   Wendy Mogel, *The Blessing of a Skinned Knee* (New York: Scribner, 2001), 38.

156   Eliyahu Eliezer Dessler, *Michtav MeEliyahu*, vol. 3, 306.

157   Moshe Mycoff, *The Empty Chair: Finding Hope and Joy; Timeless Wisdom from a Hasidic Master, Rebbe Nachman of Breslov*, 36.

158   Zelig Pliskin, *Life is Now* (Brooklyn, NY: Me'sorah Publications, 2009).

159   Menachem M. Schneerson, *Sichot Kodesh*.

160   Zalman of Liadi, *Tanya*, Likkutei Amarim 33.

161   Ayn Rand, *The Virtue of Selfishness*.

162   Zelig Pliskin, *Life is Now* (Brooklyn, NY: Me'sorah Publications, 2009), 53.

163   Zelig Pliskin, *Life is Now* (Brooklyn, NY: Me'sorah Publications, 2009), 56.

164   Menachem Mendel of Lubavitch, *Igrot Kodesh*, 323–324.

165   Kim Zetter, "Scientists Meditate on Happiness," *Wired*, September 16, 2003, http://archive.wired.com/culture/lifestyle/news/2003/09/60452?currentPage=all/.

28. Attitude Is Everything

166   "Is the Law of Attraction a Jewish Idea?" Tzvi Freeman, Chabad.org, http://www.chabad.org/library/article_cdo/aid/1402579/jewish/Is-the-Law-of-Attraction-a-Jewish-Idea.htm/.

167   Ayn Rand, *Atlas Shrugged*.

168   Moshe Mycoff, *The Empty Chair: Finding Hope and Joy; Timeless Wisdom from a Hasidic Master, Rebbe Nachman of Breslov*, 32–33.

169   For more examples see chapter "Emotional Resilience."

29. Expectations

170   Yosef Yitzchak Schneersohn, *Sefer Hama'amarim 5710*, 239.

171   Yiddish, "shameless audacity; impudence."

172   Adapted from Yitzhak Buxbaum, *Jewish Tales of Mystic Joy* (San Francisco: Jossey-Bass, 2002), 141–144.

173   For more on gratitude, see chapter "Be Grateful."

30. Life Is Beautiful

174 "Life is the biggest bargain. We get it for nothing," a Yiddish proverb.

175 Ecclesiastes 11:7–8.

176 Caroline Stroessinger, *A Century of Wisdom: Lessons from the Life of Alice Herz-Sommer, the World's Oldest Living Holocaust Survivor*, 206.

177 Caroline Stroessinger, *A Century of Wisdom: Lessons from the Life of Alice Herz-Sommer, the World's Oldest Living Holocaust Survivor*.

178 Caroline Stroessinger, *A Century of Wisdom: Lessons from the Life of Alice Herz-Sommer, the World's Oldest Living Holocaust Survivor*, 126.

179 David Aaron, *Living a Joyous Life: The True Spirit of Jewish Practice* (Boston: Trumpeter Books, 2007).

180 Yitzhak Buxbaum, *Jewish Tales of Mystic Joy* (San Francisco: Jossey-Bass, 2002).

181 Moshe Mycoff, *The Empty Chair: Finding Hope and Joy; Timeless Wisdom from a Hasidic Master, Rebbe Nachman of Breslov*, 59.

182 Sonja Lyubomirsky, *The How of Happiness* (New York: Penguin Press, 2008), 228–244.

183 For more on practicing mindfulness, see chapter "Mindfulness."

184   Rick Hanson, "Taking in the Good," *The Blog*, *Huffington Post*, September 23, 2010, http://www.huffingtonpost.com/ rick-hanson-phd/taking-in-the-good_b_732117.html/.

31. Put on Rose-Colored Glasses

185   Dictionary.com, s.v. "Optimism," http://dictionary. reference.com/browse/optimism/.

186   Caroline Stroessinger, *A Century of Wisdom: Lessons from the Life of Alice Herz-Sommer, the World's Oldest Living Holocaust Survivor*, 207.

187   S. Felix Mendelsohn, *The Merry Heart: Wit and Wisdom from Jewish Folklore*.

32. Be Grateful

188   Caroline Stroessinger, *A Century of Wisdom: Lessons from the Life of Alice Herz-Sommer, the World's Oldest Living Holocaust Survivor*, 209.

189   Jonathan Sacks, *Celebrating Life: Finding Happiness in Unexpected Places* (London: Continuum International Publishing Group, 2003).

190   Ocean Robbins, "The Neuroscience of Why Gratitude Makes Us Healthier," *The Blog*, *Huffington Post*, last modified January 4, 2012, http://www.huffingtonpost.com/ocean-robbins/having-gratitude-_b_1073105.html/.

191   Josepha Sherman, *A Sampler of Jewish-American Folklore*, 160.

192   "Eight Ways Gratitude Boosts Happiness," Sonja Lyubomirsky, A Network for Grateful Living, http://www.gratefulness.org/readings/eight_boosts_gratitude.htm/.

193   Geoffrey A. Mitelman, "To Be a Jew Is to Give Thanks—by Definition," *The Blog, Huffington Post*, last modified January 26, 2014, http://www.huffingtonpost.com/rabbi-geoffrey-a-mitelman/jewish-thanksgiving_b_4333641.html/.

194   Deuteronomy 11.

195   Menachot 43b.

196   Joseph Brodsky, "May 24, 1980."

197   Caroline Stroessinger, *A Century of Wisdom: Lessons from the Life of Alice Herz-Sommer, the World's Oldest Living Holocaust Survivor.*

198   "Beyond Just Desserts: A Recipe of Thanksgiving," Sara Yoheved Rigler, Aish.com, November 27, 2014, http://www.aish.com/sp/so/Beyond_Just_Desserts_A_Recipe_of_Thanksgiving.html/.

199   Babylonian Talmud, *Berachot* 58a.

200   Tziporah Heller (webinar, Jewish e-books).

201   Caroline Stoessinger, *A Century of Wisdom. Lessons from the Life of Alice Herz-Sommer, the World's Oldest Living Holocaust Survivor*, 151.

202   Talmud, *Taanit* 21a.

203   Robert A. Emmons, *Gratitude Works!*, 23–24.

OLGA GILBURD

204   The Rohr Jewish Learning Institute, *How Happiness Thinks*, 108.

205   Moshe Miller, quoted in "Gratitude," Alan Morinis, Jewish Pathways, http://www.jewishpathways.com/mussar-program/gratitude/.

33. Smile

206   Caroline Stroessinger, *A Century of Wisdom: Lessons from the Life of Alice Herz-Sommer, the World's Oldest Living Holocaust Survivor*, 209.

207   "A Rabbi Walks Into a Bar...", Aish.com, http://www.aish.com/j/j/147482125.html/.

208   Melinda Wenner, "Smile! It Could Make You Happier," *Scientific American*, August 1, 2009, http://www.scientificamerican.com/article/smile-it-could-make-you-happier/.

209   "Stress Relief from Laughter? It's No Joke," Mayo Clinic Staff, Mayo Clinic, last modified July 23, 2013, http://www.mayoclinic.org/healthy-living/stress-management/in-depth/stress-relief/art-20044456/; Ron Gutman, *Smile: The Astonishing Powers of a Simple Act*.

210   *JewishEncyclopedia*, s.v. "Badhan," http://www.jewishencyclopedia.com/articles/2320-badhan/.

211   Yisrael Salanter, *Ohr Yisrael*, 112.

212   Ta'anit 22a.

213 Marnie Winston-Macauley, *A Little Joy, A Little Oy: Jewish Wit and Wisdom.*

214 Yitzhak Buxbaum, *Jewish Tales of Mystic Joy* (San Francisco: Jossey-Bass, 2002), 210.

215 "Humor and Nursing II: Using Humor to Cope with the Challenges of Nursing," Corexcel, https://www.corexcel.com/courses/humor.nursing.two.page10.htm/.

216 Yiddish for "trouble."

217 Caroline Stoessinger, *A Century of Wisdom: Lessons from the Life of Alice Herz-Sommer, the World's Oldest Living Holocaust Survivor,* 167.

218 Yitzhak Buxbaum, *Jewish Tales of Mystic Joy* (San Francisco: Jossey-Bass, 2002), 226.

219 Caroline Stroessinger, *A Century of Wisdom: Lessons from the Life of Alice Herz-Sommer, the World's Oldest Living Holocaust Survivor,* 142.

220 Moshe Mycoff, *The Empty Chair: Finding Hope and Joy; Timeless Wisdom from a Hadisic Master Rebbe Nachman of Breslov,* 103.

34. The Power of Music

221 Caroline Stroessinger, *A Century of Wisdom: Lessons from the Life of Alice Herz-Sommer, the World's Oldest Living Holocaust Survivor,* 150.

222 Emily Saarman, "Feeling the Beat: Symposium Explores the Therapeutic Effects of Rhythmic Music," *Stanford Report,*

May 31, 2006, http://news.stanford.edu/news/2006/may31/brainwave-053106.html/.

223   Zelig Pliskin, *Happiness: Formulas, Stories, and Insights* (Brooklyn, NY: Shaar Press, 1999), 54.

224   V. Woollaston, "Listening to Happy Music Really CAN Make You Happier, Find Researchers," *Daily Mail*, May 15, 2013, http://www.dailymail.co.uk/sciencetech/article-2325004/Listening-happy-music-really-CAN-make-happier-researchers.html/.

225   Caroline Stroessinger, *A Century of Wisdom: Lessons from the Life of Alice Herz-Sommer, the World's Oldest Living Holocaust Survivor*, 98.

226   Psalms 100:2.

227   Moshe Mycoff, *The Empty Chair: Finding Hope and Joy; Timeless Wisdom from a Hasidic Master, Rebbe Nachman of Breslov*, 50.

228   Moshe Mycoff, *The Empty Chair: Finding Hope and Joy; Timeless Wisdom from a Hasidic Master, Rebbe Nachman of Breslov*, 105.

229   Moshe Mycoff, *The Empty Chair: Finding Hope and Joy; Timeless Wisdom from a Hasidic Master, Rebbe Nachman of Breslov*, 50.

230   Yitzhak Buxbaum, *Jewish Tales of Mystic Joy* (San Francisco: Jossey-Bass, 2002), 155.

231   Caroline Stroessinger, *A Century of Wisdom: Lessons from the Life of Alice Herz-Sommer, the World's Oldest Living Holocaust Survivor*, 93.

35. Choose Your Influences

232   Jenny Hope, "Happiness Is Contagious and Spreads Quickly between Friends and Family, Say Scientists," *Daily Mail*, December 5, 2008, http://www.dailymail.co.uk/sciencetech/article-1092192/Happiness-contagious-spreads-quickly-friends-family-say-scientists.html/.

36. Enjoy, Not Endure

233   Zelig Pliskin, *Happiness: Formulas, Stories, and Insights* (Brooklyn, NY: Shaar Press, 1999), 62.

234   Itzkhak Buxbaum, *Jewish Tales of Mystic Joy* (San Francisco: Jossey-Bass, 2002), 224.

235   Caroline Stoessinger, *A Century of Wisdom: Lessons from the Life of Alice Herz-Sommer, the World's Oldest Living Holocaust Survivor*, 177.

236   Ecclesiastes 9:10.

237   Zelig Pliskin, *Happiness: Formulas, Stories, and Insights* (Brooklyn, NY: Shaar Press, 1999), 64.

238   Nidhya Logeswaran and Joydeep Bhattacharya, "Crossmodal Transfer of Emotion by Music," abstract, *Neuroscience Letters* 455, no. 2 (May 15, 2009), http://www.sciencedirect.com/science/article/pii/S0304394009003279.

38. Make Room for Negative Emotions

239   Jerry D. Duvinsky, *How to Lose Control and Gain Emotional Freedom.*

240   See the section "Pleasure" in the chapter "Our Happiness Delusions."

39. Emotional Resilience

241   Caroline Stroessinger, *A Century of Wisdom: Lessons from the Life of Alice Herz-Sommer, the World's Oldest Living Holocaust Survivor,* 211.

242   Caroline Stroessinger, *A Century of Wisdom: Lessons from the Life of Alice Herz-Sommer, the World's Oldest Living Holocaust Survivor.*

243   "What is Resilience," PBS, http://www.pbs.org/thisemotionallife/topic/resilience/what-resilience/.

244   Quoted in "How Maimonides Dealt with Stress and Anxiety," David Zulberg, Orthodox Union, July 22, 2013, https://www.ou.org/life/health/how-maimonides-dealt-with-stress-anxiety/.

245   *Iz do a braireh, darf nit zein kain moireh,* a Yiddish proverb.

246   *Ven tsu a krenk iz do a refueh, iz dos a halbeh krenk,* a Yiddish proverb.

247   Robert Fulghum, *Uh-Oh.*

248   "20 Favorite Jewish Quotes," Aish.com, http://www.aish.com/sp/ph/20-Favorite-Jewish-Quotes.html/.

249   Joseph Telushkin, *The Book of Jewish Values: A Day-by-Day Guide to Ethical Living* (New York: Bell Tower, 2000), 3–4.

250   Alfred Dreyfus, *Five Years of My life: 1894-1899.*

251   Arkady and Boris Strugatsky, *Roadside Picnic.*

252   Adapted from http://fit4brain.com/649/.

253   Zelig Pliskin, *Happiness: Formulas, Stories, and Insights* (Brooklyn, NY: Shaar Press, 1999), 70.

254   "I Offered a Prayer to God," *Jewish Magazine*, April 1999, http://www.jewishmag.com/20mag/anon/anon.htm/.

255   Abraham J. Twerski, *Happiness and the Human Spirit* (Woodstock, Vt.: Jewish Lights Publishing, 2007), 57.

256   Wendy Mogel, *The Blessing of a Skinned Knee* (New York: Scribner, 2001), 58.

257   Robert A. Emmon, *Gratitude Works!: A 21-Day Program for Creating Emotional Prosperity.*

258   Zelig Pliskin, *Happiness: Formulas, Stories, and Insights* (Brooklyn, NY: Shaar Press, 1999), 104.

259   Kelly A. Turner, *Radical Remission.*

260   *Beser geboygn eyder tzebrochn*, a Yiddish proverb.

261   *Az me ken nit ariber, gait men arunter*, a Yiddish proverb.

262   Adapted from S. Felix Mendelsohn, "Perfect Adaptation," in *Here's a Good One: Stories of Jewish Wit and Wisdom.*

263   Moshe Mycoff, *The Empty Chair: Finding Hope and Joy; Timeless Wisdom from a Hasidic Master, Rebbe Nachman of Breslov*, 18.

264   Job1:21.

265   Adapted from Gary Rosenblatt, "The Ever-Dying Art Of Jewish Humor", The Jewish Week (April 24, 2012), http://www.thejewishweek.com/editorial_opinion/gary_rosenblatt/ever_dying_art_jewish_humor/.

266   Moshe Mycoff, *The Empty Chair: Finding Hope and Joy; Timeless Wisdom from a Hadisic Master Rebbe Nachman of Breslov*.

267   Moshe Mycoff, *The Empty Chair: Finding Hope and Joy; Timeless Wisdom from a Hadisic Master Rebbe Nachman of Breslov*, 92–93.

268   *Tanya*, Iggeret Hakodesh 11.

269   As told by Rabbi Moishe Winner at the Rohr Jewish Learning Institute.

270   Nachman or Breslov, *Likutey Mahoran* I, 115.

271   Yanki Tauber, "Good Thinking," Chabad.org, http://www.chabad.org/library/article_cdo/aid/2492/jewish/Good-Thinking.htm/.

272   Rabbi Aryeh Katzin at Limmud FSU 2015.

273   Adapted from Zelig Pliskin, *Happiness: Formulas, Stories and Insights* (Brooklyn, NY: Shaar Press, 1999), 44–46.

274   Caroline Stroessinger, *A Century of Wisdom: Lessons from the Life of Alice Herz-Sommer, the World's Oldest Living Holocaust Survivor*, xix.

275   *Hagigah* 15b.

276   Moshe Mycoff, *The Empty Chair: Finding Hope and Joy; Timeless Wisdom from a Hadisic Master Rebbe Nachman of Breslov*, 113.

277   Kelly A. Turner, *Radical Remission*.

278   *Regimen of Health*, quoted in "How Maimonides Dealt with Stress and Anxiety," David Zulberg, Orthodox Union, July 22, 2013, https://www.ou.org/life/health/how-maimonides-dealt-with-stress-anxiety/.

279   Caroline Stoessinger, *A Century of Wisdom: Lessons from the Life of Alice Herz-Sommer, the World's Oldest Living Holocaust Survivor*, 203–204.

40. Every Cloud Has a Silver Lining

280   Yossi Katz, "The Silver Lining," *Pathways* 5, no. 7 (5775): 1, http://www.breslov.org/pathways-parashat-vayishlach-2/.

281   For more on seeing positive in all things, see chapter "Put on Rose-Colored Glasses."

282   Marnie Winston-Macauley, *A Little Joy, A Little Oy: Jewish Wit and Wisdom*, 48.

283   Marnie Winston-Macauley, *A Little Joy, A Little Oy: Jewish Wit and Wisdom*, 34.

284 *Besser di tenoim tsereissen aider di ketubeh.*

285 "The Silver Lining," Aish.com, http://www.aish.com/ j/j/251171821.html/.

41. Enemies of Happiness

286 Ayn Rand, *Atlas Shrugged.*

287 *Regimen of Health,* quoted in "How Maimonides Dealt with Stress and Anxiety," David Zulberg, Orthodox Union, July 22, 2013, https://www.ou.org/life/health/how-maimonides-dealt-with-stress-anxiety/.

288 Proverbs 12:25.

289 Zelig Pliskin, *Happiness: Formulas, Stories, and Insights* (Brooklyn, NY: Shaar Press, 1999), 135–136.

290 See chapter "Be Grateful."

291 Rabbi Bahya ibn Paquda, *Chovot Halevavot.*

292 "Joseph Brodsky: Quotes," GoodReads.com, https:// www.goodreads.com/quotes/151641-when-hit-by-boredom-let-yourself-be-crushed-by-it/.

293 A Yiddish proverb.

294 Ayn Rand, *Atlas Shrugged.*

295 Zelig Pliskin, *Happiness: Formulas, Stories, and Insights* (Brooklyn, NY: Shaar Press, 1999), 63.

296 "Arthur Rubinstein Dies in Geneva at 95," *New York Times,* November 21, 1982.

42. Release Your Emotions

297   Quoted in "How Maimonides Dealt with Stress and Anxiety," David Zulberg, Orthodox Union, July 22, 2013, https://www.ou.org/life/health/how-maimonides-dealt-with-stress-anxiety/.

298   Leviticus 19:18.

299   Zelig Pliskin, *Happiness: Formulas, Stories, and Insights* (Brooklyn, NY: Shaar Press, 1999), 178.

300   An exercise by Kelly A. Turner, *Radical Remission.*

44. Cultivate Connection

301   Emma M. Seppälä, "8 Powerful Ways to Turn Loneliness into Deep Connection," *Psychology Today.* http://www.psychologytoday.com/blog/feeling-it/201304/8-powerful-ways-turn-loneliness-deep-connection/.

302   Adapted from Shoshana Boyd Gelfand, "Heaven and Hell," in *The Barefoot Book of Jewish Tales* (Cambridge, MA: Barefoot Books, 2013).

303   David Aaron, *Living a Joyous Life: The True Spirit of Jewish Practice* (Boston: Trumpeter Books, 2007).

304   Sara Yoheved Rigler, "Kesher Wife" (webinar, Jewish Workshops).

45. Find Meaning

305   C. Peterson, N. Park, & M. E. P. Seligman, "Orientations to Happiness and Life Satisfaction: The Full Life Versus the Empty Life," *Journal of Happiness Studies* 6 (2005): 25–41.

306   The Rohr Jewish Learning Institute, *How Happiness Thinks*, 34.

307   Ayn Rand, *Atlas Shrugged*.

308   Martin E. Seligman, *Authentic Happiness* (New York: Free Press, 2002), 185–186.

309   Psalms 37:23.

310   The Rohr Jewish Learning Institute, *How Happiness Thinks*, 67, 216.

311   Abraham J. Twerski, *Happiness and the Human Spirit* (Woodstock, Vt.: Jewish Lights Publishing, 2007), 61.

46. Practice Kindness

312 Caroline Stroessinger, *A Century of Wisdom: Lessons from the Life of Alice Herz-Sommer, the World's Oldest Living Holocaust Survivor*, 210.

313   "The world stands on three things: Torah, the service of G-d, and deeds of kindness," *Pirkei Avot*, 1:2.

314   Told by Sara Yoheved Rigler for Kesher Wife, webinar.

315   Sonja Lyubomirsky, *The How of Happiness*.

316   E. W. Dunn, L. B. Aknin, and M. I. Norton, "Spending Money on Others Promotes Happiness," *Science* 319 (2008): 1687–1688.

317   www.JewishFoodforthought.com/.

318 "Kindness Makes You Happy . . . and Happiness Makes You Kind," Alex Dixon, Greater Good, September 6, 2011, http://greatergood.berkeley.edu/article/item/kindness_makes_you_happy_and_happiness_makes_you_kind/.

319 Abraham J. Twerski, *Happiness and the Human Spirit* (Woodstock, Vt.: Jewish Lights Publishing, 2007).

320 Leviticus 19:34.

321 Ketubot 50a.

322 Joseph Telushkin, *The Book of Jewish Values: A Day-to-Day Guide to Ethical Living* (New York: Bell Tower, 2000), 336.

323 Ayn Rand, *Philosophy: Who Needs It*, 61.

324 B.L. Fredrickson, M.A. Cohn, K.A. Coffey, J. Pek, and S.M. Finkel, "Open Hearts Build Lives: Positive Emotions, Induced Through Loving-Kindness Meditation, Build Consequential Personal Resources," Journal of Personality and Social Psychology 95(5) (November 2008):1045-62.

325 Zelig Pliskin, *Happiness: Formulas, Stories and Insights* (Brooklyn, NY: Shaar Press, 1999), 153–154.

47. Verbalize Your Happiness

326 Genesis 1:1–31.

327 Chofetz Chaim, *A Lesson a Day*, xvii.

328 "The Stunning Power of Speech," Morasha, http://www.morashasyllabus.com/class/The%20Stunning%20Power%20of%20Speech%20II.pdf.

329   S. Felix Mendelsohn, *The Merry Heart: Wit and Wisdom from Jewish Folklore.*

330   Rabbi Sholom Dovber Schneersohn, *Sefer Hama'amarim 5659, 5.*

48. Stay Interested in Life

331   N. Park, C. Peterson, and M. E. P. Seligman, "Strengths of Character and Well-Being, *Journal of Social & Clinical Psychology 23 (2004):* 603–619.

332   Caroline Stroessinger, *A Century of Wisdom: Lessons from the Life of Alice Herz-Sommer, the World's Oldest Living Holocaust Survivor.*

333   Joseph Telushkin, *Jewish Wisdom* (New York: William Morrow, 1994).

334   Todd Kashdan, "The Power of Curiosity," *Experience Life,* May 2010, https://experiencelife.com/article/the-power-of-curiosity/.

335   Todd Kashdan, "The Power of Curiosity," *Experience Life,* May 2010, https://experiencelife.com/article/the-power-of-curiosity/.

49. Act It Out

336   Moshe Mycoff, *The Empty Chair: Finding Hope and Joy; Timeless Wisdom from a Hasidic Master Rebbe Nachman of Breslov,* 101.

337   Moshe Chaim Luzzatto, *Path of the Just.*

338   Menachem Mendel Schneersohn, *Igrot Kodesh*, 324.

339   Jane Meredith Adams, "The Pessimist's Guide to Being Optimistic," *Prevention*, December 2, 2011, http://www.prevention.com/mind-body/emotional-health/pessimists-guide-being-optimistic/.

340   Pesachim 50b.

341   Zelig Pliskin, *Life Is Now* (Brooklyn, NY: Me'sorah Publications, 2009), 47.

342   Zelig Pliskin, *Happiness: Formulas, Stories, and Insights* (Brooklyn, NY: Shaar Press, 1999), 117.

51. Take It Easy

343   Yitzhak Buxbaum, *The Light and Fire of the Baal Shem Tov*, 138–139.

344   Zelig Pliskin, *Happiness: Formulas, Stories and Insights* (Brooklyn, NY: Shaar Press, 1999), 228.

345   Abraham J. Twerski, *Happiness and the Human Spirit* (Woodstock, Vt.: Jewish Lights Publishing, 2007), 68.

52. Be Patient

346   Sarah A. Schnitker and Justin T. Westbrook, "Do Good Things Come to Those Who Wait? Patience Interventions to Improve Well-Being," in *The Wiley-Blackwell Handbook of Positive Psychological Interventions*, ed. Acacia C. Parks and Stephen Schueller, 155–159.

347   Jennifer Roberts, "The Power of Patience," *Harvard Magazine*, 2013, 40–41.

348   Genesis 37–48.

349   *Mit geduld boiert men durch afileh a kizelshtain*, a Yiddish proverb.

350   Levi Yitzchak of Berditchev, *Pitgamin Kadishin*, a Yiddish proverb.

53. Pause

351   Genesis 1–2.

352   David Aaron, *Living a Joyous Life: The True Spirit of Jewish Practice* (Boston: Trumpeter Books, 2007), 130.

353   Moshe Mycoff, *The Empty Chair: Finding Hope and Joy; Timeless Wisdom from a Hasidic Master, Rebbe Nachman of Breslov*, 14.

354   David Aaron, *Living a Joyous Life: The True Spirit of Jewish Practice* (Boston: Trumpeter Books, 2007), 143.

355   See chapter "Get Your Priorities Straight."

54. Do Not Clutter Your Life

356   *Tsu shain iz amol a chissoren*, a Yiddish proverb.

357   Gerald Epstein, *Healing Into Immortality* (New York: ACMI Press, 2010).

358   *Vos tsu iz iberik*, a Yiddish proverb.

55. LET'S DO IT: Introduction to the Section

359　Adapted from www.fit4brain.com.

56. Settle but Struggle

360　Adapted from the parable "The Fisherman and the Businessman."

361　See chapter "Get Your Priorities Straight."

57. Change Your Behavior

362　Moshe Mycoff, *The Empty Chair: Finding Hope and Joy; Timeless Wisdom from a Hadisic Master Rebbe Nachman of Breslov*, 16.

363　Gerald Epstein, *Healing into Immortality* (New York: ACMI Press, 2010).

364　Sara Yoheved Rigler, http://www.aish.com/sp/ph/20-Favorite-Jewish-Quotes.html/.

365　Abraham J. Twerski, *Happiness and the Human Spirit* (Woodstock, Vt.: Jewish Lights Publishing, 2007), 126.

366　Exodus 24:7.

367　The Rohr Jewish Learning Institute, *How Happiness Thinks*, 148.

368　Moshe Mycoff, *The Empty Chair: Finding Hope and Joy; Timeless Wisdom from a Hasidic Master, Rebbe Nachman of Breslov*, 44.

369   Midrash Shir HaShirim 5:11.

370   *Pirkei Avot* 4:2.

371   *Chagigah* 9b.

372   http://fit4brain.com/7475/.

58. Do It Now!

373   Leora Kaye and Hanan Harchol, "Study Guide for Episode Nine: 'Faith,'" http://jewishfoodforthought.com/wp-content/uploads/2014/05/Faith_StudyGuide.pdf/.

374   *Pirkei Avot* 2:5.

375   Joseph Telushkin, *The Book of Jewish Values: A Day-to-Day Guide to Ethical Living* (New York: Bell Tower, 2000), 39.

376   Zelig Pliskin, *Life is Now* (Brooklyn, NY: Me'sorah Publications, 2009), 32.

Made in the USA
Las Vegas, NV
20 November 2023

81230610R00223